CW01091585

COME AND GET THESE MEMORIES

COME AND GET THESE MEMORIES

THE GENIUS OF
HOLLAND-DOZIER-HOLLAND
MOTOWN'S INCOMPARABLE SONGWRITERS

EDDIE AND BRIAN HOLLAND

WITH DAVE THOMPSON

OMNIBUS PRESS

London / New York / Paris / Sydney / Copenhagen / Berlin / Madrid / Tokyo

"The songwriting and producing team of Holland–Dozier–Holland was a once-in-a-lifetime match made in heaven for us all. We each brought our unique set of tools and talents to the table, and organically the collaborations became the now iconic songs that we created together. I have so much love and respect for Brian and Eddie, and will always cherish those years we worked together. And every so often we still love coming together for special projects and it's like we never skipped a day... it's always magical sitting in a room together and letting our juices flow." – *Lamont Dozier*

"You guys were the foundation that Motown was built on. Thirteen number one hits in a row, and the record still stands today, it hasn't been broken at all. I still use 'How Sweet It Is' to open up my show, and I wish you all the success in the world. God bless." – *Stevie Wonder*

"I first met Eddie shortly after I met Berry Gordy. Berry would use Eddie to sing demos for some of the songs Berry was writing for Jackie Wilson. After Berry started Motown, Eddie was one of our recording artists. He had a hit record, 'Jamie', but decided he'd rather be behind the scenes and joined his brother, Brian, and his partner, Lamont Dozier, and one of the greatest music writing and production teams in pop music history was born.
"Eddie is one of the greatest wordsmiths ever and has most certainly earned his place in music history, and he's my friend."
– *Smokey Robinson*

"HDH put The Supremes into the realm of 'superstars' by producing 12 number-one, million-sellers for us. Eddie Holland, Lamont and Brian Holland are one of the greatest producer/songwriting teams in American history. I owe these three young men my life, as they made me who I am today. Thank you, guys." – *Mary Wilson*

"The Hollands... what amazing songs they wrote! Vanilla Fudge made it in 1967 because of the great song they wrote, that we arranged. It had amazing music, lyrics and melody. All I can say is, thanks!" – *Carmine Appice*

"HDH were the sound of young America, but they were so much more than that. If Chicago was the consciousness of the US in the sixties, Motown was its hope, and HDH were the front line. They were it. They were America's Lennon & McCartney." – *Andrew Loog Oldham*

Copyright © 2019 Omnibus Press
(A Division of Music Sales Limited)

Cover designed by Ruth Keating.
Picture research by the authors.

ISBN: 9781785588679

The Authors hereby assert their right to be identified as the author of this work
in accordance with Sections 77 to 78 of the Copyright, Designs and Patents Act
1988.

All rights reserved. No part of this book may be reproduced in any form or by
any electronic or mechanical means, including information storage or retrieval
systems, without permission in writing from the publisher, except by a reviewer
who may quote brief passages.

'My Heart Wants To Try One More Time'
'One Sweet Moment'
'Whirlpool Of Emotions'
'Ode To Esther'
© 2019, Words and Music by Brian Holland and Eddie Holland

Every effort has been made to trace the copyright holders of the photographs
in this book but one or two were unreachable. We would be grateful if the
photographers concerned would contact us.

Designed and typeset by Evolution Design & Digital Ltd (Kent).
Printed in the Czech Republic.

A catalogue record for this book is available from the British Library.

Visit Omnibus Press at www.omnibuspress.com

Dedications

Brian: I want to dedicate our book to my wife, Cassandra. Also my children, Linda, Leticia, Holly, Brian Jr. and Brandon.

Eddie: I want to dedicate our book to my children, Edward, David, Eric, Christina, Edina, Craig and Lauren. Hoping it will give them a deeper insight and understanding into my life.

Also, to my nephew Johnny Terry, who is more of a son to me, and his wife, Isela.

To Maggie Jones, whose inspiration stimulated the insight that caused me to look deeper.

To Richard Davis, for holding down the fort and taking care of the accountants, CPS and lawyers, and giving me time to concentrate on this book.

To Barney Ales for so many memories and a lovely introduction to this book.

To Bishop Andrew Merritt of the Straight Gate International Church, whose wisdom and guidance gave me so much inspiration.

And very special thanks to Shirley Washington for so aggressively and consistently pushing me to complete this book, no matter what else I wanted to do, to go deep into myself even when I didn't feel like it, and for arousing memories that I really didn't want to contact. Without her, this book would never have been written. Most people would have turned away but Shirley endured my insults and rage, and always moved ahead.

Shirley, meanwhile, would like to offer special thanks to her research team, Gwendolyn Owens and Marian Michaels, and to our agent, Lee Sobel.

Dave Thompson: Thanks to my agent, Lee Sobel, for making it happen, to Shirley Washington for so much more, and to Amy Hanson, for everything else. Thanks to Barney Ales for his masterful memoir, *Motown: The Sound of Young America* (Thames & Hudson, 2018). Thanks also to Jo-Ann Greene, Karen and Todd, Jen, Oliver, Trevor, and sundry snails and fish.

"A problem is no bigger or smaller than the mind sees it to be. People cannot create problems for you, they can only create obstacles. You must create the problem in your own mind."
– *Eddie Holland*

Contents

Foreword by Barney Ales   11

Introduction   15

Chapter One Kidnap   24

Chapter Two A Family History   38

Chapter Three Boys Will Be Boys   49

Chapter Four Music Music Music   62

Chapter Five Enter the Creator   75

Chapter Six Motown Love   88

Chapter Seven The True Meaning of Royalties   100

Chapter Eight Living in a New World   112

Chapter Nine The Birth of a Legend   122

Chapter Ten Baby I Need Your Loving   138

Chapter Eleven Hitsville from the Inside   149

Chapter Twelve Diana, Mary and Florence   161

Chapter Thirteen A Baby Love Story   175

Chapter Fourteen No Stopping Us Now   187

Chapter Fifteen With The Beatles   198

Chapter Sixteen Big Decisions   210

Chapter Seventeen Storm Clouds Forming   222

Chapter Eighteen When Good Friends Fight 232

Chapter Nineteen Invictus Rising 245

Chapter Twenty The End of the Beginning 259

Chapter Twenty-One Return to Motown 268

Chapter Twenty-Two Murder Happen 278

Chapter Twenty-Three My Heart Wants to Try One More Time 285

Chapter Twenty-Four Back in My Arms 300

Epilogue Esther 306

Selected Discography

Highlights – Awards and Honours 316

All The Hits – HDH on the Hot 100 317

Chronology of Selected Compositions and Productions 329

Selected Productions 356

Solo Recordings 360

Collected Listening 364

Foreword by Barney Ales

I first met Eddie and Brian Holland at the bowling alley on Woodward Avenue in Detroit. They were kids at the time – Brian was maybe seventeen, Eddie was a couple of years older – and they were still at the dawn of their musical careers. Whereas I, at the grand old age of twenty-six, was already running a record distributing company.

I liked them both immediately, and my interest was further piqued when I got to see Eddie perform. Like I said, he was still just starting out, a slow stream of solo singles recorded with Berry Gordy as the still-nascent Motown operation came to life.

But he could sing! He was a natural, the sexiest, slickest thing on two legs. The girls went wild for him. He sounded to me like Jackie Wilson, and a lot of other people agreed. He was a reluctant performer, though. He loathed touring, hated performing, he disliked travel. He didn't enjoy crowds. We were together a lot, going from gig to gig, record hop to radio station, and he never ever caused me any problems. Always a gentleman, always doing his best to help, he was really good about everything.

I knew he wasn't happy with the life he was leading, but he never allowed it to affect his work. He was professional, through and through. And I could tell there was more to him than just a great singer and performer. I remember one time we were in San Francisco, getting ready for a performance at the Cow Palace, alongside The Marvelettes. The only problem was, finances were tight and we were only able to bring one Marvelette with us, Gladys. The idea was, we would recruit four more girls once we got into town, and they would stand in for the rest of the group.

Eddie took charge, arranging the auditions, listening to the girls who filed into the room, and putting together a group for the show. He wasn't even phased when we realised we didn't have the arrangements for the songs with us – he taught the girls what he could, harmonies, choreography, the lot, while we waited for Motown to send the sheets to us, and he was still putting them through their paces while I was frantically running around San Francisco, trying to discover which hotel the package had mistakenly been sent to. I finally caught up with it at a tiny little place in Chinatown, whose proprietors could barely understand a word I spoke.

The record we were promoting on that outing, 'Jamie', would give Eddie the massive hit that we all had been waiting for – it was a sensational disc, and I still love it today. In fact, my first granddaughter would be named after it!

But Eddie was still not happy. He wanted to stay in the music business, he wanted to stay at Motown. He just didn't want to record and tour any longer, and I have to say that performance's loss was songwriting's gain. His brother Brian had already shown himself to be a supremely gifted composer and arranger; now, with Eddie alongside him, providing the lyrics that would illustrate Brian's music, the pair were unstoppable.

As I read this book, so many memories came flooding back. Some were sparked by the tales that they tell... those all-night poker games, for instance, or the first time I heard 'Where Did Our Love Go?' It's funny, there's a story going around that, when the song was first completed, it was offered to The Marvelettes. Not true. That song was always intended for The Supremes and, when you listen to it today, you know it could never have been any other way.

Other memories sprang from my own observations. I remember what a perfectionist Eddie was, how he used to wrestle with his lyrics and how, even after a recording was completed (and already on its way to the top of the charts), he would still be thinking of ways he could have improved upon it.

'Stop! In The Name Of Love', for example. One line... no, one *word*... in that song would haunt him forever. Even as he wrote the song, he knew that when Diana sings "Leaving me alone and hurt", she ought to have sung "alone to cry". But he didn't make the change, and he has regretted it ever since. Oh, and it didn't make him feel any better the first time Berry heard the song and made the same observation. "You should have written 'cry', not 'hurt'." Poor Eddie. His expression didn't change, but he knew Berry was right. He wouldn't make that same mistake again.

Holland–Dozier–Holland became the powerhouse behind Motown's success in the sixties. I know, because I was the man responsible for taking the finished records out into the world, to play to the DJs and journalists of the day. Some songs were a hard sell, but HDH records all but sold themselves the moment the needle touched the grooves. Not even the first snatch of lyric. The opening bar! I don't have the statistics to hand, but Brian, in particular, was responsible for so many millions of records sold, whether as a writer, a producer or as an inspiration to others. And together, there was a point where HDH's music truly was the sound of Motown.

Their true importance, however, was not as a money-making machine.

Even today, I cannot think of any songwriting team in history that created as many great records as they came up with. We all know the hits, but even their B-sides and album tracks were classics, a status that is hammered home today, every time Motown digs into the vaults and discovers another song that might never even have been released at the time, but which now takes its place proudly alongside the very best of sixties Motown music.

They continued to do it, too, first with their own Invictus/Hot Wax label following their departure from Motown, and then in the mid-1970s, when they returned to pick up where they left off. I had also been away; I came back to Motown in September 1975, this time as President, and one of the first songs I heard was The Jackson 5's 'Forever Came Today'. I didn't even need to be reminded of the writing credits; I knew, from the moment it started, that Brian and Eddie were still firing on all cylinders.

This book proves that they still are. Reading *Come and Get These Memories*, I hear their voices, I hear their laughter. So much laughter, so many good times. A lot of years have passed since those halcyon days, but we remain close friends and, to me, this book is like spending an evening in their company, just listening to them talk, Brian quiet and reserved, Eddie forthright and joking. I think you will feel the same way.

Barney Ales, 2019

Introduction

Although this book has two storytellers, there are three voices to be heard, exactly as there were three voices in many of the songs that we wrote: Brian Holland and Eddie Holland, of course, and Lamont Dozier, the equal partner in the music that delighted and, we are often told, helped to define a generation.

Together, we three were responsible for more songs than we can even remember. Together, we changed the ways in which people listened to pop music, what they demanded of it.

No matter where time and life have taken us, how many different avenues we have travelled down, together we are inseparable. Holland–Dozier–Holland long ago ceased to be a mere identity; it became an entity in its own right. According to the statistics a click away on the internet, Holland–Dozier–Holland is one of the most successful partnerships in modern musical history.

It's not our intention to repeat those statistics or even to refer to them again. They are ours, but they don't feel like ours. It was not us who sent this song to number one or that one to number two; nor did we give this hit to Rod Stewart and that smash to Phil Collins.

Neither was it we who handed out the gold discs or the songwriting awards. That was all the work of others, and it is they to whom those statistics belong, the people who caused those events to come to pass. All we provided was the raw material.

At the same time, however, we know the quality of our work, in the same way we're aware of the quality of the artists we chose to record it. We know, because that's what we set out to achieve: the best songs for the best singers, accompanied by the best musicians, for the greatest record label in the world. And that is what we accomplished.

We cannot claim to recall our every composition. Time and again as this book came together, a question would arise regarding one song or another. It might have been a massive hit. It may have been a minor one. It might even have been one that was filed away in the legendary Motown (or, later, Invictus and Hot Wax) library, not to see the light of day for decades to come. 'The Boy From Crosstown', for example. 'Love (Makes Me Do Foolish Things)'. 'I Like Everything About You'. We would look at one another and shake our heads.

"Sorry. I don't remember."

Brian: When I write songs, I write them. I don't go back and try to remember. I'm the same with events, dates, things like that. I want to keep going forward.

Of course, certain songs stick in our minds, not only as musical favourites but also as emotional and personal touchstones. We are well aware, too, that there are people out there for whom others are equally important. We know that and we are thrilled when they tell us why.

But please understand. We wrote a lot of songs through the 1960s and 1970s, and we are still writing them today. If we could remember every single lyric that was ever set to music, every single tune that was given its own special voice, we would scarcely even be human. We'd be computers. And, no matter how advanced computers get, how adept they become at doing everything a human can do, and doing it better too, there is one thing of which we are certain. A computer could never write 'Baby Love'… 'Bernadette'… 'This Old Heart Of Mine (Is Weak For You)'… 'Where

Did Our Love Go'. It wouldn't even know where to start. Certainly it would not have gone on to write the hundreds of other songs we have completed in the years since then.

For many people, however, the name Holland–Dozier–Holland remains synonymous with the years we spent at Motown in the 1960s. That is largely what this book is about.

It isn't a straightforward history. There have surely been more books published about Motown than any other record company – maybe any other company – in the world. Some were written by the people who were there, some by people who wish they were there, and some by people who… well, who's to say where they found their information. But there is nothing so frustrating as sitting down to read a book that claims to tell the story of your own life and times, and discovering little more than rumours, lies and speculation. In fact, one of the first things we asked our co-writer, Dave Thompson, when we started work on our story was, "Have you read any of the other Motown books?"

"Yes," he replied cautiously.

"Then do us a favour," we requested. "Forget everything you have ever read."

Our intention is not to detail every lyric, every session, every record we made. Nor is it to outline every meeting we attended, every discussion we had, every battle we fought.

Motown, through the years we were there, was a working environment, exactly the same as any other. People are people, whatever situation they find themselves in. But it was also a magical playground. Of course, it was a place where success was valued highly… that's what we were in the business of doing, creating hit records. But it was a place where creativity was valued even higher than that. We wanted hits, but we wanted *great* hits, *memorable* hits. If a song didn't make everybody prick up their ears and ask "What's that?", then we didn't want to know about it.

Famously, Motown founder Berry Gordy Jr. convened monthly Quality Control meetings, where every new recording would be evaluated by the ears he trusted the most. But, beyond those meetings, everybody who worked at Motown, no matter their role or the position they held, knew the standards we were aiming for. If you didn't meet them every time, believe us, you'd hear about it from someone – and, very often, their word would be sufficient to send you back to the drawing board.

That quest for perfection… that is what this book is about. Of course, we talk about our early years growing up in Detroit, discovering first music and then our particular musical talents. We follow our paths from street corner singers to Top 40 songwriters. We go beyond that as well, to the music that we continued to make in the years after we left Motown.

But it is the years we spent at Hitsville that flavour both the story and our appetite for telling it. Non-performing songwriters do not, after all, lead the most thrill-a-minute, hedonistic lifestyles. Or at least we didn't. We were generally too busy writing songs. Therefore, it's the songs that bring a framework to the story, as much as our interactions with other people, artists and otherwise.

Again, we cannot remember every song we ever wrote. We do recall those whose creation was somehow out of the ordinary, or whose subsequent success made them memorable. The stories that we tell around them, we believe, are those that illustrate precisely why this one particular moment in time, on this one particular street in Detroit, is as beloved today, more than half a century on, as it was when those records were still new releases.

We ask just one thing of you as you sit down to read this book. Please remember, we were no more than kids at the time. We were still learning how to write, just as we were still learning how to live. We got a lot better at both.

Eddie: It bothered me for years when people would tell me I was a great songwriter. As far as I was concerned, I was still learning.

All of the big hits we wrote in the sixties, The Supremes, The Four Tops, all of those, they were my early work. I'd only been writing songs for two, three years. Even when we left Motown, I'd only been writing for five years. You know from reading any author or listening to any songwriter, the first five years is when they are still finding themselves.

So, it bothered me when we received an award for such and such a song that we wrote back then. I knew I'd only just begun. I never agreed with it. It always embarrassed me. The other thing was, I knew it was an acquired skill. It wasn't a talent I believed I was born with.

I sat down and I taught myself how to write songs. I went to four or five people I trusted, people in my neighbourhood, people around Motown, and I asked them, "What do you look for in a song? What is it about this song that makes it so magical, whereas that song isn't?"

I gathered all this information. The only thing I brought to the process was knowing how to do that, how to relate to it. I never felt I was a great songwriter. I was not a poet. I'm a better songwriter now than I've ever been but I didn't feel that way then.

I remember once, Brian said to me, "You're a songwriter, aren't you?" I thought about it. In my mind, I said, "I think so," but I don't think I actually answered him. Yes, I was writing songs but it wasn't planned. It was a euphoria, an almost hypnotic thing that drew me in and made my pen move.

Besides, if it wasn't for the melodies that Brian was bringing to me – and I've told him this many, many times – I would never have written those lyrics. I became so involved and engrossed in his melodies. That's why I had to write pages of lyrics, pages and pages, before any of them made sense.

Whatever the reasons, however we chose to view what we were doing, we were good at what we did. People say we were among the best. It still takes us by surprise today.

We were invited to London in 2004 to receive the Ivor Novello Special International Award. It was our first time there. For years, The Four Tops would say, "Man, you should go to England. They love you. We mention your name and people get so excited." I couldn't believe it.

We realised that the UK has a far greater appreciation for writers and producers than America. Here, the focus is on the stars, the singer. Whereas in Britain, they want to know who wrote this, who produced it. We flew there and we got a taste of it. That taste was – they treated us like royalty.

People were coming 40, 50 miles in the rain, driving all that way for us to sign an album sleeve for them. I was shocked! "Why the heck would you drive this far to get me to sign a record?"

Brian, Lamont and I attended an engagement at a nightclub. People were queued up to listen to us talk. They were treating us like we were celebrities and we'd never been treated like that. Even when we walked down the street, people recognised us. We'd never had that in America.

We'd never had it. We never wanted it. Fame was not anywhere on whatever list of ambitions we may have had at the time. A job well done, yes. The knowledge that people loved what we did, yes. Songs that other artists would want to sing or even record their own versions of. Yes.

But fame, for the sake of being famous? Never.

One of the funniest things that ever occurred to us was at the BMI (Broadcast Music, Inc.) Awards in 1966. We'd won Songwriter of the Year for the past two years, but had never attended the ceremony itself. This year, we decided to show our faces.

It was a really strange situation. We were seated at our table. People kept coming over, looking at me, and then walking away. Not merely looking, either – some of them actually stood there and stared.

Three, four times this happened, until finally one man spoke.

"Are you Eddie Holland?"

I said yes but he didn't reply. He continued staring. Later, I sought him out and asked him why.

"Because we didn't think you existed," he replied. "Nobody has ever seen you before. We all thought that you were Berry Gordy, writing under a pseudonym!"

For us, it was and still is about the creative process. As we write these words, work is afoot to recreate our lives and music for the stage. We never set out to find fame. Regardless, it finds you.

We want to thank you for taking this journey with us… sharing the "where were we, when and what" of what we were doing, and igniting memories of the "where were you, when and what" of the first time you heard 'Baby Love', 'Stop! In The Name Of Love', 'Where Did Our Love Go', 'Baby I Need Your Loving', 'I Can't Help Myself (Sugar Pie Honey Bunch)' and so many others. The unbelievable euphoria of those halcyon days, both yours and ours.

We invite you to 'Come and Get These Memories', just as we also invite you to continue this incredible journey with us.

Eddie and Brian Holland, 2019

Brian, Eddie and Lamont are joined by The Pointer Sisters, among others, at the Lifetime Achievement Awards ceremony.

My Heart Wants To Try One More Time
(Music by Brian Holland; lyrics by Eddie Holland)

Time after time
I tell myself (that) I want you out of my life
Night after night
You still invade my thoughts that stay till morning light
All the hurt you put me through
I tried to find the good in you
You made it hard to live with you
But love keeps on needing you

I say love go away
But love wants to stay
Just keeps holding on
Love has a mind of its own
You see it's out of my control

'Cause my heart wants to try, one more time
Just one more time

Love has a way of forgiving all the hurt
That lives so deep inside
Love has a way of finding memories I've tried to hide
I keep reaching out for happiness
But ending up with something less
You left and took the best of me
Then love took the rest of me

I say love go away but it stubbornly stays
Just gets stronger and stronger every day
You see it's out of my control

'Cause my heart wants to try, one more time
Just one more time

This heart of mine
Refuses to let you go
Living with memories
Are more painful
Than you'll ever know
I guess my heart knows me
Better than I know myself
I can't fake it

I can't take it
The thought of losing you

'Cause I want this man
I need this man
This is my man
And I want to stay, I want to stay
'Cause my heart wants to try, one more time, one more time,
     one more time
Just one more time, just one more time

Chapter One

Kidnap

Eddie: It was the most significant moment in my life, and not only do I not remember it, I was not even aware of it until I was nineteen years old. Until the day I asked my mother what was the worst thing that ever happened to her. She replied, it was the day that I was kidnapped.

But to me, reflecting on her story then, and looking back on it today, the kidnapping was merely the prelude to something far more meaningful. The fact that I was found again.

For if I hadn't been, not one line of the story that my brother Brian and I are about to tell would have occurred.

I would have been raised and grown up with other parents, siblings and friends. My entire life would have been utterly altered. I would never have known Brian or my sister, Carole. Would never have met Berry Gordy and Lamont Dozier. Would never have written those songs. Nothing in this book would ever have happened.

But I *was* found. I *did* know those people. We *did* write those songs. All because my mother got me back.

This is the story she told me.

It was a beautiful spring day in April 1940, an early taste of sunshine after what had been a typically bitter Detroit winter.

My mother had thrown open the windows of the house we shared with my grandmother, Ola. She parked me in my stroller outside the front door, so I could catch a little sun. Every so often, she would look out to check on me while she went about her daily routine. The morning passed by without incident. Just another day.

Until she looked out and my stroller was empty.

She burst out of the house, onto the street. She was hysterical, looking this way and that, crying, screaming uncontrollably at the top of her lungs. "Where is my baby? Oh God! Where is my baby? Help, somebody help!" Other neighbours were streaming out onto the sidewalk.

Her pleas for help were answered almost immediately.

An old man living across the street had seen the entire episode unfold. He was sitting on his front porch when he saw a woman approaching our house. She glanced into our yard and spotted the stroller; took a few steps towards it, and saw me laying there. Then, as fast as she could, she scooped me up into her arms and took off down the street, not running, but walking faster, her illicit bundle cradled in her arms.

The neighbour continued watching as she walked a few blocks further down the street and into a house.

He called from across the street. "It's okay, Mrs Holland. I saw everything." He started pointing down the street, telling her where the lady had gone. My mother asked him which house. Then she ran as fast as she could, into the woman's yard, banging on the front door. "Give me my baby! Give me back my baby!"

The woman came to the door. "She looked into my eyes," my mother told me. "She knew that I knew, and she said, 'I have him.' She disappeared into the house, then came back and handed me my baby."

My mother said she had never felt relief like that in her life. She was so happy to get me back. She couldn't even be angry. She held me to her breast, feeling her heart rate finally slow, the adrenalin subside. But she had to ask. "Why did you take him?"

Eddie: "I was just a baby. I don't even know how old I was here."

"Because he's the most beautiful baby I've ever seen," the woman replied. "I was walking by, saw him, and I couldn't help myself. I had to have him. I'm so sorry."

My mother was stunned. She didn't even know what to say. She simply turned and carried me home. And that's the way she described the worst thing that ever happened to her.

I cannot even imagine what went through her mind, but 19 years later, the memory of that discovery still set her heart racing. I could still see the panic in my mother's eyes as she relived that awful moment. But talking to her, it was ancient history. It was not something she thought about very often. I was sorry I put her through the pain of remembering.

For me, however, who had never heard this story before, it was as though it had just happened… and was still happening. All that day and deep into the night, and even today, all these years later, I sometimes reflect and cannot shake that story from my mind.

What if the neighbour had not seen that woman grab me? What if she had not lived down the street but had come from a different part of town altogether? What if my mother had never found me? Where would I be now? What kind of life would I have led?

I cannot answer those questions and I don't want to. She *did* find me. That is what I focus on. My mother found me, and it was the most important thing that has ever happened to me.

Our mother, Evelyn Virginia Everett, was the eldest of four children. She was born in 1917, in the town of Comer, Georgia. Her brother, James, arrived the following year and in 1921, the twins, Dorothy Marie and Richard, were born.

The family had moved to Detroit by that time, one of thousands that trekked out of the American south in the years that followed the First World War, in search of work at the automobile factories that were springing up around the city.

As I grew up, I discovered that many of my friends could tell a similar story. Their parents or grandparents, too, had fled the south, where life was hard and money was sparse. Many of them moved north. The assembly lines at Ford, Chrysler, General Motors and Packard promised better opportunities than anything the south had to offer. Ford was also offering equal pay to blacks and whites, regardless of skin colour.

Not that Evelyn's father, Howard, had any intention of taking a job in any of them. He did work there for a short time, but he found it too confining.

Howard Everett was born in 1892, and worked on his father Richard's farm until the army called him up in 1917. His real loves, however, were tailoring and music. He could make you a suit as soon as look at you. That's how he earned his living. Then, to relax, he would sit at the piano, playing spiritual tunes.

He was a stocky man, a familiar sight around the bars of Comer. And the town itself was booming, a small place with very big ideas. It was still a young town, almost exactly the same age as Howard. It was incorporated on January 1, 1893 and took its name from one of the first settlers to live in the area, a Mr A. J. Comer, a century before.

At that time, the place was known as Honey Pond and, by the end of the American Civil War, Comer's blue-eyed, fair-skinned descendants owned the entire area. They grew cotton for miles around, and the area flourished. There was a railroad, farmland and everything a modern town could need. So the locals set about creating one. Hotels, schools, stores, blacksmiths, cotton gins, fertiliser plants, a newspaper – Comer had it all.

Howard's parents, our great grandparents, Richard and Millie Everett, were certainly impressed by it all. Sometime around 1890, they left their home in Pleasant Hill, 100 miles away, and took the Comer Road to this exciting town-to-be. There they raised their family and their first grandchildren, too, before Millie Everett passed away in 1919. Then, when Richard followed her to the grave in March 1921, Grandfather Howard made the decision to sell the farm and move north to Detroit, Michigan.

Grandma Ola and Grandfather Howard on their wedding day.

Howard was married now, to a local girl five years his junior, named Ola Smith – apparently she was no more than fifteen or sixteen when they wed.

Ola was the eldest of five children and, when her mother had died, it was Ola who'd had to take responsibility, but not only for her own siblings. Her father, Jerry Smith, soon remarried a girl barely a few years older than Ola and, in quick succession, there were four more babies to be cared for. Ola got on well enough with her stepmother, a lady with the magnificent name of Texas Smith, but the burden had been too great. She had decided to leave home and get married.

Now it was time for Howard and Ola to leave Georgia, so they did. They packed up their belongings, gathered up the children and took the train 740 miles north to Detroit.

They did not make the journey alone. Ola's brother, Gordon, travelled with them; and, over time, other members of the family – including Texas and her now-grown-up children – would join them in Detroit. Gordon even moved into the house next door to Ola and Howard on Lumpkin Street, in the north of the city, and his three children, our cousins George, Roberta and Hattie Elizabeth, would become our greatest playmates while we were growing up.

Evelyn's sister, our aunt Dorothy, and her husband Richard Dean were also in Detroit, and their son James would be another close cousin. Many of Grandfather Howard's 15 brothers and sisters were soon in the city as well.

Life wasn't bad at first. Howard had savings – some $3,000, or the equivalent of $40,000 today. It was enough to buy the family home, and it kept them buoyant, too. But then the stock market crashed and the Depression set in. His savings were completely wiped out.

Ola quickly found a job at the Ford factory. In fact, most of the family worked there, and most of Detroit as well. Even our mother, long after she finished high school, worked at Ford for a time, and who did she meet while she was there? A young man named Berry Gordy Jr.

Our grandfather Howard, as I've mentioned, worked for Ford a short time, but he had no interest in clocking in and out every day. Life, he believed, was for living, and you could not do that in a factory. Not when you could earn money making suits for whoever wanted one, and spend your free time playing piano and whistling. He loved to whistle! Walking down the street, he would reach up, pluck a leaf from a tree or bush, put it to his mouth, and the most remarkable sounds would come pouring out. We could never, ever, learn how to do that, no matter how hard he tried to teach us.

So Howard went about his life, happy as can be, with just one dark cloud hanging over him.

Ola!

She hated what she saw as his random, careless lifestyle, and never knowing how much, if anything, he'd contribute to the family budget in any given week. Particularly with four children to raise.

Putting even greater strain on Ola and Howard's marriage, their son Richard, Dorothy's twin, was diagnosed with epilepsy, following a fall while he was still a toddler. One day he was playing on the porch and Ola, who was watching him, had to turn away for a few minutes. While she was gone, he climbed onto a balcony, slipped and fell, and hit his head. At a time when medical care of any description was out of the reach of many working class families, Richard passed away when he was just fifteen.

Ola never forgave herself for the death of their son. She never spoke of him, though. All the while we were growing up, we would see pictures of the twins in the cabinet. We recognised Aunt Dorothy, but not the young man alongside her. I asked who he was – Ola never answered. But she would visit his grave every Memorial Day.

Eddie: I was fifteen years old before I found out who he was, when I happened to ask my cousin George. He simply said, "That's Dorothy's twin."

⋆   ⋆   ⋆

Some time in the mid, maybe late 1930s, our mother met and married our father, Edward Holland Sr. He was older than her, born in North Carolina in 1915. His family had also moved to Detroit during the 1920s.

A widower (his first wife died in childbirth), Edward worked as an auto mechanic and he was one of the best around. He could strip an engine and have it back together and purring perfectly without even breaking a sweat, we were told. He also worked as a bump and body painter for a while, but the thing he was best at was making money.

He was the kind of guy who was high living. He would play golf, go horseback riding, boating, fishing, hunting. He was never short of cash. The only problem was, he wouldn't spend it on his family.

We know very little about his family background, only that his mother (our grandmother Mary's) father, Lawrence O'Bryant,

Our parents on their wedding day.

was half African-American and half Creek Indian, and worked as a linesman throughout the south; and her mother Molly was mulatto, mixed with a little Irish and Cherokee, and kept a very strict household. She also absolutely dominated her children, to the extent of telling them what they should name their own kids!

But Grandmother Mary was strong-willed as well, so when Will Holland came around, she married him, even though he was old enough to be her father. Anything to get away from her mother.

Will left the south first, heading up to Detroit in the hope of finding work. Mary and their son, Edward, our father, were left behind, expecting Will to send for them once he had settled. Time passed, however, and they didn't hear a word. Finally, Mary's brother passed on a rumour that Will was now living with another woman.

Leaving little Edward with her brother, Mary made her own way north, to discover the rumours were true. Not being the kind of woman who would take any such nonsense from a man, she promptly left Detroit and moved to Chicago, where she quickly secured work.

Learning what had taken place, Will Holland, meanwhile, hired two of his associates to travel back down to North Carolina to seize the boy. Then they brought him back to Detroit, where he lived with Will and his new partner. Our father, who was seven or eight years old at the time, used to ask the woman where his mother was. Cruelly, she would respond, "She gave you away. She didn't want you."

It was a lie – Mary had had no choice. But it would be 10 years before Edward saw his mother again, by which time she had earned, and saved, sufficient money to return to Detroit and buy a house… in cash. Edward moved in with her and could not have been happier. But the damage to his relationships with women had been sealed.

Mary, too, carried the guilt from that lost decade, locked deep inside of her and endured throughout the remainder of her life.

Eddie: I was the recipient of all the love our grandmother Mary had not been able to bestow upon our father. She really spoiled me and I became the centre of her life. Grandmother Ola was a disciplinarian and very strict. Grandmother Mary was the complete opposite. She always doted on me by telling me how beautiful I was. Ola, on the other hand, would never say that to me, or even allow anyone else to say it in front of her. She didn't want it to go to my head. She felt it spoiled children.

We were all born about 16 months apart, Eddie, Brian and our sister, Carole. Our parents, however, did not remain together for long. They loved each other but they didn't get along. They were both such headstrong people, and Dad could only take so much fussing. He didn't like people interfering with his life and telling him what to do. He would simply do whatever he wanted, coming and going as he pleased.

He was a very handsome man as well, and women found him extremely attractive. They had trouble keeping their distance from him and he had trouble keeping his distance from them. Finally our mother couldn't put up with his misbehaviour any longer, but with all her fussing, he left.

He went to live with his mother, our grandmother Mary, for a time, and he remarried, to a lady named Ossi. This marriage lasted around four or five years before he divorced and moved to Chicago, where he married for a fourth time.

Eddie: My first memory as a child is about my father although, unfortunately, he isn't in it. My mother, Brian and I were living on Goddard Street, in Detroit. I must have been about three years old, and I remember looking out of the window, waiting for my father to come and pick me up. He and our mother had already separated by that time, but he was supposed to be coming to see me that day.

I was crying because he was already late. I must have stood in that window all day. But he never showed up and I was very hurt. Even today, I sometimes wonder if maybe that's the reason I have

Grandmother Mary and her son, our father.

a problem with trust, particularly because my mother always said that on the occasions when our father was around, he was the parent I was most drawn to. He had such a magnetic personality! He fascinated me. He would drive around Detroit on his Harley Davidson with his motorcycle club.

Growing up, I would stay with him at his mother's, sometimes for a week or so. I enjoyed being with him, hanging out together, visiting his friends or other relatives in the evening. Or he would take me out to get a haircut (I hated that!), or to buy new shoes.

He had a way of talking and laughing that appealed to me so much, and when I grew up, I was amazed by the strength of his personality.

Brian: I don't remember much about our father, apart from the motorbike rides. He had a big Harley Davidson motorbike, and he'd come by and take us for the most hair-raising rides on the back. "Get on and hold on tight," he'd say and then zoooooom. You'd feel it in the pit of your stomach, and forget holding tight – you'd be clinging on for dear life.

Years later, we discovered that our father owed our mother a fortune in child support payments. It wasn't until he remarried that he started making regular payments, and that was only because Ossi, his wife, made certain that he did.

He would visit from time to time, and he and Evelyn obviously reconciled occasionally, because 16 months after Brian was born, our sister Carole Ann came along. Uncle James once said Dad would come round long enough to get our mother pregnant. Then he would be gone again.

So that was our family, fractured in places but still bound together by love and respect. Everyone getting by as best as we could.

These were happy times. Of course we kids got up to all manner of mischief but that's what kids do. You're learning about your surroundings, you're testing the boundaries of what is and isn't permissible, and you're trying to find your place in this world that you suddenly find yourself a part of.

Eddie: Poor Carole! She had a doll that made this crying noise. She loved that doll so much. But I wanted to find out how it worked, so I picked it up, went behind the bed and took it apart. I don't know what I expected to find, maybe a tiny baby that sat there and cried when you pressed the button. All I found was machinery. I was so disappointed, and of course Carole was in tears as well because I'd broken her favourite toy.

Brian: Most of my early memories are of Edward because he was always a problem for me. We shared a bedroom, we had bunk beds, and when I was really little, he'd do things to bother me all

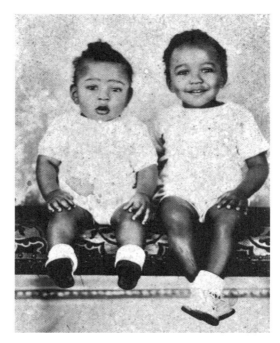

Our strong bond started early on.

the time. I was constantly running to our mother and complaining "Yay, Yed do" – I couldn't pronounce his name at the time, so he was Yed. But I suppose it's what big brothers are for, to bother you. Help you grow up.

Eddie: Brian, when he was little, would follow our mother everywhere, all around the house, even to the bathroom. So, when she closed the bathroom door and left him outside, I would creep up on him and pinch his legs.

Mother would call through the door, ask what was going on and if I'd made him cry. I would say, "No Mama, I didn't." But Brian would always tell on me. He'd say, "Yay, Yed do," which meant "Yes, Eddie did it." She thought that was so cute."

Brian: I don't remember much else about my early childhood, but I do recall listening to someone reading in the paper about all the bombing of Japan. This would have been when I was around three, and that really stuck in my mind. I didn't understand that we were at war, and had been since the year I was born. I just didn't like the fact that we were over there killing people. I was gazing up at the sky all the time, to make sure they weren't coming over to bomb us back. I was convinced that they would. I didn't realise how safe we were, that they didn't even have planes that could reach Detroit, so it was absolutely terrifying.

One memory that I suppose you could say was key, though, is of these little parties that Mama used to give, when she would wake me up to ask if I wanted to tap dance for the guests. Of course I always said yes.

Chapter Two

A Family History

In 1943, we moved again, to a house a few blocks from Grandmother Ola, on Melrose Street. Carole had arrived by now, and Mama rented out our spare rooms to a couple on condition that they would help take care of us kids while she was at work.

We remained there for about a year and a half, before we moved again, this time to 8 Mile Road in Ferndale, which is a suburb of Detroit. It was a great neighbourhood but the school system was appalling, one of the worst in the city. Consequently, our mother was growing increasingly worried about Brian's education. He would be starting school that autumn.

One day she was talking about this with Grandmother Ola. Between them they hatched a solution. Brian could go and live on Lumpkin Street with Ola and our uncle James.

Brian: That's the first house I really remember, and those were the days that I cherish because I loved her so. I even started calling my grandmother 'Mama' – if I hurt myself I would run in and say "Mama…" and she always came to my aid. I still think about her today. Someone sent me some pictures of her quite recently and I keep them in my phone, look at them now and then.

Brian around the time he moved to Lumpkin Street.

Lumpkin Street was what you'd call a blue collar neighbourhood. Most of the people living there worked in the factories. They took great pride in the way they lived. There was very little gang activity. The entire area was well maintained. The houses and the streets were clean, garbage got picked up, gardens were kept nice.

People were doing well for themselves. They weren't 'rich' by any means, but compared with other parts of the city, they were comfortable. Ola always had a car and, when it got old, if she had enough cash at hand, she'd trade it in and get a new model. With our cousins next door and the people across the street, it felt like home.

Ola and Howard had parted by now. All the while they were together, the only thing Ola wanted was for Howard to take what she regarded as a 'real job' at one of the auto plants, but he wouldn't do it, he didn't want to do it.

He did try – he worked for a time as a machine operator. But he hated every minute of it, and finally he quit. He went back to doing the things he loved doing and eventually, and inevitably, Howard and Ola parted. Apparently, the final straw came when Ola bought my mother a piano and Howard allowed it to be repossessed. There was no going back after that.

He still lived there for a time but they were in separate rooms. Divorce followed and Howard went to live with his sister a couple of streets away. We would still see him fairly regularly, though, because he would drop by to visit Ola every now and again, probably because she was such a terrific cook.

Those were strange visits. They wouldn't speak to one another. Howard would simply walk into the house, go into the kitchen, inspect whatever was cooking on the stove and help himself to a plateful. He would exchange a few words with us boys but that was it.

Or, if there wasn't any food being prepared, he would go to the store, pick up some hamburger meat and then cook it up himself. Except he didn't fry it like we thought you ought to. He would boil it in water. He was a heavyset kind of guy, and whether it was for medical reasons, or his way of trying to lose weight, he could not eat fried food. So he would boil his hamburgers. We thought that was very strange.

Brian: I attended Davison Elementary, on East Davison Street. I really don't have much to say about school, though. I wasn't street-smart, but I wasn't gullible, either. I was too busy daydreaming about being a rich boy. I wanted to be rich. When you're not from the rich side of town, you're constantly thinking, "How do I get a bit of money to do this and buy that?" So that's what I would do; I'd concentrate on daydreaming about being rich. I even renamed myself. Instead of being Brian Holland, I was Brian *Van* Holland, because people with a Van in their name, they were all wealthy.

Eddie: The years I was living on 8 Mile Road were some of the happiest of my life.

I became the local marbles champion… I still remember the day I discovered the game, I was walking home from school and

I saw some kids playing. I watched for a while, then asked one of them if he would loan me three marbles. By the time the game was finished, I not only returned the three he'd given me, I had a dozen more of my own.

Brian was now living on Lumpkin with Ola and I missed him so badly. Of course Carole was around, but I was never as close to her when we were kids as I was with Brian. I still enjoyed myself, but our mother was also growing concerned that her sons might be growing apart. So finally she suggested that I go to live with Ola as well. And that is how I came to enter a world that was as far removed as it possibly could be from the happy-go-lucky life I'd grown accustomed to.

Grandmother Ola was as strict as any teacher. Part of it, where we were concerned, was due to the fact that our father was still not paying child support. It meant Ola had to take over as the head of the family, looking after our mother and looking after us.

Eddie, Carole and Brian.

She was our grandmother after all and, in those days, that was a very special relationship. She knew more, she'd lived more, she understood more. Naturally, everybody went to her for advice and support. She was an older lady from the south, opinionated and fair-minded at the same time. The way she raised her children and grandchildren was exactly the same way her parents had raised her. She wouldn't take any back-talk from any of us.

Ola was really clever, as well. She wanted to protect us and keep us out of trouble. We were in a good area but we were still close to those parts of town where kids were brought up differently, to put it politely, and she didn't want that for us.

It was Ola who taught us the foundations of what became our personal principles. She was independent and proud. For example, if our clothes had holes in them, we wouldn't wear them and she wouldn't force us to. A lot of kids we knew couldn't say that. But she kept us looking presentable at all times.

We had all the clothes in the world. All the food in the world. Ola had more food than you could imagine and, again, not everyone in our neighbourhood was like that. But she made sure that we never went hungry. In fact, one of Ola's strictest rules was that we were forbidden ever to eat at somebody else's house. "I have food here," she'd tell us, "and more than enough for both of you. You don't need to be taking other people's food when you have plenty here at home."

Eddie: The only exception to that rule was Grandmother Mary. Although Ola cooked lavish meals every day, there were times when she cooked something I didn't like. So, I'd ask if I could go to visit Grandmother Mary, because she would cook me whatever I wanted. My favourite meal was breakfast, and Grandmother Mary would make it for me whatever time of day it was!

We were not spoiled, but we didn't go without the things we wanted. For example, for a long time there was no television in the house, so whenever we wanted to watch a particular programme – our favourite shows were things like *Gunsmoke* and *Perry Mason* – we'd go next door to our cousins' house and watch it there. They didn't mind. Both families were in and out of one another's homes all the time. But the idea of us going to somebody else's house simply to watch television for hours on end struck Ola as somehow disrespectful, even though she understood why we did it.

It bothered her for a while. On the one hand, a television was an extravagance. Although there were two pay cheques coming into the house every week from Ola and James, neither of them cared for what they considered frivolous purchases.

But, on the other hand, she could see that we enjoyed watching it. Finally, she made a decision. One Saturday, she told Uncle James to go down to the store and buy the biggest television he could afford.

Eddie: I went with him. The one he decided upon was enormous, a 25-inch screen. I'd never seen one that big – at that time, a 16-inch screen was considered luxurious. Aunt Dorothy's television had a 6-inch screen! But James bought it, we set it up and that meant we could watch TV at our own house (and invite our cousins over as well!), and Grandmother Ola could keep an eye on us at the same time.

So yes, we got a lot of pampering and a lot of attention. But Ola and James also taught us very strict rules about the difference between right and wrong.

Eddie: I was walking home from school one day and I found this beautiful toy truck. It was right on the corner, lying there all shiny and colourful, so I picked it up and took it home. Grandmother looked at it and asked me where I got it.

"I found it on the street."

"Well, you go put it back exactly where you found it."

And I did. I didn't like the idea, because I knew the next person along would pick it up and take it for themselves, but I did it.

* * *

Ola could be hard on us, but she was never strict for the sake of it. She was bringing us up to be disciplined in our thinking, but crucially, she would never interfere with what we were actually thinking. For example, she knew we were listening to secular music, and singing it as well. But she didn't interfere, even though she didn't like it.

She did have her ground rules, though. No profanity. No slang. If we said 'kids' when we were talking about other children, or called somebody a liar, she didn't like that. It was disrespectful.

She used to give us chores, dusting the tables and the ornaments, cleaning the windows, you name it. She had us washing the dishes, sweeping and mopping the floors. Every Saturday, we'd have to clean all the wooden baseboards. She was out all day working, so of course she didn't want to come home and have to clean her home as well. We had to participate. One of her favourite expressions, and most fervent beliefs, was "An idle mind is the devil's workshop".

Eddie: I didn't like doing the ironing, and I remember telling her that when I was about thirteen years old. How I'd rather do almost *anything* other than ironing the clothes.

She replied, "You're going to have to learn to iron your own clothes at some point," and I said, "Never." She just laughed and said, "You wait…"

All of this was good, though, because we learned, very early on, that if you have a job to do, you do it well. At times we'd be doing our chores and Ola would come up behind one or other of us and say, "No, no, no, you have to do it over," and we would, because we knew we wouldn't be allowed to go out to play until she was happy.

Besides, she had no hesitation about letting us know if we hadn't done what we were supposed to do, or if we hadn't done it to her satisfaction. If we disobeyed her, she'd have us go out into the front yard and collect some switches – thin, flexible branches from a bush. We'd have to clean them off, take off all the leaves and twigs, and bring them inside to her.

She'd look them over, run her fingers down the switch to make certain it was to her satisfaction and give it a couple of practice swishes through the air. Then she would whack us a few times. Not too many, just enough to remind us that we had to pay attention to what she said. But it kept us on our toes. It let us know that we had to get up in the morning, go to school and when we got back from school, we had a choice. We could either clean the house or we could clean the switch.

Brian: I'd clean the glasses to the point that if I saw a single smear, I'd put them back in and wash them again.

Eddie: I remember when I was thirteen I heard Ola tell my mother, "Edward is too old to spank. He's at the age now when you can talk to him and reason with him." And that was music to my ears! But until then…

The switch was not the worst punishment we could face. Even more terrifying was Uncle James's shaving strap, the leather belt he'd sharpen his razor on. That thing was mean.

We didn't get it very often. Usually, whatever the problem was, Ola would sort it out herself. But sometimes, she figured we needed a stronger reminder, so she would sit us down and make us wait until James came home from work.

Uncle James was a strong guy. Even waiting for him was terrifying. But then he'd walk through the door and Ola would tell him what was going on, what we had done to deserve our punishment.

He would look us up and down, and then speak. "Okay," he'd say, "come into the back room and pull down your pants. I don't want no pants." Then he'd trap your head between his legs, with his arm around your butt, and pick up his belt. That was the worst. It only lasted for about 10 seconds but it felt like an eternity.

Brian: It was awful, but it taught me, "Brian, you'd better not do nothing wrong. You'd better stay on the straight and narrow."

Even when I was older, all my friends would be smoking, drinking, hanging out at the pool hall, but not me. I told myself, "I'm staying away from all that. I'll do anything I wanna do, but I don't want to get caught up in that."

One thing I never did, though. I never cried before I got the whupping. I would cry during the whupping and after the whupping, but when they said, "You're going to get a spanking today," I'd never cry. What was the point? I'd do enough of that when he hit me. Don't rain before the storm.

As a rule, we were treated equally. If there were treats to be handed out, both of us would receive them, and it was the same with our chores and the same with our punishments. However, there was one area where there definitely was an imbalance.

Eddie: I always thought Ola disciplined me a little harder than she did Brian, and that was because she felt that the eldest should have more responsibility. Uncle James felt the same way and so did our mother. During those years when we were living with Ola, our mother would come to visit and she'd take me to one side and say, "Baby, you know you're going to have to look out for your brother, because Brian is not going to look out for himself."

That made a big impression on me, not only at the time but in the future, too. It explains a lot about what happened later, when our dispute with Motown blew up, but it also explains why we were, and remain, such a good team.

At the time, of course, I didn't want to know, I didn't want to hear it. It was so unfair. Why should I have to take responsibility for Brian? Why couldn't he take it for himself? I used to get really annoyed about it. It felt as though I was being held to a completely different set of standards and, of course, I was. But even then, I knew why our mother said that, and why Ola and James spent so much time and energy reinforcing it. Because I was the big brother, and what do big brothers do? They look out for the younger one.

There were definitely occasions when we'd do something wrong, both Brian and I, but I was the one who got punished for it. I'd ask why and they would explain – very patiently, because I asked that question a lot – that Brian followed my lead. I was his big brother, which meant he would do what I did and learn from what I taught him.

So I had to behave well for both of us, even though there were only 16 months between us. He and I thought in different ways, our attention spans were different, our attitudes towards other people were different. Ola and James understood that long before I did, and although I still didn't think it was fair, I sensed that they were doing it for a reason so I dealt with it. In fact, I was proud of it.

There was one occasion, however, when the roles were completely reversed.

Brian: I always looked up to Edward as the older brother, as the protector, really. We were so close – we've always had a symbiotic feeling towards one other. If he feels pain, I'm gonna feel it too, in a certain kind of way.

What bothers him bothers me too. And vice versa. There was one time when Edward got into a fight with some kids at school, and told me, "Man, don't you go to school today." He wanted to protect me and keep me from getting in trouble, because he knew I'd say something to them. He said, "Let them deal with me."

Sometimes, though, I would protect him too. Like the time I kept him from getting a beating from Ola.

Eddie: I remember that day so well. I was talking with Grandmother and even when I was a kid, I was always very opinionated and I spoke my mind. Ola said something that I disagreed with; she criticised me for doing something, when I'd seen her do the exact same thing. So I asked why it was all right for her and not for me. She replied that it was different because she was grown. To which I responded, "Being grown does not make it right. Being grown doesn't make it right at all."

She got so mad, as angry as I'd ever seen her. She grabbed a belt and, as I walked away, she roared, "I'm gonna kill him!" And then she came after me – oooh, she was sizzling!

Brian: I'd been watching them go at it, and the moment Ola snapped, I stepped in between them. She was so mad! She shouted at me, "Brian get out of the way this instant. Do it!"

But I stood my ground. I wasn't going to move, not for anything on Earth, because I couldn't stand to see Eddie get hit. So Ola took the belt and whup! She hit me across the arm as hard as she could.

I didn't cry out. I took it.

Eddie: Ola looked at him, watched him for a moment or so. Then she lowered the belt and walked away. I was so relieved because, if she'd gotten hold of me, she would have whupped me to death. I'd still be laying on that floor today. I didn't express myself again until I turned sixteen. That's when my attitude changed; I didn't feel like a little kid any more.

Chapter Three

Boys Will Be Boys

Eddie: The worst question anybody can ask me is, "What were your influences?" Not because I can't answer it, but because it's never the answer they want to hear.

They're expecting me to name songwriters, Rodgers and Hammerstein, Burt Bacharach, Lennon and McCartney, whoever. But the truth is, it's none of them. I appreciate them, I respect them, and I love what they did and the songs they wrote.

But the people who truly influenced me, who made me what I became and the person I am today, weren't for the most part they songwriters or musicians or anything to do with the music industry. It was family, and not only direct blood relations. You often hear people say that "it takes a village to raise a kid", and that is exactly what happened to me.

Although we saw our mother regularly and our father occasionally, so far as we were concerned, our true parents were Ola and James. They were the ones who raised us, they were the ones who taught us right from wrong. And they were the ones who the neighbours would report to if either of us stepped out of line.

For instance. Walking down the street together, nobody in sight. One of us swears, or takes the Lord's name in vain. It didn't matter where we were on the street – we could be five houses down, we could be two streets across. Neighbours, neighbours of neighbours, they all knew who we were, and it didn't matter that we didn't know who they were. There wasn't a thing we could get away with without Ola hearing about it, and usually before we had even returned home.

We'd walk in the front door and Ola would be standing there waiting, and you could tell from the look in her eye that something new had displeased her. Or, occasionally, had delighted her. The neighbours passed on good reports, as well.

It was a strange feeling, knowing that wherever you went there were eyes focused on you, a vast underground network of twitching curtains, surreptitious glances, muttered conversations and furtive phone calls. You would never have guessed that behind that beautiful rose bush, a neighbour lurked.

The most dangerous places, however, were people's porches.

Porches were the nerve centre of Grandmother's spy ring. Every house had one and every family used it, whether it was a grand screened-in affair or simply a rickety platform occupied by a couple of old chairs. There they'd sit, passing the day away, and all the time they'd be watching, watching.

You hear a lot these days about how neighbourhoods no longer have a sense of community; how people can live in the same house for years and never once say hello to the family two doors away. The loss of porches is a big part of that, at least in African-American areas. Yes, people have decks out behind the house, but that's the key thing – they're behind the house. Porches faced the street. You would sit there and hail your neighbours as they passed by, or they'd cross your yard to say hello to you. And there were eyes on everything all the time.

Porches fostered friendship but, more than that, they created community. The village that raised a kid.

Eddie: One night, walking down the street, humming songs, as Brian and I often did, I uttered a curse word. From behind the rose bushes I heard a voice that said, "Does Mrs Everett know you talk like that?"

I glanced towards the porch for a person that I never did see, and answered, "No, Ma'm." I was so startled. I was so afraid that she would tell my grandmother.

When I got back home, Grandmother never said anything to me or Brian. But all I could think was, "I will never say another curse word ever again."

For many years I never did.

Being allowed out on the street was a relatively late development for us. For a long time, Ola forbade us to even leave the house once we arrived home from school, not until she returned from work. So that's what we did. We stayed indoors.

She relaxed slowly. As we grew a little older, she'd say, "You can go out on the porch." A little bit older than that, we'd be allowed to play in front of the house but we couldn't leave the yard. The day we were given permission to go out onto the street, all the way down to the corner, that was a really big deal.

A lot of kids our age were going down to this place called the Center, where everyone would gather. There were basketball courts and pool tables, things like that. But we couldn't visit those places, and even when we were older, they weren't places we felt any inclination to frequent. Ola was programming us, teaching us a certain kind of discipline.

Besides, we had a lot of friends. Next door to us were our cousins, but we had so many relatives in the neighbourhood, and they knew all about us long before we went to live at Ola's. And, of course, there were friends from school. But we also discovered one of the dynamics that has balanced our relationship ever since.

Eddie: Brian was the one who had a lot of friends. He was always much more outgoing than I was, and much friendlier. I didn't like having many people around me, I didn't feel comfortable. My feeling was, you go your way and I'll go mine.

The kids in the church, for instance. I got to know them but they weren't what I called friends. We socialised at church picnics and stuff like that, but then we'd say goodbye and I wouldn't see them until the next time some function brought us together.

But I amused myself. My cousin, George Smith, lived next door, and I'd go over to his house or he'd come over to ours and we'd play little games together. Or we'd join in with his sisters playing hopscotch. It's a girl's game, but I was watching them one day and they were having so much fun that I joined in.

Then there were the kids across the street, the Bridges. We'd play things like tag, running down the street or hitting a ball with something.

But there was never any temptation to get into trouble, because I didn't want to disappoint my grandmother and my uncle. It was very important to me how they regarded me, and I didn't want to do anything to bring shame on them, or upon myself.

When I was about eight or nine I started walking to school with a bunch of other kids who used to run into this one store and steal cakes. Now, I loved cakes, and it looked so easy that I was really, really tempted to do the same thing. I wanted those cakes so badly. But it kept flashing through my mind, if I was caught, or if my family heard that I was doing something like that, it would utterly crush them. I would humiliate them and, no less importantly, I would humiliate myself.

Ola was our biggest influence when we were children. As we developed into teenagers, however, Uncle James took over in a lot of ways.

Eddie: Uncle James was tough but he was also very smart. One thing he said that really struck home was, "Whatever you do, whatever is in the streets will still be there when you finish school."

He wanted me to learn from the mistakes he'd made when he was my age. He was a very bright man but he had never fulfilled his potential. He worked at Ford like everybody else, and it was only now, when he was older, that he was able to branch out. He was studying architecture at Lawrence Tech, which is something he should have done years before. He had been good in school. But he was more interested in clothes, music, shoes, the things in the street, and that was a major mistake.

The other thing he told me, when I was around thirteen or fourteen, that made an impression was, "You have all these girls chasing you now but, one day, you're going to ask those girls out on a date and they're going to say, 'Oh Edward, I would love to go out with you, but right now I'm seeing Doctor so-and-so, or Lawyer so-and-so,' someone who's making a lot of money." James said whatever you do, get your education. That gave me a lot to strive towards.

It was Uncle James who showed me how to organise things in my mind. He taught me that you didn't have to know everything about something, so long as you knew enough to be able to explain it. Get a feel for something and be able to build on that. It might not always be the accepted way of doing something, but if it worked, then it worked. You didn't need to master everything – like he said, that is what experts are for. But in order to be able to rely on the experts, you had to have a feel for what you were doing.

He would loan me books to read, things like Socrates, Plato and Aristotle, the great Greek philosophers. As a rule, I didn't care for what I considered history, and the African-American in me may have had something to do with it. The stuff in the history books, it wasn't my world, it wasn't my people. I wanted to understand the world *I* was in, not the one that other people had been in. I learned more from my grandparents than I did from history books because they *were* my history.

But those old philosophers weren't history. They were talking about humanity and life itself, and those things are timeless. I know I didn't fully understand them. But I had a feel for what they were saying, and I learned enough to be able to hone in on certain things as I grew older.

That wasn't all I read, of course. When I was a little younger, I loved the magazines where they would take stories from literature and put them in comic book form. I'd read those. And *Tales from the Crypt*. I'd wait until it was dark and I went to bed, and I'd read them then. For some reason, I didn't enjoy them during the daytime.

I also went through an Al Capone phase, darkly fascinated by the violence but intrigued, too, by the glamour that hung – and still hangs – around his name. How public opinion often rates a man not by what he actually does but by what he represents, be it power, money or plain bravado, the ability to brazen one's way out of any situation no matter how hopeless it might appear.

They were not qualities I envied. But I fervently wanted to understand them, and that quest seemed to dovetail exquisitely with the books my uncle gave me.

He would always talk to me about school and learning, about life and people, but like Ola, he never really pressured me about anything, except that I should always do what was right. So long as I walked the line, there was not a lot of pressure. They trusted me to do the right thing, because that was how they brought me up.

As long as I was responsible, and I was looking after Brian – I asked my uncle once, "Why do you never tell Brian all this stuff?" He said, "Because you have to be the one. You're the oldest, and you've got to be responsible.' And I've felt that way ever since.

That's why, if there's one thing I've always believed, it's that no man can ever be what you'd call a 'self-made man'. I know there are people who like to say that's what they are, and some very successful and powerful people, as well.

But I disagree. Everybody is a product of their environment and, more than that, they're a product of all the people around them, the good ones and the bad ones, and the standards to which those people held them.

No way in the world was I self-made. My family played a part in my development, our neighbours played a part, my teachers played a part. A little later, Berry Gordy played a part. All the things that shaped and moulded me at a very young age, they are what made me. They are my influences, and they are Brian's as well.

Ola's most inviolable law was that we should always go to church. Our mother was a very devout Christian, and that's the way we were brought up from the start. Ola, however, reinforced it.

We attended Davison Avenue Baptist Church, a short walk from the house, a couple of times during the week and twice on Sundays. Our grandfather Howard and a couple of his friends had started the church, and it was certainly the most important thing in Ola's life. Of course, she expected it to be the most important thing in ours as well.

It wasn't, but that didn't mean we could treat it with anything less than the utmost respect.

Brian: That church was such a big thing in our neighbourhood. I don't want to say people worshipped it, because of course that's what they did, but they worshipped the very act of going to church, too. It was the only thing that mattered.

Ola introduced us to this new routine gently.

Eddie: I went to Sunday school long before I understood what it was. In fact, the first time Grandmother mentioned it, I thought she was mistaken. "You don't go to school on a Sunday," I told her, but she shook her head. She said, "No, this is *Sunday* school," and I didn't understand it at all. I was five years old at the time.

Very soon, however, we were deemed ready for 'the real thing'.

Every Sunday morning, we would have to get up, wash and get dressed, and then put on a suit and tie. We had a special Sunday suit and special Sunday shoes, separate from our everyday ones. We'd put on our Sunday outfit, go to church, and when we got home, we'd be sent to take it off and then in the evening we'd have to put it all back on again for the next service.

The services weren't short, either. The first one would start around 10 in the morning and we'd be there until something like 3 in the afternoon. Then we'd be back there at 5 and that would last until around 8. It was endless.

Brian: You want to talk about something boring? I couldn't wait to get out, and then as soon as I did, it was time to go back again. I did a lot of daydreaming in church, even if it was only about getting out and going to play somewhere.

It was torture. You'd be there and you'd have to be quiet as a mouse – don't sneeze, don't laugh, don't make a sound, don't fidget, and the moment you are told all the things that you cannot do, that's all you want to do. And if you did do something wrong, like whisper "I want to get out of here" to your brother, somebody – you might not even know them – would pinch you. Hard.

Brian, our cousin James Dean, our sister Carole and Eddie on Lumpkin Street.

Eddie: I enjoyed church! I was around my cousins and my friends, and we would be in the choir, go out on the Sunday school programmes together... they kept us relatively busy and we were together, and that was important.

At Christmas, we had to recite poems in front of the congregation and I was pretty good at remembering those poems. Grandmother would give Brian four or five lines to learn but I'd take four or five verses, because I could remember stuff like that really well. That may have been my moment.

It was music that was the church's greatest attraction, though.

Brian: Beginning when I was about seven, I would follow Ola to church, where she attended choir practice and I would watch the lady who was playing the piano. I'd watch her hit the keys. I'd say, "Well, how is she gonna play the white keys versus the black keys?" I was very curious about that.

Then, after everybody left, I would go up to the piano and start playing. I would play the black keys and then I'd play the white keys. I quickly learned how to differentiate between them, and I even learned how to play this one song that Edward and I would sing all the time, '(He's So) Wonderful', which Sam Cooke recorded early on with The Soul Stirrers. I really loved that song.

We had always been surrounded by music. Our mother, Evelyn, liked to sing. One night, Ola even woke us up so we could listen to her on the radio; the church that she attended was having one of its services broadcast live, and mother was one of the featured soloists.

Eddie: I was so inspired by hearing her that I immediately joined the school choir. There's no doubt in my mind that Brian inherited his musical abilities from our grandfather. That was where he got his natural ear for music. Just like I got my voice from our mother.

*   *   *

Our love of music, however, probably came from Uncle James. He couldn't play a note, but he knew more about music, both history and technique, than anyone we have ever met. He was also a devout record collector.

He bought everything, all kinds of records. Count Basie, Bing Crosby, Nat King Cole, Ella Fitzgerald, Frank Sinatra, Sarah Vaughan, Dinah Washington – you name them, he had them. He didn't care if they were black, white, Mexican, German, whatever. If they were hit records, he had them. He didn't care about genres, either. True, he didn't particularly like R&B, but everything else, he adored. Pop, jazz, big band, show tunes, anything – and that's where we learned our music.

He loved pop. Once we started writing songs of our own, that was what we were drawing on, that pop mentality. We weren't aiming for any genre or market; we didn't care about that. That attitude was 100 per cent Uncle James's doing.

There's no question about it, it was one heck of a collection and it would remain with us forever, and the greatest thing about it was, he was happy to let us play the records when he wasn't around.

Uncle James.

He wanted us to love music as much as he did. His only instruction was, whatever records we played, we had to return them to the correct sleeve when we were finished or else there would be hell to pay.

Every once in a while, one would get broken – these were the old shellac 78s, and they were so fragile that it really didn't take much for one to have an accident. Particularly if two boys happened to be wrestling on the floor, close by a carelessly placed disc.

"What happened to this record?" James would ask, and we'd be, "Oh, we don't know." And very often, we'd be telling the truth. We didn't know. Sometimes, all you had to do was look at a disc and it would shatter. Or, at least, that's how it felt to us.

Uncle James's music taught us what we liked and school filled in the gaps.

Brian: Apart from becoming rich, my other favourite daydream was music. I'd be sitting in class and they'd hand out the assignments, and I'd half do them. I'd get a B or C. Mathematics, I was pretty good at; I could always add and subtract, divide, I was good at that. But when it came to English – aah, I didn't learn.

Instead, I'd be tapping rhythms out on my desk.

The teacher, Mrs Platt, would come over and ask, "What are you doing?"

"Oh, nothing."

"Well stop it."

Then after a couple of these exchanges, she'd tell me to hold out my hand. "You're doing wrong" – and BAM! She'd hit my hand with a ruler. BAM! And if you snatched at the ruler and tried to hold it, she'd turn your hand over and hit you on the knuckles even harder. BAM!

Davison School had an excellent music programme, probably because it was so integrated. Statistically, it didn't look it – it was about 70 per cent white, 30 per cent African-American. But that 70 per cent was made up of a lot of different nationalities – Ukrainian, Polish, Italian,

Irish, all of whom would sing different songs or put on different plays. The whole time we were there, we had music teachers showing us new things, new songs, and it was so inspirational.

Eddie: I was open to everything, but the music that most penetrated my mind was gospel and pop. People would play the blues but I didn't like it at all, so it was gospel and pop. Even the little ditty songs they'd teach when I was tiny, songs about the merry-go-round and the wheels on the bus, I can remember them all now. They've never left my mind.

Brian: I never had formal piano lessons, I learned to play by ear. I did have vocal lessons at school but not to any great degree. I had enough to say I liked music, and I loved the chorale that we had every year at Christmas. They'd give you robes and a candle, and you'd go down all the corridors, singing Christmas songs. And you'd get out of class, which made it all even more exciting.

I think what made the biggest impact on me were the classical music concerts we went to at elementary school. Strings and violins. I was so impressed. I loved the bells and the oboes and the bassoons and the timpani. That was the most unbelievable sound. When I walked out of there, it was like heaven. It had an indelible effect on me, the whole time I was writing.

I did try to learn other instruments but they're bad memories. I tried to play every instrument I could and teachers constantly knocked me down. I tried the violin; I tried the cello one time; I tried the drums… oh, I made so much noise on the drums that people around the neighbourhood complained.

I even tried the French horn, which I loved. But my music teacher said, "Well man, you are never gonna be able to play the French horn."

I said, "Why not?"

He said, "Your lips are too big!"

That put me off completely, so I tried the tuba because I thought that might be better. But I didn't like the sound of it. I do have the rudiments for some of them, the drums more than any of them and the piano more than that, but I'm not good.

Eddie: I never had Brian's musical talent, but when it came to singing, I was good at that. I remember one day the music teacher heard my voice; he looked at me and said, "Boy, you have such a beautiful natural tone in your voice, but you can't help it. You inherited those tones from somebody in your family." He asked me whether anyone else in the family could sing. Of course I told him about our mother.

Like our grandfather, she never benefited from her talents, materially anyway, but she didn't really want to. Howard was happy playing around on the piano, Mother was happy singing in church.

But sometimes I'd be talking to Uncle James about singing, showing him what I could do, and he'd stop me and tell me where I was going wrong, or if there were other things that I should be doing. He knew this stuff. He didn't use it for himself but he handed it to me. He taught me about rhythm, he taught me about tone. And I'd practise the things he told me.

Things which Brian seemed determined to undo.

Brian and I were singing together in the church choir by now. He was around twelve years old, and already he was hearing music in a very different way to the rest of us. For example, when he was singing, he would always change the harmonies to fifths and sevenths. It would be completely off note to what was being sung, and I would constantly elbow him, trying to make him stop. It was going to get us into trouble. "Stop doing that," I'd hiss.

He would stop for a moment but then he'd start right up again. Later he told me it was because he loved the sound of the chord, and I suppose other people must have as well. He certainly never got into trouble for doing it.

Those moments, I later realised, were the precursor to Brian's destiny. The stars had started to align.

Chapter Four

Music Music Music

If you were at all interested in music, the mid-1950s were an incredible time to be growing up, especially if you had an Uncle James, forever bringing new records home.

The first half of the decade was dominated by pop, show tunes and novelty songs, and we devoured them all. But, beginning around 1955, other sounds started to creep in – what the white disc jockeys referred to as 'rock'n'roll' but which we thought of as another kind of pop. It just had a harder edge.

There was no way Kitty Kallen would ever sing a song like 'Heartbreak Hotel'. No way Frank Sinatra would ever croon 'Be-Bop-A-Lula'. True, Pat Boone did cover 'Tutti Frutti', and that's the way it had always been. When black records (or 'race music', as it was known at the time) reached a certain level of popularity, the industry would get white people to cover them.

Now, however, the radio played Little Richard's original almost as often as it played Pat Boone's cover, and there was a lesson there for us, whether we understood it or not: there is a difference between a singer who simply sings a song and one who lives it. It might not be apparent in pure musical terms – in fact, very few people could argue that Pat Boone's records were not played, sung and recorded with far more finesse and precision than Little Richard's. But sometimes, those qualities are not the ones that matter.

The performance itself speaks far louder than any of them, and that, to us, was the most important ingredient. Little Richard performed, and suddenly we noticed that there were a lot more performers on the radio.

You had always heard music on the street, playing in stores, filtering out of bars, coming out of automobiles as they motored by, the radio blaring through open windows. But now you found yourself listening to it, and reacting to it as well.

We started experimenting with the radio at home, spinning the dial to see where it ended up, and there were a lot of stations to choose from, not only broadcasting out of Detroit and its environs but from across the lake in Canada, too. You never knew what you would hear. Yes, there were a lot that we would quickly move away from, the non-stop chat, sports or religious stations. There were foreign language stations for the different European communities that had made Detroit their home, and stations that focused exclusively on jazz and old-time music.

But there was also WCHB, Michigan's first African-American-owned station, pounding out a non-stop diet of R&B on 1440 AM, and that became the dominant sound, whether in our home or elsewhere, as we visited friends or walked around the neighbourhood.

Names we had scarcely heard of in the past, people like Hank Ballard and James Brown, suddenly they were everywhere. Jackie Wilson was another one – he sang for Billy Ward & His Dominoes at the time, although we also knew him as a cousin of Uncle James's wife, Helen (they married in 1950). We'd never met him, but we'd hear about him every now and then, and suddenly we were hearing him everywhere.

Eddie: Somebody else I really liked was Little Willie John, because he was someone I actually knew well. He was a couple of years older than me and he lived not too far from us. I used to run into him on his way to Cleveland Intermediate School when I was going there. He was a mischievous kid. I would be walking down the street with my cousin, George Smith, and Willie would come running past and knock the books out of his hand.

He also carried two knives, fishtail knives, and he would make these noises and you knew to get out of the way, because that was a warning that he was about to throw one of the knives. He would aim the first one at George's lunch. George would leap back and then the moment he'd reach for his food again, Willie would throw the other one.

He was also dating a girl across the street on Lumpkin, so I would see him there, too.

I knew what a great singer he was. He was always singing in the auditorium, school talent shows, things like that. He was such a creative, gifted singer, he truly was. Technically, he was a better singer even than Jackie Wilson, and he had a better ear for music as well.

Levi Stubbs, who went on to join The Four Tops, was really good friends with Willie, and when we worked with Willie's sister, Mable, a few years later, she told us how the two of them would often enter the same local talent contests.

Each time Willie would win, until finally he suggested that he and Levi should never enter the same contests because Levi would always come in second. This way, they could both become first-placed winners.

Eddie: Nobody was surprised when Willie got the deal with King Records, or that Johnny Otis was such a big fan of his. I was very impressed, though. At fourteen years of age, it was almost as though he'd lived 20 years ahead of himself.

Suddenly, R&B was getting onto the pop charts. Rock'n'roll had knocked down a lot of the old racial barriers, and you started hearing all these people on the radio that would never have been played before. Clyde McPhatter & The Drifters, Billy Ward & His Dominoes… and, of course, The Coasters, who were the biggest of them all. In fact, our brother-in-law, Carole's husband, Johnny Terry, later (in 1963–1965) sang with The Drifters, so we always had a lot of affection for them.

Eddie: I remember the first time I ever heard Johnny's voice. I was in the car with Berry, Mabel John, who was Little Willie's sister, and Robert Bateman, on our way somewhere, and 'There Goes My Baby' came over the radio. The car went silent. I had never heard a record like that before, or a voice like that, either.

Detroit itself was alive with music, hundreds of bands and dozens of record labels, rising and falling so fast that many of them barely even played a show or released a record before everybody involved had moved on. But so many of the names who would later shape the scene of the sixties, at Motown and elsewhere too, got their start during these turbulent years, and some of the most exciting performers that we ever saw, as well.

Eddie: All across Detroit at that time, different movie theatres would stage shows featuring local artists, both amateur and professional. The groups would tour the city and play these shows, and it was so entertaining.

Of course I saw Little Willie John many times. Ike & Tina Turner at the Park Theater, that was the first time I saw them. The Turbans, Stanley Mitchell & The Tornados – they were a great group. That's where I met William Weatherspoon, who later came to Motown. He wrote 'What Becomes Of The Brokenhearted' with our cousin, James Dean, and after we left the label, he joined us at Invictus.

There was The Diablos, who were probably the most popular band at that time, and The Royal Jokers, with Willie Jones. Out of all the amateurs at that time, I thought he was the best singer in the city; he had a voice very similar to Clyde McPhatter's, but Willie's was better. And Albert Hamilton, who had so much promise as a singer, and started recording under the name Al Kent. His brother, Bobby, was also very musical; he could arrange, he could write... Jackie Wilson's 'Am I The Man' was one of Bobby's.

Brian: We were developing our own musical tastes and they were all over the place. I could sing R&B songs as a teenager. Listening to Clyde McPhatter, The Drifters, people like that, was fun. All my friends had the records and they danced to them. I loved listening to The Flamingos, The Soul Stirrers, all the spiritual groups... and the greatest singer of them all, Ira Tucker of The Dixie Hummingbirds. They were a gospel group; they'd been around since the 1920s, but almost every singer who you wanted to listen to, everyone from Jackie Wilson to James Brown, took something from them.

Black music in the fifties would have been completely different without The Hummingbirds, and they were still having an impact in the 1970s. Paul Simon recorded 'Loves Me Like A Rock' with them, and Lynda Laurence, who was in one of the later Supremes line-ups, was Ira's daughter. But nobody could sing like Ira.

Eddie was more into things like Jackie Wilson and Little Willie John. But he was also listening to Mario Lanza and Enrico Caruso, and developing his vocal technique from them, the way they could hold a note, or squeeze that extra ounce of emotion into a lyric that nobody else could have managed.

As far as pop music was concerned, for me, Nat King Cole was the greatest thing ever, and I don't care what anybody says. People look back now and they say he wasn't as great as Sinatra, but Frank couldn't hold a candle to Nat King Cole. That guy had hit after hit after hit, and even when he had the hit A-side, they'd turn it over and he'd have the hit B-side as well. He was the greatest thing ever. I listen to him all the time.

Sam Cooke was a fantastic singer, and I really liked Johnny Mathis. I always thought of him in the same light as Nat King Cole, although Nat was so much smoother. But Johnny was good, and also, he was managed by a woman, which was really unusual at that time, a white woman – which was great for him because she could take him into places that a black man couldn't ordinarily go. In fact, when he first started, we always thought he was white.

We started noticing something else. There were groups forming all around the neighbourhood, doo-wop harmony groups who would meet up on the street, on the corner, on the porch, wherever they could, and they'd stand there and sing.

Some were good, some less so. You'd be out walking and every so often you'd see a police car pull up alongside a group. The officers would sit and listen to them for a few minutes. If they liked what they heard, they'd drive away. But if they didn't, they'd tell the kids to break it up and then watch as they dispersed – usually towards another street corner, where they'd carry on singing. Other times, the neighbours would chase groups away because they were singing too loud.

But it looked like so much fun, and soon we were singing with them.

Brian: I sang a lot of church music at first. We had a little church group, me and a couple of guys I knew. We did a few shows entertaining the people, singing spiritual songs and R&B. And I had another group a little later on, we'd do R&B songs, the big hits, so by the time I was fifteen or sixteen, I was doing a lot of singing.

Eddie: Brian learned quickly how to do all the harmonies, and that amazed me. It totally baffled me, how and where he learned it.

One of our cousins, John Roberts Thorton, was putting a group together, and he asked Brian and I to join. That's when it really became noticeable to me that Brian's ear was better than everybody else's.

John could hear the music really well also, and he would teach us the harmonies. But what I realised very quickly was, John would always have to give me my note twice, because all I was doing was going by memory. But Brian didn't have to be taught twice. When the chord changed, Brian would automatically change with it.

I also saw that John kept looking at Brian – he always had sort of shifty eyes anyway, but this was really noticeable. He'd look over at Brian, and then he would look at me and say, "Brian really knows what he's doing."

On another occasion, there was an older vocal group in the area, guys who were around seventeen, so they were three, four years older than us. They were really having trouble with their harmonies, so I told them my brother could help them out.

"How old is your brother?" they asked.

"He's fourteen."

"No way. You don't know what you're talkin' about." But I knew Brian could do it.

For the next two or three years, we would be out there singing on street corners. We had different groups, people would come and go, names would change. One group was The Quailtones, with our friends Sonny Sanders and Freddie Gorman – they even cut a record on Josie Records, 'Tears Of Love', although we weren't there for that.

Brian: Another group was The Fideletones, with Sonny and Freddie again, and a guy named Bosco. He had the lowest voice you've ever heard. It was so bassy! I used to have a lot of fun thinking about it, what we could do with it, which songs would allow him to really let rip.

I wasn't the lead singer, though. I sang one song, a Brook Benton number. We actually recorded a single for the Aladdin label, 'Pretty Girl', but I don't think it was ever released.

None of this was what you would call serious. We didn't sit around dreaming that we'd be discovered and whisked off to stardom. It was for our own entertainment, hanging out on the corner, messing around. It was a lot of fun.

Our favourite corner was at Lumpkin and Modern, by Miss Pippins' grocery store, probably because the store sold ice cream, cookies and candy. We'd sing, we'd snack, we'd sing some more. It was a great time.

Another corner that we enjoyed singing on was just down the street from a gentleman named Mr Eugene Humphrey. I remember him well because, if we were singing too loud, he would actually get up from his bed and run down the street. "Eddie, Brian," he'd yell. "You guys can sing but please sing lower. I can't get to sleep and I have to go to work in the morning." We would scatter and find another corner to sing on. It was, after all, 10 or 11 o'clock at night!

Unfortunately, it was also time for one of us, at least, to start thinking about a future beyond such distractions.

Eddie: I never really knew what I was going to do once I graduated high school, but I knew what I *wasn't* going to do.

I couldn't have been more than nine, maybe ten or eleven years old, and I used to sit on the porch watching our neighbours as they came home from the factory. They would be dragging themselves along, literally looking as though they could barely take the next step. I'd be wondering how they were even going to make it the last few feet home.

That started me thinking. I didn't know what I was going to do when I grew up, because I was still a kid. But the more I thought about it, and the more I watched our neighbours struggling home, I was adamant that I was never going to do that kind of work. I didn't want a life like that.

I was now attending Wilbur Wright High, on Warren Avenue. It's not there any longer, it closed down in 2005. Around this same time, I also started talking to one of the teachers at school. He was the typewriting teacher, a really smart man. He loved psychology and he was fascinated by President Roosevelt – the second one, the one who led the United States through the Second World War – and he would talk about how Roosevelt was the perfect example of a man who could talk to anyone. He was always on their level; it didn't matter if they were the richest businessmen or the most impoverished, Roosevelt understood how they thought and how they lived, and he could identify with it.

We talked not so much about what I was going to do after I graduated but about how to make the most of the talents I had, so that whatever job I ended up in would be the one I wanted to do. And he taught me things that have stayed with me my entire life, and that I have applied all my life.

He taught me how to talk to people, and the impact of words. The way you talk to one person this way and another person another way, not so you could take advantage of them but so you could arrive at an understanding.

How to decide for yourself whether someone had an open mind or a closed mind. The little tests that you give people when you talk to them, feeling your way around their attitudes and mindset, until you can create a common ground on which to deal with them. And I practise that to this day.

I graduated when I was seventeen, and I went straight into night school to study accounting. I was fourteen when I first decided that might suit me, and the only reason was, somebody told me that if you're an accountant, you don't have to sit in an office from nine to five. You travel around, you do audits, you visit clients. There was a brief period when I also considered becoming a doctor. Somebody else suggested that, because doctors earn even more than accountants. But I never could stand the sight of blood, unless it was in *Tales from the Crypt*, so I put that to one side straight away.

So I started studying, but was this what I really wanted to do, more than anything else in the world? No. Even though I had set my mind on qualifying, my thoughts were never still. I was forever trying to figure out who I was.

Even when I was very young I always used to wonder "What am I here for?", trying to get a feel for what life actually meant. "How long have I been here? What have I achieved?" I was questioning everything. I don't know why those things kept going through my mind but they did, and I allowed them to.

The one area where I felt secure, as though I already knew the answers, was in my relationships with girls.

Growing up, I sensed that females always paid attention to me. A lot of that came down to the way in which I was raised. Even though Ola could be strict, she still doted on me, and so did the other women I was around, Mother, Grandmother Mary, various aunts, cousins and so on.

That instilled me with a certain amount of self-confidence. I remember Ola once telling Uncle James, "Edward gets an awful lot of calls from girls. I thought you got a lot, but he gets even more."

I had a lot of girlfriends, friends who were girls, but one thing I learned very early on was never to use the term 'going steady' with any girls I was seeing. Everybody else did, but I didn't want to

A high school picture of Eddie, dedicated to Grandmother Mary.

because it committed you, and I didn't want commitment. I didn't like feeling that way. I would become friends with girls, but we were never 'going steady', because I noticed that when I was their friend, it didn't make any difference anyway. And by me being their friend, they felt more comfortable than if we were acting like boyfriend and girlfriend all the time.

But I *did* commit. I'd been spending time with Almetta, the girl who lived across the street, and the reason that came about was simply because I was fifteen and, as far as I was concerned, I was the only virgin in the whole school… if not the entire world.

So we started seeing one another, sleeping together and, of course, the inevitable happened. Almetta became pregnant with my first child, my son, Edward Jr.

Nobody really said that much about it. I guess, being in the neighbourhood, they could see me going back and forth across the street and hanging out at Almetta's all the time, so they weren't surprised.

I did get a lecture from Almetta's stepfather, and somewhat from my grandmother and my uncle, but not much of one. They knew they didn't have to say a lot for me to understand. None of them liked the situation but their attitude was, what's done is done.

Meanwhile, without a word to any of them, I had decided to do the responsible thing. I asked Almetta to marry me.

In truth, it was not the most conventional proposal. My position was this. I told Almetta I would marry her, but only if I could continue to act and live as an individual. I knew she couldn't carry on living at home because her stepfather was kinda tough on her, and I didn't want her to have to go through that. At the same time, though, I had only recently turned seventeen and I didn't want to get tied into some kind of domestic situation.

I explained all of this to her and she agreed. I also told her that I didn't want any more kids because I could barely take care of myself at that age, and she said okay to that as well. And that was it, we were engaged.

But, of course it wasn't as easy as all of that sounds.

I went to my mother and told her what we were planning, and she had a fit. "No, absolutely not."

Ola didn't like the idea, my uncle didn't like the idea. He told me, it didn't matter what Almetta and I had agreed, I would end up having a lot of children and that would be it for my life. I'd never have a chance to find out what life was. I argued with him and told him that wouldn't happen, but he was adamant. "You say that now, but you'll find out it won't work that way."

I didn't care. I went back to my mother and asked if she would sign the papers for us to get married, because I was still only seventeen.

She said no.

So we waited until I turned eighteen, then Almetta and I went down to the county building, got married and didn't tell a soul. The first our families knew about it was when Ola saw the marriage announcement in the newspaper.

She went straight to our mother. "Evelyn, did you know Edward got married?"

Mother was as shocked as she was. "No, he never told me."

Of course, she then started fussing. "Why didn't you tell me? I would have wanted to be there with you."

I said, "Why should I ask you when you'd already refused to sign for me?"

Brian: I said to Edward, "Man, you're married? Does that mean you're going to move out of our room?"

It was around this same time that we moved back in with our mother. We were older and didn't need somebody looking after us all the time, and she wanted to spend more time with all of her children together. The only problem was, she didn't have the money.

Eddie: But I did. Over the years, I had secretly saved every cent I had. My allowances, birthday gifts, Christmas gifts, odd jobs, everything, ever since I was a young child. I was seventeen, and I had $2,500 stashed away.

Eddie with son Edward on Clements Street.

I asked Mother how much she needed, she told me $1,600. So I went to my room and I gave it to her.

She couldn't believe it. "Where did you get all this?" I explained to her how I had saved it, and that was it. She had found a place on Clements Street, on the corner of La Salle, with two bedrooms, a living room, a dining room, a kitchen and a bathroom. It was huge by our standards, and we all moved in – our mother, my brother and sister, and Almetta and I.

It was in the midst of all this, with us singing our hearts out on street corners, and Eddie discovering the responsibilities of parenthood, that a man named Berry Gordy entered our world.

Or, more accurately, we pushed our way into his.

Chapter Five

Enter the Creator

Eddie: Teddy Johnson was a friend of mine, one of the very few people who I did actually acknowledge as a friend, as opposed to merely somebody I hung out with. I liked him a lot.

We met, I think, through singing. His group and mine must have encountered one another somewhere, and Teddy and I bonded. He often used to walk through the neighbourhood where I lived and, whenever he had the opportunity, he would stop by the house, to say "Hi", and find out what I'd been doing. Other times, I'd join him walking, and we'd amble up to Conant Gardens.

Back in the 1860s, Conant Gardens was the centre of the local anti-slavery movement, and now it was one of the most prosperous African-American neighbourhoods in Detroit. It was fascinating to see how, for some people, the American Dream could come true, regardless of skin colour.

Teddy loved music as much as I did. I remember when he stopped by to say, "Look, Aretha Franklin is singing at this church. Do you want to come with me?"

Aretha was still in her mid-teens, still singing gospel at New Bethel Baptist Church and a few other places around town, and I tell you, I had never walked so far in all my life! It had to be six or seven miles, just to hear Aretha, but it was worth it. I'd heard so many good things about her but I'd never seen her, so we went to this church and I was amazed as I watched her perform. She was electrifying. The part I remember best was when she started doing this up-tempo, sanctified dance, the sort of thing you'd sometimes see in a Baptist church but different as well. I loved the way she was moving, stepping and kicking. I would have to wait a long time to see anything like that again!

Not in my wildest dreams would I ever have imagined that, just a few years later, I would be on the same stage as Aretha.

It was my first ever engagement at the Apollo Theater, around the same time as I had my hit 'Jamie'. Aretha actually went on before me and I stood in the wings, waiting for my turn. I watched as she performed, still as electrifying as ever, and wondered how I was ever going to follow that. She finished her performance and

Eddie's friend Teddy Johnson, without whom...

the crowd was going wild, and I saw her walking in my direction although I was also looking out at the stage, waiting for them to give me my cue to come out. Aretha walked right up to me, planted a big kiss on my lips, as if to say "good luck", and then she kept on walking back to the dressing room.

I managed to get through my performance and, all in all, it was very exciting. But that was the highlight.

I would never really get to know Aretha, not until much later. Both Brian and my sister Carole knew her because they would go to the same skating rink, but I was always very sorry that I didn't get to know her a lot better, because I admired her so much.

Eddie: One evening, Teddy stopped by the house; he had an audition downtown with an entrepreneur named Homer Jones and, although I hadn't seen him for a while, he wanted to know if I'd go with him.

Although I wanted to support him, I really wasn't in the mood to go out. I made some excuse, probably something about not having the bus fare, and I remember looking around to make sure our mother hadn't overheard me. She knew I always had money, and would want to know why I was lying. But Teddy said he'd take care of that and, because I couldn't think of any other reasons to keep on refusing him, I agreed to go along.

Teddy had always been seduced by the entertainment industry. He really was not a singer, but he believed he was. He had a love for it. Mr Jones, however, seemed impressed. Teddy ran through his paces, and it looked as though he had passed the test.

Then Mr Jones spotted me and, assuming that I was along to audition as well, he asked me if I was ready. I explained that I was there to keep Teddy company but he asked if I could sing.

"A little."

Mr Jones suggested I let him decide that for himself, and he asked what songs I knew. A few people had told me I sounded a little like Jackie Wilson, so I started singing one of his songs, 'Christmas In Heaven'.

I was barely through the first verse when I noticed people coming over from different parts of the theatre to listen, and I wasn't even halfway through the song when Mr Jones told me to stop. "Okay, that's enough. Wait here, I'll be right back."

He returned with a management contract, handed it to me and asked how old I was. "Seventeen," I said, so he told me to take it home, have my mother sign it (a legal requirement) and return the document to him at his office. He didn't say another word to Teddy.

I couldn't believe it. I don't remember if I'd actually heard of Mr Jones before this; I don't believe so. Later, somebody said he'd once had some kind of involvement with Little Willie John, back when Little Willie was first starting out in the early 1950s. As far as I was concerned, however, a real-life manager wanted to sign me up to be a real-life singer.

I was thrilled. Teddy, on the other hand, simply looked embarrassed, a little taken aback and probably very disappointed. He certainly didn't say a word to me on the bus ride home, and I didn't say anything to him. To be truthful, I was embarrassed too, and didn't know what to say or how to begin to handle this situation. It wasn't until the bus reached my stop and I got up to leave that I finally spoke, and that was to say, "See you later."

Teddy didn't even look up. He mumbled, "Yeah, yeah," and the bus pulled away.

I had my mother sign the contract and a few days later I was at Mr Jones's office. He put my contract in a file then took me over to where a pianist was waiting. He nodded, and the pianist started playing a song for me to try. It was 'Laura' – Frank Sinatra would later have a hit with it, but a lot of other people had sung it since it first appeared in the 1945 movie *Laura*.

It's a nice enough song if you like that kind of thing, and it was certainly popular. But to my ears, it was saccharin and corny. I did my best but I couldn't begin to put any heart or enthusiasm into the song. I didn't want to sing like that. I wanted to sing hip stuff, and I told Mr Jones that.

He spent an hour that afternoon, and another hour a few days later, trying to marry me to that song, until at last, my message got through.

"I'll tell you what," he said. "I know this guy who writes songs. He'll have some songs you'll want to sing."

He scribbled a name and address on a piece of paper and a few days later, I took the bus there. I knocked on the door, and a young man – he appeared to be in his late twenties – opened it and glanced at me. He didn't say a word.

"Are you Mr Berry Gordy Jr.?" I asked.

He looked at me cautiously. "Yes."

"Mr Homer Jones sent me. I was told you had some songs for me."

Berry was puzzled. "I only have songs for the people I manage. I don't have any songs for you."

And as far as Berry was concerned, that was the end of the conversation. But I remained standing in his doorway, staring at him, and I was not budging. Berry stood there staring back at me, and all the while my mind was whirling.

There was something about this guy that I liked. I don't know what it was and I can't explain it to this day. It was that feeling you sometimes get when you meet somebody and you instinctively know they are, or will be, a part of your life.

Plus, he had songs, and I wanted them. If 'Laura' was anything to go by, Mr Jones certainly didn't have any.

Berry was growing uncomfortable, I could see that. But I still wasn't going anywhere. He politely invited me in.

He asked me what songs I knew, so I told him 'Christmas In Heaven'.

"Isn't that a Jackie Wilson song?"

"Yes," I replied.

"You can sing Jackie Wilson songs?"

Again, I said yes.

He looked surprised. I didn't know this, but it transpired that Berry himself was writing for Jackie Wilson at the time. In fact, he was writing for a lot of people. "Okay, let me hear you sing it."

With Berry seated at the piano, I began to sing 'Christmas In Heaven'. Again people started appearing from other rooms to listen – his sister, Loucye Wakefield, who also lived there; a cousin or two. One person even came out of the bathroom to listen.

This time, I was allowed to complete the song. The end result, however, was the same. Berry wanted to manage me.

I mentioned my freshly signed contract with Mr Jones, but I also told him, "Berry, I want you to manage me." I figured that If Mr Jones had to send me to Berry Gordy to get songs, why would I want to be with anybody else?

Berry asked to see my copy of the contract, and said he knew Mr Jones and he'd take care of it. And sure enough, he did. Shortly after, I would sign with Berry, who became my manager.

The audition was over, but I still wasn't going anywhere. I sat on the couch and, although I could see Berry's mind was moving on to other things, we started talking.

Somebody came to the door; he got up to let them in, and introduced me to Janie Bradford, a striking African-American woman with a short hairstyle and the sweetest smile.

"We're going to the movies," Berry said.

"Okay," I replied. Obviously I was supposed to take that as my cue to leave but instead I remained seated. We talked a little more, but I could see Berry growing more and more perplexed. How was he ever going to get rid of me? And, more importantly, did he want to? Finally, he announced that he and Janie were getting ready to leave.

Again, I sat there. Again, he stared at me. Finally, he spoke.

"You know, I didn't think I'd like you at first but you're a lot different to what I was expecting. You're actually quite likeable. Do you want to come to the movies with us?"

Of course I said yes. That connection – I'd felt it, and so had he.

"Come on then."

From that day on, I spent as much time with Berry as I could, and the instant liking I'd taken to him only intensified as time passed. He was bright, he was smart, and although he was almost exactly a decade older than me, sometimes he behaved like the youngest person in the room. I especially enjoyed being around him when he found, saw or heard something that excited him. Like the most ebullient teen, his enthusiasm took on an almost physical weight. It was impossible to avoid being bowled over by it.

I'd go to his house simply to hang out, meet his friends and his family, and be made to feel as though I was a part of the family. We'd visit his parents, and Berry would come visit me at home. My mother recognised him immediately, the boy she'd worked with at Ford's.

They'd got on well back then, and they got on well again now. She was as comfortable as I was about me spending so much time with him, and they remained close.

In fact, decades later, I discovered that Berry had loaned her money. He and I were in the middle of negotiations over something, when suddenly he turned to me and said, "Eddie. You ought to be ashamed of yourself." I asked why, and the story came out. Our mother had gone to him to borrow some cash. Not to me, not to Brian. To Berry. And it took me a while to figure out why, but in the end, I did. Our mother loved to go to the track, and she loved to spend money. A lot of it. Finally I got her to promise me she wouldn't keep doing it, wouldn't keep asking us for money and then spending it at the track. So she went to Berry instead!

I adored the Gordys. They were so different to any family I had ever met. They were so demonstrative, forever hugging and kissing one another. Even the guys would kiss one another on the cheek. I was in total awe of the sheer love and devotion that family placed on permanent display. Such a contrast to mine.

Yet we weren't that different from one another. Like my family, Berry's hailed from Georgia, a small town called Milledgeville and, like mine, they moved to Detroit in the 1920s, in search of a better life.

They found it, as well. Despite an early setback when Berry's father, Berry Sr., lost their life savings to a property scam, the family was soon overseeing a minor property empire, a range of flourishing businesses, a printing company and even a savings and loans company, the Ber-Berry Co-Op. Founded by Berry's eldest sister, Esther, it was to this co-op that Berry would turn for the $800 he required when he came to launch his musical career.

Berry loved his family, and all that they had achieved, but it wasn't for him. Berry lived and breathed music. He told me once about the day he was working with his father, who was also a skilled brick mason, and who fully expected his son to follow in his footsteps.

Suddenly Berry picked up a brick, threw it to the ground and said to his father, "I can't do this." And he walked off the job.

I asked him, "What did Pops say?" (we all called the elder Mr Gordy 'Pops').

Berry replied, "He didn't say anything."

I've always believed that there comes a pivotal point in someone's life that sends him or her in the direction they want to go. Earlier, I spoke about the struggle of being in search of myself, looking for the awakening, the spiritual arousal that I knew awaited me somewhere. I still hadn't found it, but merely being in Berry's company made me feel that it was a little bit closer. I guess we were all on that same journey, beginning with our leader Berry Gordy – and what a leader he became.

I didn't know all of Berry's struggles through the years before he finally experienced that epiphany. But I do remember one of the things that signposted, literally, the direction he was to take. We were standing on Woodward Avenue one night and he pointed to a sign depicting the figure of a handsome man in a white suit, poised, holding a baton. It was band leader Stan Kenton, and he said that impressed him.

Berry had found the path, but he was still searching for direction. What became Motown was still a long way away at this point – I don't believe he had even dreamed of such a thing. His sisters, Gwen and Anna, would have their own label, known as Anna, up and running long before Berry made a move in the same direction.

An early Eddie promo shot, taken shortly after meeting Berry.

But he had his management company, he had his growing songwriting portfolio, with people like Janie and his business partner, Billy Davis (who was also dating Gwen) writing alongside him. He was a wizard in the studio, recording the songs he'd later license to different record labels, and with hindsight, it is easy to see that everything Berry did and said was pointing him in one direction, towards an enterprise that would bring all of his interests – management, composition, publishing, recording, everything – together under one umbrella. And I wanted to become a part of it. In fact, I already was.

I was not the sole focus of Berry's attention, of course. He was working with other singers and musicians. One time I went over to Berry's and Jackie Wilson was there. It was the first time I met him, and it was such a thrill. Even better, after that, I'd be invited (or maybe invite myself) along to watch while he and Berry rehearsed together. In fact, I was there the day Jackie announced he was going on the road, and asked Berry to join him as pianist.

My heart was in my mouth. Berry and I were rehearsing a lot now; we had demos piling up, and he was talking about me getting a record out. The last thing I needed was for him to disappear on tour for weeks, or even months, on end.

I have rarely felt so relieved as I did when Berry, without actually saying no, made it clear that he wasn't especially enthusiastic about going on the road. It meant that my career was still on track.

My first record was released in April 1958. I was a little disappointed that we weren't recording one of Berry's own compositions. Instead, I was handed a song that The Jordanaires, Elvis Presley's background singers, had recorded for the movie *Country Music Holiday*, called 'Little Miss Ruby'. Berry's song 'You (You You You You)' was the B-side, and I much preferred that one. 'Little Miss Ruby' was a corny, corny song; I didn't like it at all. But the publisher was adamant that I cover it, and I would always do what I was told.

We would be recording it in New York City, at Mercury Sound Studios, and would you believe, we drove there, 600-and-some miles in the dead of a viciously cold winter, in Jackie's Cadillac Eldorado. He was recording something in the same studio at the same time, so it made sense for us to travel together. No matter how thrilled I was to be spending so much time with Jackie, however, it was the longest car ride I'd ever had. The journey took 11 or 12 hours, and I simply wasn't accustomed to being in a car for that amount of time. Sitting there with nothing to do, with Jackie on one side of me and his driver on the other, crushed in the middle between them, all I wanted to do was sleep.

Finally, I asked Jackie if he'd mind switching places with me, so I could at least lean my head on the window.

Of course he said no, but he could see me nodding off, my head bobbing around, so he told me I could put my head on his shoulder. That surprised me, because a lot of people don't want your head on their shoulder. But I wasn't going to say no.

Even so, the journey felt endless – cold and dark and snowy – and the entire experience was so horrible that it stopped me wanting to ride in a car for a long time after. I did get over it, of course, and later I'd join Berry on some of his trips to New York, either for recording sessions or promotional jaunts. But it would be a long time before I was able to enjoy travelling again, and it only took the smallest incident to remind me of why.

For example, a couple of years after that endless ride to New York City, I was on my way somewhere to promote a record with Mary Wells. We were travelling by prop plane, and halfway through the flight I felt the aircraft suddenly plunge towards the ground. We slowed our descent soon enough, but what startled me the most was when the stewardesses screamed and dropped to their knees, I looked at Mary, seated to the right of me, and she didn't look scared at all. So I made up mind that I couldn't be frightened either, because Mary was so calm. But deep down inside, it scared the bejesus out of me.

I would not fly for a long time after that. Even when I moved from Detroit to California in 1974, I took the train. The journey was four days but I enjoyed it, I really did. I had good company and it was spectacular, watching the country passing by. But I'll never forget what Levi Stubbs said to me shortly before I left Detroit.

"You're on your way to California by train? You're going to be on your way for a long time."

Finally, we arrived in New York City and we made our way to Mercury. The great arranger Don Costa had been recruited to work on both Jackie's song and mine, but what should have been an exhilarating experience turned out to be deathly dull.

The entire process was so mechanical, so dispiriting. Even though Berry had joined us there, it was nothing like the fun we used to have in the studio in Detroit. And listening to the music, I might as well have been back in Homer Jones's office, gritting my teeth while the pianist pounded out 'Laura'.

I was surrounded by session singers and musicians, and I cannot complain about their ability. They read the charts, they sang the songs and they played everything perfectly. It sounded really good. But what it didn't sound was soulful. The music didn't have any substance to it; it was too sterile, too slick, too clean. The musicians and the backing singers hit all the right notes in all the right places, but there was not an ounce of feeling in any of them.

Not that it mattered. The single didn't go anywhere, which didn't surprise me, and I didn't particularly care, either. I was enjoying myself hanging out with Berry and everybody else, and of course everything was a new experience.

First record, first live show, first tour, first girl backstage… all my life I'd been searching for something I wanted to do, to find my niche, and I wanted to make money. Music, which I had always adored anyway, suddenly felt like the best way I could achieve that.

My family agreed. Even Ola. She was so supportive, and she always would be. One time I was at the Graystone Ballroom. The show was being broadcast on the radio, and I spotted my cousin George. I said, "Great, you came down," and he said, "Oh, the whole family was here – did you know Ola came down?" I was so shocked, but George continued, "Yeah, she came by, she was sitting in the audience, and when your name was announced, and people roared, and those girls were screaming, she said, "There goes the sheikh!"

After I came off, she had apparently left. She never said a word to me about it and I never asked her. But, in her heart, she wanted to see her grandson and what he was doing. When I was on *American Bandstand*, she also never said anything to me, but I later found out that she called all our relatives to tell them to watch.

But what of Teddy Johnson, the friend whose unwitting request for moral support had put me in this position?

Well, our friendship survived but it was never the same again. On the occasions we ran into one another, which were seldom, he'd always be very friendly. He didn't come around too much and I can't say I blame him. I probably wouldn't have, either.

The last time I saw him was sometime around 1962. Four years had passed since that fateful afternoon at Homer Jones's audition, and although nobody would ever have mistaken me for a star, I was now recording regularly, touring a lot and doing all the things that Teddy probably still wished he could do.

Almetta, baby Edward Jr. and I had recently moved into our own apartment on La Salle Boulevard, and Teddy dropped by with a friend. We were sitting there, and they were both looking around the flat, because it did look good, nicely decorated, well furnished.

All of a sudden, the friend asked me, "Hey man, you smoke?"

He was talking about marijuana, and my answer was no. Never had, never would. But this guy, this complete stranger, fixed his eyes on me, gestured around the apartment, and asked, "How can you enjoy all this if you don't get high?"

Back then, I didn't know how to answer him. Today I could, because I never depended on marijuana (or any other drug) for anything. I was already happy enough. At the time, however, his question really threw me, and whatever conversation we might have been having beforehand fizzled into silence.

They stayed for about an hour, then left, and after that? I was very, very busy; Teddy was doing his own thing, whatever that was, and we drifted apart. Besides, I was living in a different world. I would never see him again.

But I do occasionally wonder what might have happened if, the day Teddy asked me along to that audition, and I lied that I didn't have the bus fare, if he'd shrugged, said oh well and gone alone?

Throughout our lives, things happen that we cannot control, events or occurrences whose consequences we cannot ever conceive, almost as if a higher power is directing them. And, as far as I'm concerned, that event with Teddy is the most pivotal of them all for me. I have never forgotten that, but for the sake of a few cents' bus fare, the rest of my life might have turned out to be very different.

Chapter Six

Motown Love

Eddie: I enjoyed singing but I could take it or leave it. Being in the studio was fun, it was interesting. Being in that little booth, it was exactly the same as being on the street corner, or in the shower, singing for myself.

What I didn't enjoy was everything that went along with it.

I disliked the travelling, I disliked performing on stage. I didn't like the cheap motels where we'd put up for the night, or the crummy buses that we were jammed onto. I didn't like the crowds, the expectations, the atmosphere.

Maybe at first I found those things exciting, and I certainly enjoyed this newfound sense of freedom. All of this was a new experience for me. But it was a curse as much as it was a blessing.

Anything I do, I like to know what I'm doing *beforehand*. Including school plays, I'd never been on stage more than three times in my life before, and in this situation I was an inexperienced, unrehearsed amateur. I was completely naive; I knew nothing, and the worst part, I wasn't learning much, either. Instead, I was being herded around like cattle for 24 hours every day, being told when to sleep, when to sit, when to sing, when to do everything. And very quickly, I realised I hated it.

I'd never been an especially sociable person but this was torture. It doesn't matter how pleasant your travelling companions are, after a couple of weeks with no company but theirs, when everything they say is simply a variation on something they said a few days before, it gets tiring. I have never been so uncomfortable. I had no life at all. It was buses, crowds, more buses, more crowds. Over and over and over.

I could have quit, but that, to my way of thinking, would not have been any better. I've always believed you can't stop doing something simply because you don't like it. You have to make the best of the situation until something else comes along that maybe you enjoy more. Ola taught me that.

So, over the years that followed, I made a lot of records, because that's what you did, and I tried my hardest to get a hit record, because that's also what you did. But I didn't enjoy it.

All I dreamed of was escaping the straitjacket. But how?

It wasn't a creative thing. It wasn't as if I was desperate to do something else. I didn't have any musical ideas of my own. All I could do was sing along with the band, and that's all anybody expected of me. I can remember being on stage at the Apollo, looking out into the crowd and asking myself, "What the hell am I doing up here?"

I didn't let it show. In his book, *The A&R Man*, our band leader, William 'Mickey' Stevenson*, is another person who says I sounded like Jackie Wilson, and adds that I was as good looking as Jackie too. In fact, maybe even better looking because I was younger. And he wrote a terrific passage, describing one of the shows we did together.

"Now picture this. Eddie [is] dressed in this great-looking all white outfit, right down to the shoes, baby. The brother looked like a walking angel. He had the girls backstage eating out of his hand. [Then] he would step out on stage and give the girls in the audience that big smile of his. As the girls screamed and hollered, that's when I would start the intro."

* We all called him Mickey.

But somewhere else, in another of the books about Motown, I read that I suffered from stage fright, and I don't know *where* that idea came from. I didn't have stage fright and I wasn't frightened. I simply didn't like my job. There's a very big difference.

I remember one show in particular.

I was at home and had probably already gone to bed when the phone rang. It was Berry. Willie Jones, the singer with The Royal Jokers, was at a nightclub somewhere, and I've already mentioned what a great voice he had. Everybody said so. But Berry wanted people to hear how much better *I* was.

"Just take a cab," he told me, "and get yourself down here." So I did what he asked, came down to this nightclub, and he told me to get up on stage and sing one of the songs he'd written for Jackie Wilson.

It went well – people were still always surprised that I could sing Jackie's songs so well. But I happened to glance over to where Willie was, sitting in the corner, and he was just staring at me! I didn't even look to see how other people reacted. But I saw the look on Willie's face.

Then I came off stage, got another cab home and went back to bed.

There was one saving grace to my career as a live performer.

I didn't understand why, but there were a lot of girls who came backstage at the shows, and they were always impressed to be with people who sang. You'd leave the theatre and you'd have this girl on one arm, that girl on the other, and that was interesting.

I learned some things, too, but the most important thing was that I gained tremendous respect for performing artists. I realised that the work they did, although it looked like fun, was difficult. It was trying, it was a real job. It took a lot out of them and it heaped a lot of responsibility on their shoulders.

Apart from that, I didn't care for any of my on-the-road experiences. In fact, the only other thing I enjoyed about this period was introducing Berry to my brother.

Very early on in our friendship, I had told Berry about Brian's gift for harmony, his ear for music, and how he was already singing in vocal groups with kids years older than him.

Of course, Berry was sceptical. "How old did you say he was?" he would ask, and I'd say fourteen, fifteen, whatever.

Berry always came back with the same thing. "Oh no, no, no. No fifteen-year-old can do that."

Berry did finally agree to set up an audition for Brian, but only to shut me up.

Brian: The first time I met Berry Gordy Jr. was when Edward took me to a record hop at the Graystone Ballroom in Detroit. He'd told Berry that I knew music, and that I could sing, so Berry said, "Come to the house and let me see what you can do."

A few days later, I went to the house that he shared with his sister, Loucye, and sang for him. I didn't do a particularly good job, probably because I was so nervous, although Loucye liked me well enough – she was working as a government bookkeeper at the time (later, she would do the same job at Motown), and there weren't enough hours in the day for her to look after the house as well, not with Berry around, so she took me on as a housekeeper.

She needed one. Berry was a bit of a mess, to put it mildly. He never cleaned up after himself, never picked things up once he'd put them down. You could literally trace his progress around the house simply by following the trail of discarded glasses, balled-up paper and half-eaten sandwiches he left in his wake. My job was to pick up after him, and her, for that matter. Loucye was an absolute chain smoker. I don't think I ever saw her without a cigarette, so there were a lot of ashtrays for me to empty.

She was also a hard taskmaster, but after Grandmother Ola, that was nothing new to me – not even when she insisted on teaching me how to make military corners when I made the beds. Plus she paid me a few bucks a week, and that's how I became so close with the Gordy family. I was there all the time – even more than Eddie – and the more time I spent talking with Berry about music and songs, the more he came to realise that maybe I could be useful.

Eddie: Brian was spending so much time at Berry's house that even our mother hardly saw him. But she quickly discovered that he was not going to school, so finally she marched down to Berry's house to find out what was going on.

Brian: I was supposed to be passing into the eleventh grade at Central High School, but I never went. I'd skip school to go to work with music.

Berry found out first, and asked me, "Why aren't you at school?"

"Well, I don't wanna go to school."

Then Mama found out, and she went to talk to Berry. "This boy has got to go to school," she said, so he called me in and said, "She's right. You have to."

Brian during his high school days.

So I very begrudgingly agreed and, for a short while, I did as I was told. But I still didn't like it. I was a lot better with music than I was with a paper and pen. All I wanted to do was play. And, in the end, they gave up talking to me about it.

Eddie: Brian told our mother that he was learning more from Berry than he ever could in a classroom. And for some reason, she didn't say a word. I was surprised he was allowed to get away with it, because our mother was always after me about finishing high school and going to college. Instead, it turned out that I was the only one of the three they would put that pressure on – it all comes back to me being the example that Brian and Carole had to follow.

Brian didn't get the same treatment, and part of that is because our mother knew he was right. Musically, he was vastly superior to me, and anybody else his age. He had our grandfather's ear for music. Anything he heard, he could play. There was very little that he could do apart from music, and going to school wasn't going to change that.

Brian: Berry was never impressed with my singing. He did like my writing and melodies, though, so he suggested that I try working with Janie Bradford. He had a lot of lyrics that Janie had written – in fact, she had so many lyrics that Berry simply didn't have time to write to all of them. So he introduced us, because he knew it would move the different projects a lot faster if there were someone else who could help write these songs.

We asked Janie for her recollections of this period. "We were all still teenagers," she said, "and immediately bonded like family. The Holland brothers seemed to develop a sense of responsibility for me, and of course I took full advantage of it. Once the dollars began to roll in from their various hits, at each royalty period, my hand was stuck out for my share, just like their bill collectors.

"However, Eddie, being the smart one of the three of us, would tell me in confidence that Brian had just got his royalty cheque. A smile as big as all outdoors would caress my face; I would thank him and then set out to find Brian and hit him up for a few dollars.

"It took a few royalty periods for me to catch on that Eddie was ensuring he wouldn't have to give me any money, because Brian would have already shelled out."

Before any of that could happen, of course, Berry needed to take one final step. One last push before he was ready to roll.

Eddie: I was over at the house, sitting in the kitchen with Berry, when Loucye came in from work. She barely even said hello before telling Berry to wash the dishes. I was embarrassed, and I couldn't imagine how Berry felt. But he never batted an eyelid. He got up, walked to the sink and washed those dishes.

He moved out shortly after that. I don't know if the two things were related but Loucye was very stern, very businesslike – she reminded me of Ola in a lot of ways. I knew with Berry being so creative, so bound up in his own world of schemes and dreams, and so busy defining himself, there would be conflict.

Berry moved in with his girlfriend (who later became his wife), a singer and songwriter named Raynoma Liles. We called her Rae. She'd been writing songs since she was about twelve; she was now in her early twenties and she had about a hundred of them.

She could also arrange music, which was something Berry didn't have such a handle on, and she had a good business sense, too. Rae was the instigator behind the Rayber Music Writing Company that she and Berry formed in 1958, her idea being that songwriters and producers would want professional demos and, for a fixed fee of $500 per song, the company would record the songs they brought to them.

But Berry wouldn't just make the record. He would also take it to various dance parties to test the response. Then, if he thought it stood a chance, he would try and place it with a record label. He knew $500 was a considerable sum in those days, but he gave his clients a lot of bang for their buck.

He believed in the records he was making, but even more than that, he believed in keeping busy. He was one of those people who actually made work for themselves; even when he took 'time off', he would be writing a song or recording a backing track, making a demo. The more the business took off, and the busier he became, the happier he was. That man would have gone without sleep and eating if he could, simply so he could keep on working.

Eddie: One example. My mother overheard me saying I didn't have any proper stage clothes. She told Ola and shortly after, I got a call. Ola wanted to see me. She didn't say why but that didn't matter – when Ola wanted to see you, you went.

I arrived at the house and she was sitting in the kitchen, smiling. She told me to hold out my left hand and started counting $5 bills

Eddie's first onstage engagement after Ola bought him the suit;
"I think it was the Graystone Ballroom."

into it – $5, $10, $15, all the way up to $50, $60, piling them up on my palm. And still she didn't say a word. But I knew what she wanted me to spend it on, and I did – a beautiful light-beige silk suit, which is what I wore on stage.

Berry liked that suit a lot, and shortly after he moved in with Rae he asked if he could borrow it. I said yes, why not. It was only hanging in my closet. Besides, it was Berry, the only person I would have ever loaned my clothes to.

I brought it over, he put it on, I left. The next time I saw him, he was still wearing it. I happened to come by another time and he was *still* sitting at the piano in my pants.

"Berry," I said. "You're ruining my pants."

"Yeah, yeah." He got up, took the pants off, handed them back to me. Then he sat back at the piano and continued playing. He was so caught up in 'the zone', a riptide current of activity, never noticing the water, only the force driving him. That creative high, that pure moment, that hypnotic energy which drives you to your ultimate goal… perfection. He didn't hear any outside noise. Nothing except what he was doing in the moment. Taking the pants off and returning to the piano was purely a mechanical action.

The only other time I experienced something like that was years later, when Brian was at the piano composing the music to 'Reach Out I'll Be There'. Suddenly, something he played triggered an emotional response in Lamont. He pushed Brian aside without a word, and played what became the second half of the melody.

I, too, was caught up in the emotional impact of the melodies Brian was creating. But now I was watching two artists riding that musical riptide, and creating the most exciting sound on Earth.

Berry locked himself into making the music, and in the meantime Rae was advertising the company everywhere she could. It was one of those ads that drew a singer named Marv Johnson into Berry's orbit. Marv came over with 'Come To Me', and the first time Berry and Rae heard the song, they knew it was something special.

Berry recorded it, and when he played it back to the rest of us – Rae, my brother, Janie, other people who were around at the time – we all agreed it was a smash. He then took it to various dance parties and record hops, and the audiences went wild. He even took it to New York City, disappearing off for a couple of weeks, without a single phone call back to Detroit to let us know how things were going, or where he was staying. He devoted two weeks to playing that record to everybody who would listen, and when he came back, he had a deal with United Artists.

It was a great one, as well.

What is a great deal? A great deal is a good deal that works, and work it did. It was such a very smart arrangement. Not only did it allow Berry to continue working out of Detroit, it also allowed him to launch his own record label, Tamla.

It was brilliant, absolutely brilliant. And unheard of, too. Other producers had launched their own labels through a major company but they were always based in one of the industry hubs, New York City or Los Angeles. Never a place like Detroit.

It was a smart move, though, because while Detroit was an important market, it was very hard to break. But Berry believed that a local record, on a local label, was always going to make a bigger impression on the DJs than yet another new release from the same old major labels, and he was right. 'Come To Me' was a hit.

Not long after, I was sitting at home when I heard a car horn honking in the street below. I glanced out of the window and there were Berry and Rae, proudly showing off the proceeds of their first hit, a white Bonneville convertible with a red interior. Red was never my favourite colour, but I must admit, it was a beautiful automobile.

Berry may have been buried in his work but the rest of us still had plenty of playtime, as Janie – again – remembers.

"One evening after work, Miss Rae and I decided to have a girls' night out. Because we would be leaving directly from work,

I was still dressed in my work clothes and since Berry and Rae lived upstairs, I went up there and began to raid her closet – remembering that Rae was about a size 2 and I a size 10.

"But thanks to the Detroit winters, you can always find a knit outfit that stretches a few sizes. So I put one on and away we went. The next day, someone said to Eddie, 'Do you believe that Janie can wear Rae's dress?'

"Eddie replied, 'No, I don't believe that she can. But I do believe that she would.'"

Although Rae would depart Motown in 1964, her importance to Berry's early career can never be exaggerated. It was Rae who brought Marv Johnson to his attention; it was Rae who helped Berry form both Tamla and his publishing company Jobete Music (named for Berry's three children by his first wife, Thelma); and it was Rae who found the building that became Hitsville USA.

A large house that had once been a photography studio at 2648 West Grand Boulevard in Detroit, it would become the nerve centre of American pop music for the next 10 years or more.

Eddie: When Hitsville opened its doors, the only finished producer that walked through those doors was Berry Gordy, with all his experience, all his philosophy about songwriting, all his understanding not only of the business but also of human nature.

For example – when a record label sends a record to a disc jockey, it's merely one of dozens, even hundreds, he's received that week, and no way does he have the time to sit there and play through every one.

So, DJs would 'audition' each track, playing a few seconds of the intro to see how it felt. And that was all. They'd know immediately whether or not the record was something their audience would want to hear. It might be two-and-a-half minutes long, but if you couldn't grab the DJ's attention in those first eight or nine seconds, you were finished.

Berry was convinced of that. Concentrate on those first few seconds. And we followed his lead without question. He was the main producer, and the rest of us were pieces of clay that he was moulding and shaping into what we became, and what we are today. Berry loved talent, especially raw talent, but even more than that, he enjoyed nurturing it. If you were good when you walked through the Hitsville door, you became great. All we had to do was learn.

Hitsville came together quickly. Upstairs was Berry's living quarters, although it was eventually taken over by offices, once Motown was really up and running. The head of A&R, Mickey Stevenson, had what used to be the master bedroom. The other bedrooms became rehearsal studios and writing rooms.

Berry already had plans to install a recording studio, the place that became known as the Snake Pit. The control room and tape library would devour the dining room. He converted the front room into the reception. There were tape recorders and pianos in almost every room. Only the kitchen was left untouched but that didn't keep us out of it; not with Miss Lillie's chilli bubbling away all day!

However, it didn't take long before we had outgrown the premises. Barney Ales, the head of the sales team, once joked that Motown was "the only high rise that went sideways", and it was true. Jobete Music was moved into its own offices next door at number 2644. Berry established his own headquarters at number 2650.

The original Hitsville would always be the heartbeat of the operation, though. The place where we learned what became our trade.

Chapter Seven

The True Meaning of Royalties

Brian: What I wanted to do was write songs. I kept practising on the piano, learning to play different chords, and Janie was always encouraging me, pushing me to try different things, constantly handing me new lyrics to try and put a melody to. Berry was doing it too, but he also had other ideas.

He was full of enthusiasm, always wanting to be in the studio recording something new, and all of a sudden, he started asking me to join him. I was hanging out, probably writing, tinkering around on the piano, when he burst in. He was looking for an engineer for a session he was about to start, and he asked me to do it. I said, "But Berry, I'm not an engineer," and he replied, "What do you mean, you're not an engineer? I need an engineer and you're it."

One of my very first times in the studio was when Berry and Eddie recorded a jingle for a wine commercial, called '(Where's The Joy) In Nature Boy?', and also 'Shock', which became Eddie's second single.

Eddie: Boy, did I record a lot of junk.

Brian: '…In Nature Boy' was written by Joe Howard, who was a disc jockey over at WCHB – I think Berry thought that would help it get local airplay. It came out on Kudo, a little label that operated out of the United Artists building in Detroit, but it was strange, because when the record was released, it wasn't even credited to Eddie. Instead, the label said "Briant Holland With The Band".

After that, I started writing with everybody, and doing a great deal of engineering as well. Janie was my partner a lot of the time, and Berry, but also Gwendoline Murray, one of the singers Berry used a lot, and Robert Bateman, who was a friend of mine from way back.

The next thing that happened was, I started to see the records chart. Marv Johnson recorded 'All The Love I've Got', which I wrote with Janie and Berry, and it got to number 63. Then Barrett Strong hit with 'Money', which Berry and Janie wrote, and I was on that too.

Because Rae was such a great arranger, Berry allowed her to put together the people who played and sang on everything. So she had Robert Bateman, myself and Sonny Sanders from The Quailtones, and we became The Rayber Voices. We were the background vocalists on a lot of Berry and Rae's early recordings, including 'Money'. I also sang background with The Andantes and occasionally I would play the tambourine, because Berry liked the church feel that I'd get.

Rae put together another group called The Riverboys, which was The Rayber Voices plus Gwendoline Murray. A little after that, Sonny Saunders, Robert Bateman and I, with our friends Chico Leverett and James Ellis, formed The Satin Tones. In fact, we became the first band Berry ever signed to the Tamla label.

We also sang at different venues around Detroit, and that was my first time singing a lead part in public, at the 20 Grand, a nightclub, bar and bowling alley on the corner of Warren Avenue and 14th Street in Detroit. That place would become a Motown legend. So much business was done at the 20 Grand. Even after Motown took off, you could walk in there any night of the week,

The famous Rayber Voices. (L-r) Robert Bateman, Gwen Murray, Brian and (seated) Rae Gordy.

and if there wasn't a Motown act on the stage, there'd definitely be a few in the audience.

But I was a lot like Edward in this respect. I really didn't enjoy singing in public. In fact, I hated every minute, every second of it, although not as much as Edward did, because he played a lot more shows than me. But I didn't want to be exposed like that. The moment I got on stage, I knew I didn't like it. I didn't want to be in the public view.

Anyway, between the studio sessions, the writing and the hanging out with Berry and Janie and everyone, I was around a lot, watching as all of Berry's ideas started to come together, coalescing into what would become Motown. I even remember the day we moved into Hitsville, although there wasn't much to move, I don't think, just some furniture and filing cabinets.

As for Edward, I didn't see much of him around that time. They kept him on the road a lot, and when he wasn't on the road, he'd want to be out enjoying himself.

Eddie: I would be out in the street, staying out and doing… whatever they call it. I wasn't a family person. This was my chance to enjoy my freedom after being stuck out on the road, and I made certain that I did enjoy it.

Brian: For me, on the other hand, the office was my life. Janie was there, Robert Bateman, Freddie Gorman, Smokey Robinson, they were all there, although they didn't actually *work* there, not officially.

I did. I had an actual job, and was collecting a pay cheque. Every bit of $12 a week. In fact, I was the only employee for a long time! People like A&R head Mickey Stevenson, songwriter and producer Norman Whitfield, even Edward, they came later.

Other people started coming around. James Dean, my mother's sister's boy, he worked there; again not as an employee, but he wrote songs. Musicians like Earl Van Dyke and Benny Benjamin, a lot of the people who stayed, a few who didn't.

It was regular work; people were coming from all over to work with us, to do this song and that song – it became a real workhouse. And Berry kept us busy, which was all I ever wanted. I was so happy doing that, producing and writing. I wanted to be around music.

We didn't even need to go out to eat. Not with Miss Lillie's chilli simmering away on the stove.

Of all the groups with whom we are associated as writers, individually or collectively, chart success insists that The Supremes and The Four Tops will forever be at the forefront of most people's minds. But there were many others with whom we scored hits, long before we became a team, and it quickly became apparent that writing hits wasn't a job. It was also the greatest rush you could ever experience.

Brian: My first big hit was 'Please Mr. Postman'. Oh my God, I felt like the guy who jumped off the Empire State Building and landed. I felt so good. The first time I heard it on the radio, I was so elated and so taken aback. It was really great – can you imagine? I was like a young boy in a new shiny car. And it was all thanks to The Marvelettes.

Gladys Horton, Katherine Anderson, Georgeanna Tillman, Juanita Cowart and Georgia Dobbins first sang together at Inkster High School in suburban Detroit. They initially came to Motown's attention after finishing fourth in a local talent contest – which is peculiar because the prize, an audition with the label, was intended only for the top three groups. One of the girls' teachers, however, was adamant that The Casinyets (as they were then called) deserved a second chance, and so it proved.

Auditions at that point were a two-tier process. First an act had to prove they were good enough. Then they had to present us with an original song that was likewise Motown worthy.

The Casinyets succeeded on both points, wowing everybody at their audition and presenting us with a song of Georgia's, 'Please Mr. Postman'. To add some poignancy to the situation, we were also informed that Georgia was about to leave the band for family reasons. Motown's job, then, would be to give her the greatest leaving present we could think of. A hit single.

Brian: It was Georgia who had the idea for the song, and the group brought it to Robert Bateman and me. We had started producing and writing together – we were known as Brianbert – and we ended up rewriting the verses and finishing the song with Freddie Gorman. Then we took it into the studio, and boom!

We cut the song, and everybody loved it. Berry changed the group's name to The Marvelettes, and everybody loved that as well; it really was the greatest name for a girl group at that time. What amazes me, though, is how fast this all happened. The group's audition was in April 1961, the record was recorded in

August… Marvin Gaye played drums on it… and, before we knew it, we were on the radio.

The first time I heard it, I couldn't believe it! And they would play that song over and over again. It was the most exciting thing I ever felt. I was so elated and gratified. There was nothing else that could have made me feel better; not even having sex with a great woman could match that feeling.

It started going up the chart, and suddenly there was all this talk about which record would hit number one first, 'Please Mr. Postman' or 'Ya Ya' by Lee Dorsey. Those two were battling it out, so I asked all my family and friends to call the radio station – uncles, aunts, cousins, everyone, call and demand they play our single. I had everybody calling, even the minister at church. And I told him, next time he talks to Jesus, have him call too!

Then, bang! 'Postman' went to number one. It was Motown's first ever chart topper, and Berry was so happy that he signed Robert and me as producers. He wasn't going to take a chance on us going somewhere else after we had a number one record.

So that was it. We'd had the first big hit. Now it was time to really get the Motown machine going. Berry already had the vision and the people in place. Now he was piecing together the apparatus he needed to make it reality.

Berry's modus operandi when it came to hit singles was simple. If a writer, or writing team, had a hit with an artist, they were expected to write the follow-up as well, or at least they would get first refusal.

Even this early on, Berry wasn't thinking in simple terms of creating a record company, but of creating a signature sound, in the same way that Phil Spector did. He was already putting together a house band that would play on every record, a team of producers to work with them and our own studio to work in. Using the same writers for a group was a part of that same process.

The only thing we had to be careful about was not to try too hard to be different, or not try hard enough. Which, unfortunately, was exactly what happened with the next Marvelettes single.

Brian: 'Twistin' Postman'. That was a downer, that was not very good. The idea was good, but the record was not. It was at that time when the twist was the big dance, everybody was doing it and, of course, everybody was making records out of it – 'Do The Twist' and 'Let's Twist Again' – so we thought of 'Twistin' Postman'.

We cut that record and it really didn't do well. Top 40. But Berry said have another go, and that's when Robert, Mickey Stevenson and Gladys from the group came up with 'Playboy', and that was a good tune. It was not as big as 'Please Mr. Postman' but it was a good tune.

The difference between the two songs was that 'Playboy' appealed to the teenagers because of the subject matter. It had the intimate, sexy, girlish appeal, whereas 'Please Mr. Postman' was more relatable to a larger audience. It was a part of our existence. It had a much larger appeal.

It also taught me an important lesson. When I listen to The Marvelettes today, I still don't believe any of their records were as big as they could have been, and the reason for that is… people. If people like a record, they buy it, and if they don't, you have to start all over again. You should always listen to the people.

It was Robert Bateman who set up Motown's first recording studio. He knew somebody over at WJLB radio, and they were throwing out an old tape machine. Robert was able to get it, and he put it in the basement at Hitsville. Robert did a lot for Motown in the very early days – he was writing, producing, engineering, singing, anything that needed to be done, he'd be there to do it.

He even drove Berry and Rae and their parents to Toledo when they decided to get married; drove them home when they had a huge fight on the way there and called the whole thing off; and then back again when they reconciled and decided to go ahead with the wedding anyway.

He was brilliant in the studio. If Berry thought he was good with a razor blade, splicing tape for edits, Robert was even better. He was also responsible for auditioning a vocal group called The

Primettes that Smokey Robinson introduced to Motown – they sang The Drifters' number 'There Goes My Baby' for him, and that was the first time Berry heard the young ladies that would become The Supremes.

But things weren't happening fast enough for Robert, and a dispute with the engineering department was the final straw. He went on to have a very successful career at Capitol Records and elsewhere; he worked with Wilson Pickett and Solomon Burke, and when Florence Ballard left The Supremes and went solo, Robert was her producer. One really strange thing, though: the day Robert died, October 12, 2016, was also the day Sonny Sanders passed away.

Brian: One of the first things Berry decided to do was form a Quality Control department, and that was one of the duties he passed on to me.

There were only a select few of us who went to the meetings – you couldn't get in unless you were invited – so there'd be Berry, who ran it, me and Billie Jean Brown, who Berry made VP of Creative Evaluation, which was the post I eventually took over. But what that meant was, if Berry couldn't make it to a meeting, Billie Jean would take charge. She had very good ears, and if she brought something to Berry's attention, he would pretty much go along with her.

Other regulars included Smokey Robinson and Mickey Stevenson, and every meeting worked along much the same lines. The producers, myself included, would press up acetates of everything they'd worked on since the last meeting, and play it to the room. Quality Control would listen to it, we'd evaluate the performance and then we'd write down what we thought the record needed to make it even better – more bass, more treble, the vocals aren't up high enough, whatever. Then we'd send it back to whoever made it with our recommendations. It was like the Ford Motor Company, or any other quality control office: our job was to make certain that the product was as good as it could be.

We also discussed what should be an A-side, what should be a B-side, what should be put to one side for later. Or, if two writers came up with a song for the same group, Quality Control would choose which one would be released, although if you'd had the last hit, you'd have priority, unless someone had a song that really was superior. But the most important consideration was, what would make a great-sounding record.

Berry always had the final decision. He was the commander-in-chief, and usually he'd go along with our recommendations. But every so often, Quality Control would choose something for a single and Berry would overrule them.

New faces were constantly arriving on the scene. Some stayed, some merely passed through. But one became integral to our future careers.

Brian: The first time I met Lamont Dozier was in the studio. I actually met his first wife, Anne (although her real name was Elizabeth), before I met Lamont himself.

Lamont was signed to Anna Records at the time, which was Gwen and Anna Gordy's label, but Anne worked at Motown, packing records, and I'd often stop to talk with her. After Berry took over Anna, Anne said to me one time, "My husband Lamont is coming over here to sign an artist contract and a producer's contract. You should meet him."

I'd already heard some of Lamont's music and I liked it; in fact, he had a really nice single out on Anna called 'Popeye The Sailor Man'. The kids loved it, and it was doing really well until King Features, who owned the rights to the original Popeye character, threatened to sue. So Lamont recut the song as 'Benny The Skinny Man', but it wasn't the same.

I knew Lamont was in the building that day, so I went off to look for him. I found him sitting at the piano, tinkering with something he was writing. I liked it, as well, and I told him so. "Hey man, you know what? That sounds good. Maybe I can help you with it?" And he said, "Sure, let's work on this song."

I told him I had an idea for the bridge, if he was interested. He said okay, so I had him move over on the bench and I showed him my idea. And from that day on, we began to write together. The first song we wrote, along with Freddie Gorman, 'Darling Forever', would soon be recorded by The Marvelettes and, a little later, by Marvin Gaye.

I loved writing with Lamont. He was a very congenial, affable person, and though we had different ways of writing, when we came together it was seamless. For example, I liked writing beautiful melodies, and softer, more sensual love songs – all the pretty parts, I put those in there. Lamont would put in the more rhythmic things. He was especially great at creating the shuffle tracks. We had different strengths, and that's how we gelled and got along so well.

Eddie: Lamont used to be a drummer and he understood syncopation. A lot of people couldn't sing his melodies because of that, but he could. He was a unique composer. Instinctive. He wrote from the heart, and the strange thing was, Lamont suffered from depression to an extent, and some of his greatest songs came out of that.

Lamont Dozier was born on June 16, 1941, and raised in the Detroit projects. Like us, he grew up surrounded by music – his father, Willie, had similar musical tastes to our uncle James, a lot of pop leavened with a little jazz, while his aunt Eula was a talented piano player, like our grandfather Howard, and had a vast classical repertoire.

The young Lamont sang in the Baptist gospel choir, again like us. And his grandmother, who was a choir director at church, also raised him. It was she who taught him to make sure to always enunciate the words he was singing, and always sing the right words so that the song retained the meaning it was supposed to have.

Another strong influence on Lamont was his elementary school teacher Edith Burke. He talked about her a lot, how she assigned the students to each write a poem and promised to put the best one on the board at the front of the class. Lamont was eleven at the time and he came up with 'A Song', a poem about how a song can make different people feel different things.

It was an incredibly deep thought for a boy that age, and it stayed on the board for a full month. That was what spurred Lamont to get into writing; that and his love of musical theatre – Rodgers & Hammerstein, Rodgers & Hart, people like them. *My Fair Lady* blew him away. So did *Singin' In The Rain*.

By the time he was thirteen, Lamont was singing in and writing for a group called The Romeos, one of whose members knew somebody who was thinking about starting a record label. The guy owned a few drug stores, so he had the wherewithal to finance it. He signed The Romeos to Fox Records and they released a couple of singles, 'Gone Gone Get Away' and 'Fine Fine Baby', which became a local hit. Atlantic Records stepped in, bought out The Romeos' contract and rereleased 'Fine Fine Baby' nationally. Unfortunately, it didn't do too well and Atlantic never came back for more. The band broke up when their bass singer, Don Davenport, left to join The Laredos.

Lamont's next band, along with another of The Romeos, Ty Hunter[*], was The Voice Masters. That was the band that took him to Anna Records – their single 'Hope And Pray' was the first release on the label and the follow-up, 'Needed', was the second.

The Voice Masters released a couple more records on Anna, and when the group broke up, Lamont remained there as a solo artist, so when Berry bought up Anna, Lamont came along as a part of the deal.

Brian: I would write with anybody. I was honing my craft and I was enjoying it. People might stop me in the corridor, "I've got a lyric

---

[*] Years later, when the Invictus label was formed, Ty was one of the first people to be signed.

I'd like you to look at," or, "Wait, don't get in the car yet, I've got something to show you."

That still happened, only now they were stopping both Lamont and me, and soon we were writing together almost exclusively. We wrote a lot with Freddie Gorman but there were others – Janie Bradford, James Dorsey, Henry Cosby, our cousin James Dean. If somebody had a lyric, or needed a melody, we'd always take a look at it, and if it worked, it worked. That was my thing. I loved music so much that I helped everyone. You didn't have to give me anything, you didn't owe me anything, all I cared about was the music – "Let me help you, let me help you."

We started producing together as well. Robert Bateman had left Motown by now, so it was natural that I'd gravitate towards Lamont in the studio. One of the first things we produced together was his original version of 'Fortune Teller (Tell Me)', in April 1962.

We worked with Mary Wells, Kim Weston and The Primettes, the girl group that was renamed The Supremes, very early on, and things started developing from there. We did Stevie Wonder's[*] first song, 'Contract On Love'. Lamont and I wrote it with Janie, then Lamont and I produced it. The Velvelettes, Mable John[**], Freddie Gorman, Marvin Gaye… the list goes on.

---

[*] Stevie was called Little Stevie Wonder back then. He was just eleven years old when Berry signed him to Motown in 1961.

[**] Blues singer Mable John was Little Willie John's older sister, and was the first female artist to be signed to the Tamla label.

Chapter Eight

Living in a New World

Eddie: The first single Berry ever released through United Artists was 'Come To Me' by Marv Johnson. The second was 'Merry Go Round', which Berry wrote and produced for me, with Brian and The Rayber Voices on backup.

It didn't do badly, either. It got a lot of airplay in Detroit, and because Marv's single was taking off as well, Berry was able to make a deal with United Artists for them to release our next few records. I wasn't crazy about any of them. 'Because I Love Her', 'Magic Mirror' and 'Why Do You Want To Let Me Go' were all written by Berry, so they had that going for them, but there was nothing there that I would have chosen to sing. I did what I was told to do.

When my contract was up with United Artists, Berry signed me to Motown, which was now up and running full time. I thought maybe I'd have a little more say in what I was singing. It certainly looked that way – one of the first songs I was offered was 'Jamie', written by Barrett Strong and Mickey Stevenson, which I really liked.

But I wasn't sure about it. Barrett himself was originally going to record it, but before he did, he left Motown and moved to New York. Mickey called and asked if I wanted to record it, and I told him how much I liked it. But I also said, "Listen, I don't want to be recording somebody else's property."

Mickey assured me that it wouldn't be a problem; he also reminded me that if I didn't do it, somebody else would. Nothing went to waste at Motown. So I said okay and, later, Barrett said how much he liked my version.

So the record was released and was doing okay and picking up airplay. But Berry decided it ought to be bigger.

Up to this point, Berry had always handled promotions himself, and he had the R&B stations sewn up. But, even after 'Please Mr. Postman', he was having a lot of problems getting onto the pop stations.

For example, there was a station called CKLW in Windsor, just over the water in Canada, and it had always had a big impact on the Detroit scene. I went up there with Berry one time, when he was plugging one of my earlier releases; it was pouring with rain and we were sitting in a restaurant across the street from the station when Berry said, "Wait here, I'm going to see if I can get this record on the playlist."

Half an hour later, maybe a little longer, he came back and said, "I can't get it done, they won't play it. They said I've got to go R&B first."

Now, however, he had this guy named Barney Ales working for him, a white guy, and what he didn't know about pop radio wasn't worth knowing. He was Motown's head of sales – before that, he'd been in promotions at Capitol Records, so he knew the pop market inside out.

'Jamie' was about to be released, so back I went to CKLW to see the station head, only this time I was with Barney. And, of course, I let him do all the talking. But I was paying attention, and every so often I'd see the radio man look over at me, and Barney would be talking to him, then he'd look at me again and Barney would still be talking.

Finally the guy said to me, "Okay, I'm going to tell you something. I'm going to play this record, but not because of Berry Gordy or Motown. I'm playing it because Barney asked me to."

Gladys Horton, Barney and Eddie on a trip to San Francisco.

I was, "Wow!"

He was as good as his word. Indeed, not only did he play it, he played it four or five times in a row – they'd play it through, back it up and play it again. And again and again. I couldn't believe it. You don't hear it any more, because radio is so streamlined and formatted, and it wasn't that common back then, either. Every so often, though, a disc jockey would be excited enough by a new release that he'd want to hear it again and again, like a kid who's brought home a favourite single. And 'Jamie' was one of those releases.

'Jamie' ended up being a hit – number six on the R&B chart, number 30 on the pop listings – and by Motown's standards at the time, that was big.

However, my lifestyle didn't change too much. I was still riding buses from place to place for 10 minutes on stage, still singing four or five songs a night and then waiting around, always waiting around.

But I was sure that, although royalties took a while to trickle through, once they started, I'd be raking the dollars in. I don't know how much I was expecting, but I'd probably already spent it in my head, several times over.

At last the big day arrived. I was with Brian, outside the Hitsville building, and we'd just picked up our royalty statements. I knew there would be money. Maybe a lot of money. I couldn't wait to tear that envelope open.

When I did, though, all I saw were deductions. The studio cost so much, the musicians, the producer, the arranger, the background singers, they all cost me money. *All* my money. Total deductions – however much it was. Total amount due to the artist – nothing.

All this time I'd been working towards having a hit single. I toured until I didn't know whether I was coming or going, and I appeared on *American Bandstand*. I had done *everything* that was expected of me, and when I finally got a hit, I thought I'd finally be earning.

Instead, there was nothing. Zero. In fact, I was still in debt.

I looked over to Brian. He'd received his statement too, for 'Please Mr. Postman' and some others.

"So, did you make anything?" I asked him, expecting him to sigh and come back with not much more than me. Instead, he said, "Oh yeah," and he passed his statement over to me.

I don't remember the precise figure but it was several thousand dollars, at least. And I said to myself, "Eddie, you're in the wrong job."

Brian: Edward really took those contrasting royalty statements to heart, to the point where he stopped coming around Motown altogether. He says it was around two years – that was how long it took him to teach himself how to write a song.

But really it was no more than nine months – from the end of 1961, when those royalty statements would have arrived, until the fall of 1962 – and he was still having singles released, material he'd cut with me and Mickey Stevenson, or Robert Bateman before he left Motown.

But he was hardly ever around unless Berry had a studio date booked for him, and the rest of the time he was teaching himself how to write songs.

Eddie: I'd always been fascinated by the songwriting process. Back when I was still living with my grandmother Ola, a friend of mine named Walter Lee showed me lyrics to a song. I asked him if he wrote it, and he said yes – in fact, it turned out that he was always writing. I wanted to know how he did it… how could he do it? He said it was easy.

I looked down at the page of handwriting, up at Walter, and asked, "Would you sell me this for $50?" Now it was his turn to look at me, as though I was crazy. But of course he said yes, so I handed him the 50 bucks, and I took the lyrics home. I was so impressed by what he'd done and I wanted to understand how he'd done it. I never actually used it, but I wanted to study it, which I did.

My wife, Almetta, wrote poetry too, so again, I'd quiz her about it. But it was Uncle James who really started me thinking about songwriting when he asked why I was recording so many songs that weren't hits. He was really concerned that I would get discouraged by having failure after failure, and he wanted to know why I didn't write my own songs. I told him I couldn't do it. "Yes you can," he replied. I said I didn't know how. "Yes you do," he shot back. "All you have to do," he said, "is take a copy of *Hit Parader* magazine, lift a line out of every song in there and put them together. You have a song."

I wasn't convinced that it really did work that way but I remained silent. I didn't want to argue about it.

Then those royalty statements came through and that's what convinced me to give songwriting a shot. I wanted to make money, it was as simple as that, and Brian had proved that this was how you did it. I vowed that I was going to learn how to write songs.

I used Smokey Robinson as a guideline. I thought he was by far the best songwriter around, so I took two of his songs – I don't remember which ones, although they were definitely among my favourites at the time – and I studied them.

It was hopeless. I said to myself, "This guy is really good, and it would take me a lifetime to write like he does." But what that taught me was, I needed to find my own technique, something that was unique to me. Smokey was too sophisticated, and if I tried to copy him, that's all it would sound like, a Smokey Robinson knock-off. But if I found my own style then I, too, would be unique.

I had one thing going for me. I always understood people very well. I can read them well, and when I had a certain idea, I knew how to make it accessible to people. So I applied that to my lyrics. They had to be appealing, and I later realised that was something I'd learned back in high school, in composition class.

At the time, I wasn't interested in any school. I wanted to get on with the classes, move up to the next grade and just graduate. I seemed to have picked up whatever the teacher was talking about in composition class, though, and not only had I retained it, I realised I could apply it to my songwriting.

Colloquialisms, word association, they allowed me to maintain a contrast in my lyrics and storylines, enabling them to flow. The correct use of commas – they became extremely important for me because the type of songs that we wrote were so rhythmic, and commas played a major role in the syncopation. Direct objects and indirect objects, and the way they felt. All of these elements helped me develop a technique.

The other thing I realised was, I wanted to write songs that took a very firm position. I was constantly hearing records on the radio where you couldn't understand everything they were saying, and that bothered me. I wanted to make sure that, even if you didn't understand every word, you'd not be able to hear one of my lyrics and not know what it meant. It had to communicate, and I developed a technique of doing that, which I called 'repeat-fomation', where you keep saying the same thing but in a different way.

I also realised that when you finish one sentence, you have to maintain the thought, so one line overlaps into the next and the sentiment continues on. I didn't want any lazy words. Even The Beatles, when they first started, used a lot of "yeah yeah yeah" and things like that, words that filled a gap but didn't actually advance the song. I tried very hard to steer away from that.

Instead, I found a way of using key words on certain rhythms, so it became infectious and you'd remember what it was. And that style of writing took me a long time to develop because it doesn't really rhyme. As long as you can get your lines to rhyme, you can attach any sentiment you want to them. It's easy. But I didn't want to write like that. It wasn't about the rhyme, it was about the thought and the feeling that I wanted to put across.

That made it hard to write, and it made it hard for some people to sing as well, which is why, once Holland–Dozier–Holland got going, I would personally coach the singers in how to sing each song. We only gave people the songs we thought would fit them anyway. And sometimes, the song itself chose the person.

No matter who I was working with, before they were allowed anywhere near the studio, I would have to be confident that they knew how to present the song. It wasn't any use them simply memorising the words. They had to live them as well.

All that was still to come, though – and it would, including the first time I ever went into the studio with Levi Stubbs and The Four Tops. But at that time, I was still trying to find my way, and it wasn't easy, although not necessarily because songwriting itself was proving difficult.

The people around us, family, friends, folk like that, had a very strong work ethic. You left school, you got a job, you earned a living, you supported your family. And if you didn't do that, there was something wrong.

I knew that. I saw it with Ola and Howard, and the way their marriage collapsed because Howard refused to conform to 'the norm'. And now, suddenly, in the eyes of the outside world, I was doing exactly the same thing.

Just like Ola had, Almetta went out to work every day, at a store called Hudson's. And, just like Howard, I stayed at home.

Almetta and I had moved back to Lumpkin Street, living again with Ola and Uncle James, and I know to Ola it must sometimes have felt like history was repeating itself. But I think she also understood. I was driven; I had a goal and I was not going to allow anything to distract me from it. Exactly as she had taught me. She may not have liked what I was doing, but she could read me like a book. She never interfered.

Almetta, too, left me to get on with it. Occasionally she would suggest that I find myself a job like her friends' husbands had… one of them was working at a grocery downtown and Almetta had heard there was a vacancy. Why didn't I apply for that?

"Just get out of my face," I told her. "I'm not going to work in any damned grocery store. That's not how I want to be." Plus, I knew it was the friend who had put that particular idea into her head – whether Almetta could see the point in what I was doing or not, she knew that this was important to me, and besides, she could see how much effort I was putting into it.

It made me laugh years later, however, when that same friend and her husband came to me, asking if they could borrow some money. Money that I would never have had if I'd gone along with their stupid idea.

I truly believe that songwriting… that is, the ability to write songs… is a natural talent. Either you are born with it or you're not. I also believe that I fell into the latter category.

But I was not going to let that stop me. As dedicated as any industry apprentice, learning a skill from the bottom up, I threw myself into my studies. I listened to songs and then I dismantled them, line by line, word by word, syllable by syllable. I learned why this lyric scanned and that one didn't; how this sequence of words hit you in the gut and that one flew in one ear and out the other.

I picked apart some of the greatest songs ever written, and the biggest hits as well, and worked to make them better. "What if they had used this word instead of that one?" "What would happen if, instead of starting a second verse, they had continued the themes that shaped the first one?" "Why is the chorus here, when it would sound a lot more powerful there?" I was like a forensic investigator, or maybe a mad scientist, forever experimenting, trying one thing and then another, painstakingly searching for that certain chemical reaction. A medieval alchemist, transmuting the base metal of my natural abilities into the gold of a whole new talent.

Uncle James and Helen had divorced by now; he had a new girlfriend, who would become his second wife, and we were sitting together in the kitchen. Or rather, they were sitting together; I was in the same room, at the same table, but I was in another world entirely.

Suddenly James's girlfriend asked what I was doing. I picked up the song I was working on and held it up to her. "This is going to make me rich."

She burst out laughing.

A week later, I was still seated in the same place, still working on the same song. James watched me for a while, and then said, "Eddie, you have to stop. You're going to give yourself a nervous breakdown. Please, before you lose your mind completely."

I didn't reply. I put my head down and kept on working.

Other people offered their opinions. Neighbours, watching every day as Almetta left for work, while I stayed at home – you can imagine what they thought. "Writing songs?" they'd say to one another. "What kind of job is that for a healthy young man?" Or, "That Eddie Holland. All he does is laze around the house all day, while his wife goes out to work." Or, "Music? What sort of nonsense is that?"

Music was not considered a career in those days. Music was something that happened in a universe far away, made by people a million miles from places like Lumpkin Street and beamed into their homes by some barely comprehendible technology. People had never even heard of terms like 'the music industry', let alone understood it. Saying you intended to become a musician was like saying you wanted to be an astronaut. Crazy talk.

And maybe they were right. Maybe I was crazy. And selfish and lazy and all the other things they were saying about me. But I didn't believe that, and I didn't care what they thought. I was on a mission and I knew I would accomplish what I'd set out to do. Because finally I was getting somewhere. Finally, I had a lyric that I wanted to show to other people.

All I needed was a neutral opinion, somebody to tell me what I was doing right, what I was doing wrong. So one time my brother came home and I said, "This is what I want you to do." I believed I finally had a feel for writing, so I handed him a song I'd written and asked him to take it and show it to Berry.

"But don't tell him I wrote it because he knows I don't write songs. Tell him you wrote it."

Brian looked a little unsure, but he said okay, and all through the following day I was sitting at home, impatiently waiting for him to come in at 5, 6 p.m.

"Did you show it to him, did you show it to him?"

"Oh yeah, I showed it to him."

"What did he say?"

"He said, 'Brian, you didn't write this. Janie wrote it.'"

I cannot tell you how good that made me feel. He thought my song was something that Janie would write, and I knew how good Janie was. How good Berry thought she was. And that was when I started coming back around Motown.

Chapter Nine

The Birth of a Legend

Brian: Berry was on to me straight away with that song of Eddie's. He said, "Who wrote it really?" He knew that when it came to writing lyrics, I was very limited. But I knew Edward could write because he was showing me lyrics all the time. I'd put some melodies to them, and I liked what he was doing. He was good even then.

Eddie: I didn't try to teach myself to write melodies. Or, rather, I *did*, but I quickly realised that my strength was in lyrics. At least when I compared my efforts with Brian's, which I did all the time.

I remember once I was on my way up to our office, on the second floor at Hitsville, and when I got there the door was closed. I could hear somebody playing the piano and I knew it was Brian, simply because of what he was playing and the way he was playing it.

It was a new melody… I don't remember which one, but I was so overcome, completely taken aback by all these beautiful chords he was creating. It was astounding because I'd never heard him play anything like that. In fact, it started me thinking maybe I should learn to play piano myself, but I quickly realised I could never learn to play like that, so I decided to stick with writing.

Years later, and I do mean years, decades even, I told Brian that he ruined my life. I'd decided, finally, that I wanted to learn how to read and write music, and the teacher was surprised that I'd never done it before. He asked me why, so I told him about Brian, how he could hear notes and harmonies in his head, and that I couldn't, so obviously I didn't have the ear for it.

The teacher laughed. "Oh, he's one of *those* people," he said, emphasising the word 'those'. And he explained that there are very, very few people in the world who have that ability. "Never compare yourself with your brother," he said, "because there's not many of us who could."

So I called up Brian and told him, "Brian, you ruined my life. I'd have learned music long ago if it wasn't for you." We still laugh about it.

Occasionally, a tune would come into my head, inspired by the words I'd written. 'Brenda' was one such tune, and it was all right, although I didn't do anything with it. I put it to one side, but nothing really goes to waste because years later, the song came back to me when I was looking for something to record on The Four Tops. It was completely out of the blue. "You know what would sound good with Levi Stubbs singing? 'Brenda'." And it did.

I was also testing the waters with other artists. One of the very first songs I wrote*, and had recorded, was 'Thank You (For Loving Me All The Way)'. Little Stevie Wonder recorded that one.

I didn't do much with Stevie. He was so young – no more than fourteen when he recorded that song – and he mostly worked with producer Clarence Paul. But like everybody at Motown, I was in awe of his talent – he reminded me of Brian in a lot of ways, with his ear for music. And, of course, he had a great sense of humour. Clarence told me once about how Stevie was constantly asking if he could drive Clarence's car. Of course Clarence said no, but

---

* With Mickey Stevenson and Clarence Paul.

Stevie wouldn't give up, until finally, Clarence said, "I had to let him do it."

I also remember how he could make his way from building to building at Motown without using his cane. An incredible person.

Around that time, Mickey Stevenson, Norman Whitfield and I wrote 'He Was Really Sayin' Somethin'' for The Marvelettes; I recorded 'True Love Will Go A Long Way', which was my lyrics to a melody Brian and Mickey came up with; and there was another one that I wrote with Lamont and Fran Heard, Motown's tape librarian, a lovely lady.

Fran had always wanted to write a song and have it recorded, and she mentioned that to Lamont one time. He said, "Okay, what do you have?" and she handed him 'Day Dreamer'. He and I fixed it up and then we recorded it, with me singing.

I also wrote 'Everything Is Good About You' for Barbara McNair with our cousin James Dean, and when our sister Carole mentioned that she was feeling a little left out of our newfound musical universe, Brian sat down and wrote a song with her. It was a good family affair we had going there!

My main writing partner in the earliest days, though, was Norman Whitfield.

Norman was a New Yorker who arrived at Motown – indeed, arrived in Detroit – in a very singular manner. When he was fourteen, in 1954, his grandmother died out in California. The family drove cross-country to attend the funeral. Then, as they were driving home again, the car broke down somewhere outside Detroit.

Fortunately, they had family in the city, so they went to stay with them, and they never left town again. Norman, who was already a talented percussionist, found his way into Thelma Records, a little label run by Berry's ex-mother-in-law, Hazel Coleman*, and while he started as an occasional session man, soon he was writing for the label too.

---

* Thelma was the name of Coleman's daughter, Berry's wife.

Eddie: Norman was my first regular songwriting partner, at least in terms of having records released, and of course we would continue writing together into the future.

The first song we wrote together was 'Throw A Farewell Kiss', which we cut on Freddie Gorman. But there were a lot of others – 'I Couldn't Cry If I Wanted To', which I recorded; 'No Time For Tears'; 'Bright Lights, Big City', a title we lifted from Jimmy Reed, although I'm not sure if we knew that at the time; 'The Boy From Crosstown'; 'He Who Picks A Rose'… there were a lot, but the one I remember the best was 'Too Many Fish In The Sea', which we recorded on The Marvelettes.

Looking back, it surprises me how many tracks we did together. I was writing a lot more songs than I actually realised, and many more than I remember today, and that was because I had the perfect environment in which to work.

Motown was the ideal school for me, and for everybody else, because you were around peers who were all very talented. We were constantly feeding off one another, exchanging feelings. You'd be listening to them and they were listening to you, and this was going on all day, every day. You couldn't help but learn, and Berry Gordy was our teacher.

Everything we knew, we learned from Berry. He was our mentor. But at the same time, we mentored one another. For example, I know Brian influenced Norman tremendously because Norman thought he was so exceptional. He always said that Brian cut such powerful tracks, so that's what Norman concentrated on. Making tracks that knocked you over.

I was writing with Norman, but I was also watching Brian and Lamont. They were doing a lot of production at that point, their own songs as well as other people's, and I noticed that they could whip out melodies so fast, and there was nothing they couldn't write.

The problem was lyrics. One song might have great lyrics but the next one, not so good. There was no consistency, but their melodies were so good that they demanded consistency.

Finally, I said to Brian, "You know what? You guys come up with melodies and they're great but…" I paused, and then asked, "What if you guys did the melodies, and I wrote the lyrics? We could make a lot of money. Also, if you let me write the lyrics, we'll be able to turn out records faster and produce more projects."

It sounded kinda odd to Brian. He didn't see it at first. But he thought about it, and then he talked it over with Lamont. Finally they agreed, and Brian said, "Why don't we call ourselves…" they were already known as Holland–Dozier. They added me to the end and, on that day, Holland–Dozier–Holland was born.

It was a close-run thing, though, as Janie Bradford reminded us.

"In the early days of Motown, when Holland–Dozier–Holland consisted only of Holland–Dozier, Brian and Lamont were coming up with these great tracks but their lyrics were falling short. So they asked me if I would join them as their lyricist.

"Well, I never wanted to be with a team. I wanted to stay free to write with whomever I wanted, but rather than say that, I gave them a typical Janie Bradford answer. 'Money' had just given us our first huge hit, but not only that, people all over the world were covering it. So I told them no. 'You see, guys,' I said, 'I write standards. My songs don't disappear overnight. Instead, they get covered over and over, so I'll pass.'

"Enter Eddie Holland, and Holland–Dozier–Holland was born. And now I have the bragging rights that history has proven: I gave them the opportunity to become the greatest songwriters and production team ever. Some things are meant to be, and Holland–Dozier–Holland is one of those phenomena. I am so proud to embrace Eddie and Brian as my brothers and, since I still get my share of the loot, all is well in the family."

We love Janie so much!

The first song we wrote together as Holland–Dozier–Holland was 'Come And Get These Memories', for Martha & The Vandellas. It was released in February 1963, the group's second single for Motown,

With Janie Bradford at a Motown party, collecting the company's own songwriter awards. Eddie: "We won it three years in a row, and I think they stopped doing them after that."

after Mickey Stevenson heard Martha performing solo at the 20 Grand and invited her to audition.

He handed her his card and expected her to call and make an appointment – he held auditions on the third Thursday of the month. Instead, she turned up at the front door the following morning, and announced that she had given up her job and was ready to go into the studio. Mickey was completely nonplussed, and it was even harder for him to think with the telephone constantly ringing. Finally he told Martha to answer the phone while he figured out what to do. Eight months later, she was still answering Mickey's phone!

But he did find her some work as a backing vocalist and, one day, when The Andantes – his usual first choice as background singers – didn't show up, Mickey told Martha to round up three other girls and report for duty in the studio.

Three phone calls later, Rosalind Ashford, Annette Beard and Gloria Jean Williamson, Martha's bandmates in a group called The Del-Phis, were standing alongside Martha at the mic, singing background on Marvin Gaye's 'Stubborn Kind Of Fellow'.

Mickey wanted to give them a credit on the label. But Berry hated the name The Del-Phis, and Martha wasn't keen on his suggestion of The Dominettes. Instead, she suggested The Vandellas, which she said was a cross between Van Dyke Street in Detroit and her favourite singer, Della Reese. Berry agreed.

The group's next break also came about by chance, after Mary Wells missed a session and Mickey called Martha instead. 'I'll Have To Let Him Go' became the group's first single, and in a way, 'Come And Get These Memories' was destined to be their second, even before we realised it.

Martha was in the room, taking notes in her role as Mickey's secretary, while we were writing it. She later told us "I knew it was my song" before we'd even finished it.

Eddie: I sort of inherited my place on 'Come And Get These Memories' because Brian and Lamont had already written most of it. Most of the songs didn't take all three of us to write. But the combination of the three of us was incredibly potent, even if one of us was sitting there watching.

Brian was usually involved, because his melodies were so superior to anybody else's, and his ability to produce records was second to none. Sometimes Lamont would have an idea, sometimes he wouldn't, and although I was writing the lyrics, that was a struggle because I was still learning at the same time, so they both helped me.

What made the difference was this: I could also sing the songs, and I had an ability to interpret their melodies a little better than other people. When they brought me a tune, I would sing it, sing it, sing it. I would keep working it, singing the first thing that came into my head, writing it down, then the next, and I would keep honing it and changing it.

It would take me three weeks to write the average song, using my instincts to develop a style that was a little different to anybody else. And I knew I had found it the day it was announced that everybody should come into the office and do a full day's work, every day, starting at eight in the morning. I believe it was an attempt to streamline the operation, save money and cut down on what could be seen as waste. But I believed it was the lack of streamlining and the opportunity for waste that gave the company its strength. It allowed us to experiment with our music and perfect our craft.

The idea came down from Ralph Seltzer, who was the company administrator. He was very businesslike, and he wanted us to be businesslike as well. Because we weren't. None of us 'creatives' adhered to any kind of set schedule. We would just trickle in, some at nine or ten, some at eleven or twelve, and then we would trickle out again, some at five or six, some at nine or ten. We did a full day's work, but we did it on our own schedules.

Mickey Stevenson told me I would now be expected in the office every day of the week, Monday through Friday, eight to five. I flat out refused.

"No way am I doing that."

Mickey stared at me. "Oh well. I suppose I'll have to get somebody else to write with Holland–Dozier, won't I?"

"Yeah," I said. "But they won't be as good as I am."

It sounded arrogant, I'm sure, but that's not how I intended it. I just knew that nobody else could interpret those beautiful melodies in the same way I could. Whatever his thoughts, however, Mickey didn't say another word. But I never did go in at eight in the morning, and nobody ever mentioned it to me again.

Because I couldn't be creative on the clock. Sometimes I wrote in my apartment on La Salle, sometimes I wrote in the garden, or walking down the street, or anywhere. I wrote where I wanted to, or where the idea was. I couldn't sit at a desk all day being brilliant to order, although, again, I know there were some great songwriters at that time who could.

The Brill Building people, for example. The Shirelles were one of my favourite groups back then, and a lot of their songs came out of the Brill Building, people working the day shift writing songs. Kasenetz–Katz, who scored so many bubblegum hits in the late 1960s worked the same way. But I couldn't do that. Besides, what if I woke up at three in the morning with the best idea ever? Would Motown have paid me overtime?

We had our first hit, so Martha & The Vandellas became our first act, and we wrote a string of hits for them over the years: 'Nowhere To Run', 'Quicksand' and 'Heat Wave'.

Lamont was very much the driving force behind our work with the group. What became 'Heat Wave', for instance, was a melody he always used to play when he first arrived in the studio. It was his way of warming up for whatever was ahead, and one time in the studio with The Vandellas, somebody realised they needed one more song.

"Why don't you give them that thing you're always playing?" Brian asked, and an hour or so later, they had the finished track.

Eddie: It was a very strong track, and he had the title already. The funny thing is, I thought he was cutting an old song that was also called 'Heat Wave', and asked him why, when we were quite capable of writing our own. He said, "No, I'm just cutting something. That's simply the title."

I breathed a sigh of relief. "Cut the track and I'll write the lyric."

It sometimes seems that people forget how huge Martha & The Vandellas were in 1963, and how much they contributed to putting

Motown on the map. It felt like everything we did on them went Top 10, and when you think about all the people who've recorded those songs since then – Linda Ronstadt, Ike & Tina Turner, The Who, Dusty Springfield, so many others – you begin to see what we were aiming for, even then. There's a world of difference between Linda and Tina, but Martha & The Vandellas bridged it.

The other thing about those records that stands out is the way they kept getting faster and faster. That was also Lamont's

Helping Hands

DETROIT—Claudette Robinson, petite singer with the Miracles, gets an assist with her crutches from Tamla Records topper Berry Gordy, Jr. (left), and songster Eddie Holland. Claudette is temporarily out of action as the result of surgery on her toes. Holland is getting his first taste of fame with "Jamie" on the Motown label.

One of Eddie's first ever appearances in a magazine!

influence. He heard a certain frenetic quality in the group that he wanted to capture. He knew that they could handle faster songs better than anybody else at Motown, and it was like a red rag to a bull. Faster, faster! Almost as though he wanted to find out if we could ever write a song that was too fast for them. We never did. Years later, we all laughed about that, and we agreed – a couple of them really were too fast!

So we were off and running, but we were also faced with a massive obstacle. All the big names on Motown at that time – Smokey Robinson, Marvin Gaye, Little Stevie Wonder, Mary Wells – were working regularly with other people. Or, in Smokey's case, writing everything themselves.

We did write for some of the others: Kim Weston, The Vells (who were actually The Vandellas, with Gloria singing lead instead of Martha), and The Supremes, but they tended either to be one-off sessions that would appear on albums or B-sides. Or they didn't come out at all.

Eddie: When Lamont, Brian and I first got together, we had problems getting songs released because Smokey would get all the releases. It was during that time when he was the hottest writer in the world. We'd be sitting around and Lamont would complain, "Man, we're never going to get a release." It wasn't going at all like we wanted it to, and this went on for I don't know how long – it might have been a year and it felt even longer than that.

We were getting so frustrated. We didn't want to get one song here and one song there, and maybe this and maybe that. We wanted to be doing what we ended up doing: being very, very consistent, very, very successful, and overpowering with the quality of our songs. Instead, we were sitting around, knowing we had some great stuff ready to go, and to make matters worse, everywhere we went in the building, Smokey would be there, probably writing another hit without even having to think about it.

*   *   *

We weren't completely stagnant. We were still turning out new songs. 'Lead Me And Guide Me' for LaBrenda Ben, 'I'm Gonna Make It To The Top' for Freddie Gorman, 'You Lost The Sweetest Boy' for Mary Wells. We were producing an incredible amount of material, but nothing was really sticking.

Eddie: 'You Lost The Sweetest Boy' goes way back to when I was learning. It was one of the very first songs I ever did. I rewrote that song twice. But it was so complicated. I knew what I shouldn't have done but I did it anyway. I was trying to write something I thought Smokey might write, something sophisticated like he would do, and it was a good try but it didn't quite work.

I rewrote it, looked at it, rewrote it again, looked at it, and all the while I kept thinking, "Man, you missed the sweet spot on this one." Then, when I played it to Berry and asked him what he thought of it, he agreed. "Hmmm, it is kind of complicated."

He did release it as a single, but it wasn't a hit. It was going up slowly, but then the DJs turned it over and what did they find? They found a Smokey song on the B-side, 'What's Easy For Two Is So Hard For One', so they started playing that instead.

The Vandellas aside, then, we weren't having hits. But people could see that we were trying. We were competing for a place at the top table. We weren't sitting around, quietly passing our songs around in the hope that somebody would notice them; we were actively pushing them forward, and the reason for that was, we had so many that we didn't know what else to do with them.

Eddie: I had stacks and stacks and stacks of paper for each song. Sometimes I would write lyrics I could use on another song because it tied in as well, and all I'd have to do was change it around. I didn't throw any of those scraps away, because I figured you could take anything and reshape it for a different song, so that's what I would do.

But it was always melody first, and that was one of the reasons it was sometimes so difficult. The hardest job was taking Brian's melodies, or the ideas that he or Lamont gave me, and making sense out of them. That was a very difficult job, because I had to create an image in my mind, and that's not always easy.

The other thing was, my own insecurity. I thought I was doing a good job and other people at Motown appeared to agree. But I was forever waiting for Brian to tell me because, ultimately, I was working for him. Yet I wasn't getting any feedback at all, unless we were disagreeing about something.

Brian: Oh man, we had some real knock-down battles in those early days.

Eddie: It always started in the same way. Maybe I'd need an extra couple of beats to fit the lyric and Brian simply couldn't understand why. Or he might insist on keeping a couple of beats I didn't think were necessary, because they got in the way of the words.

It happens, I think, whenever two people collaborate on a writing project. It doesn't matter how in tune they may be, there are always going to be those little things they disagree with – why did you use this word, or this note, in this place, when that word, or that note, would be better? Everybody has their own vision of how something should flow, how it should feel, where the emphasis lies or the rhythm needs to shift, and it can take a lot of work, a lot of patience and a lot of compromise to finally make it happen.

What I didn't understand back then was that Brian could hear every instrument, long before they were added. I could hear the beat and the timing, but Brian would know where the guitar was to come in and what it would sound like, where there was a drum break or whatever, and that complicated things for me.

I'd say, "Give me eight bars for a verse and two lines here or there," and he'd say, "No, you can't have a lyric there because it's in the way of my guitar" or whatever. Sometimes, he would even tell me, "Take some of those lines out of there," because they were getting in the way of another instrument, and I'd say, "No, I can't do that because it won't make sense," and he'd ask, "What difference does it make?" Or I'd tell him I needed two more bars, something like that. He would argue, "No, I want it to get to the bridge quicker. Hey man," he'd say, "it's not about the lyric, it's about the melody and the beat." And I'd fire back, "No, it's the lyric!"

We fought so hard, there were some real doozies. Years later, Brian was very happy that we did that, but at the time, he hated it. Because we would argue and argue and argue until he finally gave up – not because he agreed, but because he knew I'd never stop until he did.

Lamont, on the other hand, never argued. He hated confrontation, so he'd leave it for Brian and I to fight it out and ease himself very quietly out of the room. Plus, two brothers fighting is very different to other people fighting. I remember once, Brian and I were arguing about something and someone tried to break it up because they thought we were getting too violent, and a physical fight was about to start.

I said, "No no no, are you interfering with our conversation?" They turned to me in total shock. They thought they were doing something helpful. "You call *that* a conversation?"

What made it worse for me was, as I said, that was the only feedback I ever got from Brian. I was desperate for him to walk up and, out of the blue, say, "Hey man, I really liked that lyric," or something like that. But he never did, and it took me years to understand why. Because that wasn't where his head was: he would hear the melody, and that's what moved him. That's *all* that moved him. He could already hear the instrumentation in his head when he was writing the song, so, when he heard the finished record, my lyrics were merely another instrument.

We continued writing, we continued hoping. And one day that summer of 1963, we knew we'd finally broken through. Smokey was going to record a song we'd written for him.

According to Mickey Stevenson, 'Mickey's Monkey' was inspired by us watching him leap around the studio while he produced tracks, and joking between ourselves that he was 'doing the monkey', which was the latest dance craze.

That may or may not be true; Lamont came up with the title. But it doesn't matter either way. The fact was, Smokey – one of the greatest songwriters there ever was – was going to record one of our songs.

Eddie: The way Motown usually worked was, you'd write the song and then you'd pitch it to the producer. The artist would then record it. That was one of Motown's strongest points – the producer chose the songs, not the artist.

But with Smokey, of course, you had to pitch it to the artist as well, because he was both producer and artist. So we wrote 'Mickey's Monkey', we pitched it to him, and we didn't really expect to hear anything more. Smokey rarely sang other people's

Our mother, Johnny Terry and our sister Carole at an event in the mid-sixties.

songs. He only wanted to sing his own songs, and why shouldn't he? He could write perfectly for himself.

So, the most exciting thing about him recording 'Mickey's Monkey' was – he recorded it. Later he recorded a couple of other things we wrote, but that was after we were established. This was different. This was 1963, and Holland–Dozier–Holland were still the new kids in the room.

Plus, Smokey was such an influence on me, on my writing, forcing me to find my own unique style because there was no way I could emulate his. The very fact that he was going to do one of our songs was amazing, it really was. I was so surprised, but that inspired us to write another one for him, 'I Gotta Dance To Keep From Crying', and this time it was written specifically with Smokey in mind. We didn't know if he'd want to put it out but we hoped he'd try it.

Chapter Ten

Baby I Need Your Loving

Brian: The first time I met my first wife, Sharon Grace Pierce, she was in the hospital. Her sister, Sandra, attended Central High with me, and one time she asked me if I would go with her to the hospital to visit Sharon.

I don't remember what was wrong with her, but she was so pretty, the moment I saw her, I knew I wanted her. Robert Bateman was taking out Sandra at the same time, so after Sharon was released from the hospital, the four of us would crash around town together, and we always had so much fun.

Sharon and I remained together through high school, and finally I asked her to marry me. As for why we got married, that was because of Edward. He and I were very close and when he got married, I didn't know what to do with myself. The only reason I wanted to get married was because Edward had, and I felt left out. He'd tell me all about his little experiences and, although I don't think he was completely happy, to me, he was the luckiest boy alive, because it meant he would never be alone again.

Did I fall in love? Well, it doesn't take much for young boys to fall in love. I was sixteen or seventeen when I met Sharon, eighteen or nineteen when we got married, and at first, I enjoyed every minute of it because, when you get married, you have sex, and that's what I really loved. That's what it was all about.

As I got to know Sharon better, though, I realised I didn't particularly like her. She was a mean woman. When I first met her, things were fine, but when you get to live with someone, get to really know them, things come out that you never suspected were in there, and everything changes. Especially when you are as young as we were.

Plus, I didn't know she was also what we would call today bipolar. She had the most horrifying mood swings, and I wasn't equipped to deal with them. I don't think anybody my age, and at that time, could have been.

She used to suffer from the most awful headaches. Migraine headaches. In fact, it was a long time before I realised how severe they were. She was in such excruciating pain so much of the time,

Brian and Sharon's wedding day.

and was in and out of the Emergency Room at the hospital many, many times.

What they told me was, blood would keep going to her head, and that's what was giving her these headaches. To stop the blood from flowing to her brain, they would tie off the veins in her arms and legs, a process called arterial ligation. As a treatment, it has apparently been around since the tenth century, and the first time you see it happen to somebody, you can believe it. It looks positively medieval.

We had a little apartment on a side street of West Grand Boulevard, and I used to dread going home some nights because I never knew what I'd find when I got there. Whether Sharon would be curled up in the dark, in the bedroom, crying from pain, or what kind of mood she would be in.

So many times I got home and walked straight into a fight that I never dreamed was awaiting me. I remembered something Uncle James told me. He said, "Women change. They change on you," and he always said it was better just to love them than ever try to understand them, "because you'll never understand a woman."

He was right as well, because all of a sudden, Sharon started to not want sex as much as I did. A few times a night became maybe once a week. Once a month. Weeks could go by and we might not touch one another a single time. And if I said anything, that would be another fight – "Why do you keep pressuring me? Why do you keep on about it?"

Soon, we were barely together at all. I'm not going to make excuses for myself. I was young, I was horny and I didn't understand why, after everything had been great between us, suddenly she wasn't interested any more. All kinds of things went through my head. Did she have somebody else? Had I walked into a trap – she'd give me what I wanted until she got what she wanted... a ring on her finger? My career was beginning to take off – was that it? Was I a secure meal ticket? Linda, our first child was born; maybe that was all that she wanted, a baby. And now she had one, there was no need to go through the process of trying to make another.

It felt as though she didn't care. But not long after Linda was born, I received a letter in the mail, the dreaded "Hello, this is Uncle Sam". I was being drafted.

The Vietnam War was not yet underway, but the pieces were definitely being moved into position. The Cold War with the Soviet Union was as hot as it had ever been. US troops were stationed all over the world, often in readiness for a new conflict to erupt, and who knew where or when that might take place?

I took the letter to Berry and he read it. "Oh yeah, Brian, you've got to go into the services."

"I can't!" I told him. "I've gotten married, I've had a baby!" And Berry said, "Okay, give me the letter, I'll see what I can do."

He took the letter, showed it to one of his family members who had connections in Michigan politics, then came back and told me I was all right. President Kennedy had recently* expanded what was known as the Class 3-A deferment to include fathers of newborns.

I expected Sharon to be delighted when I told her she didn't have to worry about me being shipped off to fight in a foreign country. Instead, she responded in much the same way as when I told her I'd received the letter in the first place. She didn't really say a thing.

But little Linda gave me the biggest smile as she lay in her crib that night.

Looking back, I could and maybe should have been more understanding about what Sharon was going through. I should have read up about migraines and psychology. I should have talked to her doctor and the people at the hospital. Maybe I should have done a lot of things. Instead, I got on with my life and put up with it.

---

* In March 1963.

Divorce didn't even cross my mind. I was miserable, I was frustrated and I felt completely rejected. I felt as though I was worthless to her. But she was my wife and the mother of my child. I didn't want to stay but I didn't want to leave, either. I didn't want to be alone.

Instead, I channelled my emotions into my music. Night after night, feeling rejected and unable to sleep, I'd go out to the piano and start playing, simply to stop my thoughts from turning over and over. I wasn't necessarily writing; it was a form of therapy. It made me happy, and that took my mind off all the other emotions churning up inside me.

But one night, sitting in the dark, crying, a song did come to me. Over and over I played it, night after night, in tears, in darkness, in utter despair. It was called 'Baby I Need Your Loving'.

I had the tune, the title, the chorus – "Baby I need your loving, got to have all your loving". It was a total cry from the heart, or maybe from a bit lower than that – it was me calling out to Sharon that I couldn't live like this any longer. I loved her and I wanted her, and I couldn't understand why she didn't want me. I took the song to Edward and Lamont, and I didn't even need to tell them what it was about. They understood, especially Edward. His lyrics for that song were perfect.

Then we called in Hank Cosby to write the music charts. I'd decided I wanted strings, because I'd been listening to 'There Goes My Baby' by the Drifters, and it had the most beautiful strings on it. So we recorded the track and it sounded amazing. The only drawback was, we couldn't think of anybody to offer it to. There was nobody who felt like a good fit for the song. So we put it on the shelf, waiting for the right voice to come along.

We knew one would.

There was one other moment that year which profoundly affected us. It was when Berry announced he'd arranged to release a recording of the rally that Dr. Martin Luther King Jr. held at Cobo Hall, on June 23, 1963.

That was the night he debuted what became known as the 'I Have A Dream' speech, the one he gave in Washington a couple of months later, and it completely overwhelmed the place. Everybody in the auditorium sat in stunned silence.

It was the height of the civil rights campaign and, at that point, nobody knew which direction things were going to move. Logically, in a fair society, a democracy, the struggle should win. Particularly in the south, people were living almost as though the emancipation of the slaves had never occurred, or at least as if it somehow was optional, to be regarded or disregarded according to personal preference. That's how entrenched and vicious attitudes were.

There was no reason why that way of life should continue; no way it had a place in what we called a modern, civilised democracy. But politics doesn't necessarily believe in logic. Politicians would rather maintain the status quo than risk alienating a large group of people – particularly when that large group was mostly comprised of whites, and included a lot of very powerful people.

Whereas African-Americans… apart from people like James Farmer Jr., Malcolm X, Roy Wilkins, Whitney Young Jr., and Dr. King, who did we have standing up for us?

Eddie: There was also the feeling, again among the white community, that racism and segregation were a southern problem, and that the north had nothing to do with it. It wasn't true. One of the biggest scandals in Detroit was red-lining, which meant denying things like personal insurance to different areas, depending upon how black the neighbourhood was.

Despite this, I never felt as though I'd grown up in a racist area. There was name-calling, of course, but it wasn't aimed only at African-Americans. Every skin colour, every nationality, every religious group, there was a bad name for each of them, and that included the white, 'all-American' kids. Anything that made one person different to another had a name.

Maybe there were problems and attitudes which ran deeper than that, but I was never aware of them, and I was never the kind of person who would have simply accepted that kind of thing if I was confronted with it.

The only experience I ever had was later in the 1960s, when I bought my house in Palmer Woods, a very upscale area of Detroit. I was looking at the original deed, drawn up when the house was built back in the 1930s, and there on the page it said, "This property is not to be sold to African-Americans or Jews."

Of course, we were not immune from the struggle, not in Detroit and not at Motown. Berry himself was deeply involved – in fact, his mother, Bertha, was an National Association for the Advancement of Colored People (NAACP) activist, who was also involved in setting up the Friendship Mutual Insurance Agency, one of the few insurance companies dedicated to providing coverage for low-income black families.

There was barely a single musician at Motown who had not toured the south at some point in their careers, and they knew exactly what went on down there – the clubs that would not even hire an African-American musician or who, if they did, wouldn't allow black people in to watch them. Or the band would have to sleep on the bus because there wasn't a hotel in town that would rent a room to them.

Even radio was touched by it. The majority of people who actually worked in it, the disc jockeys and station owners, they wanted to play music, regardless of the colour of the people who made it. But their audience, and the advertisers, they had a different set of values. That's one of the reasons why there was such a divide between the pop and R&B charts. The very term 'R&B' was a form of segregation.

Berry felt so strongly about all of this. It was one of the reasons he was so keen for Motown to break into the pop market. Not for the money, although of course that was a part of it, but to try and break down the barriers between 'us' and 'them'. He loved it when a black artist had a major hit on the pop charts, and he loved it even more when a black artist from a black-owned label had one. It didn't even have to be a Motown record.

Brian: The thing that brought people together was Motown, because Motown crossed over to a lot of white people. They loved The Supremes, once they broke through, and that was the epitome of a black group becoming a part of the white world.

Then a couple more followed, Marvin Gaye and Little Stevie Wonder, so to me there was no division. Our music was universal, all around the world. Colourless. But that said, Holland–Dozier–Holland's music did appeal mostly to a white audience.

Berry was devoted to the civil rights cause. But what he didn't want us doing – any of us – was anything that could be construed as protest music.

There was a lot of it about, people like Bob Dylan and Joan Baez, Phil Ochs and Peter, Paul & Mary. An entire musical genre, 'protest music', grew up, and the civil rights movement adopted many of the songs, particularly those that were rooted in specific incidents and events. That said, it was the white section of the movement, more than the black, that sang along with them – although we would later record Dylan's 'Blowin' In The Wind' with The Supremes!

Prior to that, however, Berry counselled firmly against Motown becoming involved in that side of things, but not because he was worried about the label being accused of making trouble, or being radical. He did it because he wanted to beat the system from within. He dreamed of a day when the entire pop Top 40 would be made up of black artists, on black labels, but singing songs that appealed to everyone, whatever colour they might be.

Which is what we did.

Of course, we were horrified by what was happening. Every time you opened a newspaper, there would be another story of murders and church burnings, and wide-open discrimination on the streets of southern towns and cities.

Comer, where Grandmother Ola's family originated, is in Madison County, Georgia, and I remember how horrified we were when Lemuel Penn, who was a Lieutenant Colonel in the US Army

Reserve, decorated by his country during the Second World War, was murdered on the county line in 1964.

He was driving down the highway with two other officers, and a couple of Ku Klux Klansmen motored past and shot him dead. And the first time the killers were tried, they were acquitted. The prosecution had to appeal all the way up to the Supreme Court to get the verdict overturned and win a new trial.

You read things like that and, no matter how safe we might have felt in Detroit, you saw how close to home it was. How close to our family's roots. It would have been very easy for us to become completely overwhelmed by it all.

What stopped that from happening was our music. We buried ourselves in it. We felt so helpless about the situation, and we knew there was nothing concrete we could do. But if we could write music that was positive – love songs, happy songs, feel-good songs – then maybe we could make a difference. We were trying to keep ourselves from being angry about it, asking why a government that we all voted for, both blacks and whites, was allowing this stuff to happen.

Eddie: I wanted to make music that was maybe more pleasant and happy. I didn't want to become engulfed by what was going on because I found it very depressing. I stayed in touch enough that I had a sense of it all, but I didn't want to bury myself in it.

Years and years after, though, I saw some old films of what had been happening in the south, and I broke down and cried. It all came pouring out, everything that I had been suppressing back then, and had continued to suppress for so long afterwards. It was unlike me to cry about anything but that hit me so hard.

We were never indifferent, though. Thoughts and sentiments will always make their way into lyrics, and you don't have to be blatant about it. People will either hear what you want them to hear, or they won't.

Sometimes, of course, they heard what wasn't there. Lamont had an idea for a song, 'Jimmy Mack', which was his tribute to the songwriter Robbie Mack, who wrote 'He's So Fine' for The Chiffons but died from Hodgkin lymphoma just as the royalties were beginning to come in.

When 'He's So Fine' was honoured at the BMI Songwriting Awards in 1963, Mack's mother collected his award and Lamont felt the need to write a tribute as well, with Edward writing the lyrics.

We changed Robbie's name to Jimmy, simply because it sounded better. The song was about a girl who still carries a torch for an old boyfriend, Jimmy Mack, but her resistance is beginning to fade. If Jimmy Mack doesn't come back soon, he'll have lost her forever.

But where was he? We don't say – he might have been in prison, he might have gone back to his wife, he might be anywhere. He might even have been drafted, and that's what Quality Control was worried about. People might think we were protesting the draft. The song was shelved, and ultimately wouldn't be released until 1967.

'Nowhere To Run', on the other hand, reversed that process altogether.

Lamont had thrown a party for a friend of his who was about to be shipped out to Vietnam. They were talking, and his friend, nineteen years of age, was terrified. It was as if he knew he wouldn't be coming back, that he was going to die out there and there was nothing he could do about it. He was trapped. "Nowhere to run".

Lamont came up with the title and Edward wrote the lyrics. Two months later, this kid stepped on a landmine and was killed. You wouldn't know any of that from the song. But the guys who were out there, the men who really did have nowhere to run, they knew exactly what we were talking about, like they knew what 'We Gotta Get Out Of This Place' was about, when The Animals had a hit with it, or Bob Dylan's 'All Along The Watchtower' – "There must be some way out of here". Neither of those were ever marketed as protest songs. But they became protest songs, or anti-war songs, regardless.

With all this in mind, the Martin Luther King Jr. album was something of a departure for Berry and for Motown, both in terms of content and financially – all the proceeds were donated to the

Southern Christian Leadership Conference, of which Dr. King was president.

But it was something that Berry, and everybody at Motown, believed in so strongly, and you could also say, he knew that if we didn't put the record out, somebody else would have.

Eddie: I remember going into the offices one Saturday, it must have been early August, 1963, and Dr. King walked in to pick up copies of *The Great March To Freedom*. I was in the studio and I heard that booming voice as he came into the control room, looking for Berry.

I'd seen him before. Back when I was very young, Ola took me to a rally he was holding somewhere in Detroit – all I remember was, it was the largest crowd I had ever seen in my life. I don't recall anything else; I probably didn't recognise how important he was.

This time, I did know, and it took my breath away. I didn't actually meet him, I didn't get to shake his hand or speak to him, or anything like that.

But all I could do was stand there and look at him. It was an amazing moment for me. I was in awe.

.

Chapter Eleven

Hitsville from the Inside

Eddie: I've lost count of the number of times I've heard people describe Berry as 'lucky', as though everything that Motown became simply fell into his lap by chance.

I've never subscribed to that belief. Perhaps he was fortunate that things worked out as phenomenally successful as they did, but every step of the way he knew exactly what he was doing. If they'd known him as well as I did, they would have seen how extraordinarily intuitive he was, and they'd have understood the special gift of creative brilliance that was there all along. Yes, he's very intelligent, but he also has something that most people don't, and that is emotional intelligence. He understood music and he understood business, but he also understood people and the things that make them tick.

I have watched him since I was seventeen years of age. I grew up watching him, through his struggles and his disappointments as well as his triumphs and highs, and throughout, no matter what, he was continually moving forward. He was always centred. Even the way he put that company together, piece by piece, a little at a time over a few years, there was no blueprint; it was instinctual.

Motown's success was no accident. It grew from Berry's understanding of what both the times and the music required.

And he communicated that understanding to all those who worked for him.

There was something about Motown, the musicians we worked with, the very atmosphere of the place, which was so inspirational. We worked but it never felt like work, and although we quickly fell into a routine, it didn't feel like a routine. Every song, every session, felt fresh and new.

Brian: I would usually start writing at home on my piano. I'd play the chords and hum a melody onto tape, using a reel-to-reel machine. It came so easily to me. Then I'd bring it to the Motown office and play it for Lamont and Edward to see what they liked, what they thought.

Sometimes Lamont would add new parts to a song – he worked the same way as I did, starting a song at home, and then we'd finish it together at the office. Then, once we felt we had a strong song, we'd call in someone to write out the chord sheets for us. It was usually Hank Cosby, who Berry had known since Hank was with Jackie Wilson's band, and people like Joe Hunter and Benny Benjamin, who were also part of the Motown set-up... The Funk Brothers. And when they were finished, we'd go into the Snake Pit. We would book the studio time and I'd decide which musicians would be right for the session.

We usually used The Funk Brothers simply because they were so accomplished, so good.

James Jamerson, who I was at Central High School with, was a helluva bass player; he knew jazz and he could play any kind of music. He played with one finger, which is very difficult to do, yet he was absolutely phenomenal with that one finger. He could play really fast, and his reaction time was exceptionally quick. He also played the upright bass. When we were at school, I'd see him playing bass in the hallway. He would carry that instrument wherever he went, from one classroom to the next. He had an exceptional ear, even then; he knew how to play any song you could give him.

Benny Benjamin was a key player for us even before Motown was formed. Early on, when Berry was still a songwriter placing songs with artists on other labels, he would use Benny to play drums on his demos. Benny was another jazz musician. But he could also play anything you threw at him. He was great – we would cancel sessions if we couldn't get Benny.

For the guitars, we usually brought in two or three players. Our favourite lead guitarist was Robert White. Robert's the one who played the great guitar intro at the beginning of 'My Girl' (by The Temptations). We depended upon Robert for many sessions.

We also liked bringing in Joe Messina and Eddie Willis, who played rhythm guitar, but on certain songs, we knew we'd want to add a fourth guitar player who'd double some of the other guitar parts. So two would play certain parts, and the other two would double the other parts.

We generally had two keyboard players for the session. Johnny Griffith was one, and for piano we'd call Earl Van Dyke. He could play great acoustic piano, Hammond B-3 organ and other keyboards, and he had a feel all of his own.

Years later, we discovered that the instrumental versions he did of some of our songs, things like 'How Sweet It Is (To Be Loved By You)' and 'Nowhere To Run', were really huge in the Mod clubs in England. Those driving Hammond-led pieces were sometimes even bigger than the hit versions!

There were other musicians who played on a lot of our sessions. If the song had a shuffle beat, we'd call Richard 'Pistol' Allen to play drums, because that's what he excelled at. Sometimes we'd call in Bob Babbitt to play bass. And when we needed a percussionist, we called Eddie 'Bongo' Brown.

Most of the songs we produced would also need horns, and sometimes strings. Paul Riser was our main guy – he would do the arrangements. We'd give him the finished rhythm tracks and he would do whatever was needed. He'd write out the arrangements and give them all to Hank Crosby, who played saxophone and was the lead horn player. Hank would then call up the horn and string players.

The musicians would straggle in around noon for the session. But I would always get there an hour earlier, around 11 a.m., because I had to set up the microphones.

I usually did all the engineering – only occasionally would I have someone else in, like Lawrence Horn, who was around by that point and he and I used to hang out. I helped him when he was working on 'Shotgun' for Junior Walker & The All Stars, and if I was in the studio, he'd look in and help out if I needed it.

Lamont would usually arrive at the start of the session with all the musicians. We would give them the chord sheets, and we'd tell them what type of song it was, what the tempo was, whether it was a shuffle, and we'd guide them as they played through the chord sheets.

We aimed to record three songs in one afternoon. If the track sounded good, we'd play it back and listen to it. If there were no mistakes, we'd move on to the next song. And we worked quickly because, when our three hours was up, we knew there would be other people waiting for us to finish to start their own session. But, if we did overrun, they wouldn't disturb us, because they knew it was Holland–Dozier–Holland in there cutting.

Eddie: Once in a while we would go past the three-hour session time, but never more than half an hour or so, because we were very disciplined. And because of The Funk Brothers, and their exceptional talent. We'd never have produced so many records, at such speed, if it were not for them.

When it started getting round that we were beginning to make a lot of money, there was a certain jealousy among the executives at the label, which eventually percolated down to the musicians. One time, early on, I remember James Jamerson going to Brian… Brian was telling him the chord he wanted him to play, and James was taking the position that nobody understood. So what James did was, he'd play the wrong chord and Brian would say no. He'd call out the chord that James was playing, and then tell him the one he wanted.

But James would hit the wrong chord again, and this kept going on and on. It was James testing Brian, trying to trip him up, and it didn't happen. Finally, James played the correct chord and, when that happened, he had a whole new respect for Brian. That moment completely changed the attitude.

Brian: Once we cut the track, we'd give it to Edward, who would write the lyrics.

Sometimes we'd already have the song title. Lamont came up with some great titles like 'I Can't Help Myself (Sugar Pie Honey Bunch)', which came from something his grandfather used to say a lot when he was a kid, and it stayed with him, the way these things sometimes do. Lamont's grandmother owned a beauty shop, and his granddad used to wander in and flirt with all the customers, "Hello, sugar pie, how are you doing?" I came up with a few titles, too. But most of the time Edward would write the titles.

Eddie: When I was given a new track, I would spend many days writing. I would lock myself away. I didn't go out much – most of my life was devoted to writing lyrics.

I wrote from my own experiences, something personal that was going on in my life at the time. But I always thought that women were the most interesting subjects, and that's something I learned, in a roundabout way, from Berry.

It was the early days of Holland–Dozier–Holland and I was on my way to see Berry about something. I got to the office and realised he was in a meeting. I could hear him talking, though, and what he said was that women were the people who bought most of the records.

A light bulb went on in my head. It was one of the best pieces of information I'd ever received. Everything else went out of my mind, including the fact I was on my way to see Berry. I just turned and went back to our office, all the time pondering on what I'd heard him say.

From then on, I worked to give my lyrics what I called 'female appeal'. Everything was geared towards catching the woman's point of view, her ear, her idea of what love is like. We had all these philosophies about it – "If the man does this, then the woman should be saying this…" – and they didn't always work. We often ended up missing some piece that threw off the equation. But that little remark of Berry's caused me to better direct myself.

Of course, I had to do the research. So whenever I was with a girl, I'd ask her questions, convince her to tell me all the little secrets women usually don't tell other men. "What's this business with all the crying?" for instance, and I will never forget this friend of mine, she said, "Well, that's a game we sometimes have to play. We have to use what we have to make it work with men." And then she said, "But usually it's real."

It was a really interesting topic. She was giving me examples, all the things that she'd been through with men, and long before she finished, she had tears rolling down her face, to show me how easy it was!

I was always curious about people. Even when I was a young boy, I'd watch the dynamics between the adults in my life. Then, as I grew into my teens, I started noticing a big difference in personalities between the male and female, and it fascinated me.

By the time I hit my twenties, I realised there was a real big difference, in my opinion, between the two. I also realised that men weren't fully aware of it. That caused me to be even more curious, because I would talk to men and they had no idea about this difference. I got many ideas from conversations like that, because they were what guided the feel of the song and its emotional impact. I was always looking for that punch.

The most important lesson I learned, though, is it's not that women are complicated, like so many men like to say. It's that men are so narrow-minded and stuck in their own beliefs and their masculinity that they don't *try* to understand.

Women learn this very early on, how to conquer the man and play on his ego. And that's what I learned, and wrote into those songs. Several times, female fans would turn up at Hitsville asking to see me. I didn't know them and I'd ask them why they'd come. They'd say, "It's because you understand."

Once Eddie had completed the lyrics, he'd record his vocals onto a work tape, and arrange to meet with the artist and play it to them, so they could learn the song and rehearse it. Then they'd meet up again on the day of the vocal session, about an hour before they were due to start recording, to go over the song.

Eddie: I would produce most of the lead vocal sessions, with Brian engineering. Then Lamont would produce most of the background vocal sessions, except once in a while when he would finish the song himself. On those occasions he would produce the lead vocals.

Brian: When everything was recorded, I would do the mixing. Sometimes Edward and Lamont would be there as well, but ultimately the final mixes were my decision.

I also did the editing. We would have to cut the master tape and then splice it back together. I became really good at splicing the tape. Maybe not as good as Robert Bateman used to be, but I would watch the tape fall on the floor. Then, when I knew we didn't need that piece of tape any more, I would stomp on it, so we wouldn't mistake it for something we needed.

Once the mix was done and I was happy with it, we would play it for Berry and Quality Control. After that, even though I was on the Quality Control team myself, it was out of our hands.

Eddie: I never went to the Quality Control meetings because I didn't feel like a part of the company. But I'd always ask Brian about what went on in the meeting, what records were being picked, if there were any particular types of song they were looking for, or which artists they needed new material for, so that we knew what we needed to do next.

The other thing I told him was, when we cut the record, don't mix it immediately. Wait until one week before the release date, and the reason I'd do that was because that place was so competitive. If you put something out there a month before, two months before, you'd run the risk of someone else beating you out. But if you waited until one week before the record came out, nobody was going to come up with a better record in that time.

What was our biggest early break? So far, we'd had a few. When Martha & The Vandellas recorded 'Heat Wave'. When Marvin recorded 'Can I Get A Witness'. When Smokey did 'Mickey's Monkey'.

In terms of everything that was to happen in the future, however, it had to be The Supremes – Diana Ross, Mary Wilson and Florence Ballard.

Celebrating one of our early hits. Eddie, our mother, our sister Carole and Brian.

Brian: One afternoon Berry called me and said, "Brian, I want you to come and meet these girls." There were four of them at the time, as Barbara Martin was still involved. They were all around seventeen and they were still in high school.

The group was called The Primettes; they'd named themselves after The Primes, a local group who later became The Temptations. Robert Bateman had already auditioned them and passed them on to Berry, so we listened to them sing, and then Berry told them to come back after they graduated high school, which they did.

I liked them. I liked the way they looked. Diana – although she was Diane back then (that was her birth name, but just to be clear, we're going to call her Diana throughout this book) – always looked great to me, and she was a pleasant girl. Mary and Florence were good-looking girls too.

The first thing Berry wanted to do was find them a new name, something better than The Primettes. Janie Bradford put three names in a bag and offered it to Florence. She reached in, pulled out The Supremes, and that was that.

I was actually one of the first people to work with the group, immediately after Berry signed them back in 1961, on their very first Motown single, 'I Want A Guy', which we later recut with The Marvelettes. Berry and I wrote it with Freddie Gorman, and it was a great song. But it didn't sell anything like it should have, so Berry and Barney Ales wrote the follow-up, 'Buttered Popcorn', and that didn't sell either.

The group had more flops after that. Smokey had a go ('Your Heart Belongs To Me'), and then Lamont and I had a try. We wrote 'Time Changes Things' with Janie Bradford, and we produced it as well. It was scheduled to be the group's next single, but then Berry decided to go with 'Let Me Go The Right Way'. It took him 14 hours to get the right mix, and it still didn't happen.

Clarence Paul wrote their next one ('My Heart Can't Take It No More') and then it was back to Smokey ('A Breathtaking Guy'). It was incredible. All these great writers, the biggest and most successful names in the building, and not one of them could get a hit on The Supremes.

Before all that, though…

One day I went up to one of the music rooms upstairs at Hitsville. I opened the door and Diana was sitting on a piano bench crying, so I walked over and sat at the piano alongside her. "Hey, what's wrong?"

She told me she had just broken up with someone. I don't know if she'd ever experienced heartbreak like that before, but she was shattered. She started telling me all about it, so I suggested we take a ride out to Belle Isle, which is a small island between Detroit and Canada on the Detroit River, to relax, get away from Hitsville. It was a popular park for the locals… for young lovers. A lot of babies were made there!

But that wasn't really on my mind. I genuinely wanted to help her feel better, although I should also admit that she was one of the most beautiful women I had ever met.

Anyway, Diana said okay, so we made a date. We rode around and around Belle Isle. We talked, and I'd never felt so comfortable with someone. I really enjoyed being with her, she enjoyed being with me – we enjoyed each other. And things progressed from there…

The Marvelettes were still Motown's number one girl group at this time, and there was a lot of rivalry between The Marvelettes and The Supremes, particularly where Diana was concerned. (Florence, on the other hand, loved The Marvelettes, and even went out on tour with them after Wanda Young had her baby.)

There wasn't much difference between the two in terms of live performances – The Marvelettes had a great show, as did The Supremes. In terms of record sales, though, there was no competition.

Brian: It was around 1963 that Berry Gordy told us The Supremes needed a hit record. They'd released a few singles, but no hits yet, and he wanted to know if we had something we thought might work.

We did. The first record Holland–Dozier–Holland cut on The Supremes was 'When The Lovelight Starts Shining Through His Eyes', and it was one of those rare occasions where Edward came up with the title before we wrote the music. He told us that was what he wanted, and we had a bit of an argument about it.

I remember telling him, "Wow… man, that's a long title! Can't you cut that down some kind of way? Or maybe put some of the title in parentheses?" But he refused to do it.

Eddie: I agree, it was a long title but I really liked it. I told Brian it was simply a question of breaking up the words to fit the melody. My feeling was, you could take a melody and work it to fit anything.

That was one of the biggest arguments we had in the early days. It went on for about 35 minutes, and it was getting more and more impassioned.

Finally I told him, "Brian, it doesn't matter how long a title is. It's how the melody forms around the title that matters. If it falls in a certain way, it breaks it up anyway; if it moves in a certain way, it keeps the flow."

Boy, it was rough getting him to do that but he finally came up with it, and it worked.

I understood what he was saying, but I liked the title, and I knew he could do it with the music. So, after a little more argument, Brian finally came up with a melody that fit the title, and it was perfect! We took what other people would consider an unwieldy title and Brian's melody made it feel so much shorter.

'Lovelight…' was released on Halloween, 1963, and it became The Supremes' first hit.

It wasn't a big record, in that it only got to number 23, but it was popular enough for Dick Clark to book the group for his upcoming Caravan Of Stars tour, which would be setting out in June 1964.

What we had to do now was make sure they had another hit record to coincide with the shows.

Brian: It was right about then that Edward came to us, after he'd been to a meeting at Motown, and said, "Look, these girls are selling so many records! We should focus on them because they're the top thing at Motown now."

They weren't, not in terms of sales, anyway, but they definitely had the potential. 'Lovelight…' was doing okay so Lamont and I agreed. We still had The Marvelettes and The Vandellas, but The Supremes became our focus.

Unfortunately, Berry then made what for him was a very uncharacteristic mistake. Back before we came up with 'Lovelight…', we'd recorded another song with The Supremes, 'Run, Run, Run'.

Berry turned it down because he didn't think it was strong enough to be a single. Now he needed an instant follow-up, so he released it after all, and it turned out that his original instinct was the correct one. 'Run, Run, Run' didn't do so well (it barely made the Top 100), but while that was disappointing, we weren't worried.

We knew the next one we had for The Supremes was one of the best things we had ever written.

Chapter Twelve

Diana, Mary and Florence

Eddie: The Supremes were about to go on the Dick Clark tour and, again, Motown wanted to get a new single out to coincide with it.

I remember Brian was at the piano playing the melody, and he and Lamont were singing. We didn't have the lyrics; they were singing words and sounds, laying out the vocal melody line. But I was listening to it… the movement and feeling of it… and I said to myself, "Boy, this is a hit record on *anybody*. You don't have to be a great singer. All you need is to lay the vocal right in there with this sensuous melody, and it's a hit."

The question was, was it the right song for The Supremes?

I had very firm ideas how it needed to be sung, very sensuously, so I told Brian, "Listen, we should let Mary sing the song."

He was shocked. "Mary?" And then Lamont weighed in. "But Mary's not the lead singer."

I agreed, but I told them Mary had the softer voice, which was what the song needed. I liked Diana's voice but she usually sang in a higher range at the time.

They kept on at me. "It can't be Mary, Diana's the lead singer. You're crazy."

I looked over at Brian and Lamont, the way they were staring at me as though I had lost the best part of my senses. "Man, you got to be out of your mind." They were almost laughing. I was serious, but they couldn't see it.

I compromised. "Okay, I'll tell you what; this song has to be sung in a sensuous kind of way. Can we lower the key, so Diana can sing it in a lower range than she's accustomed to?" I knew that was the only way we would get the performance from her that the song required.

"Yeah, we could do that." So they cut it in the lower key. Then, after they cut the rhythm track, which included one of the studio hands, Mike Valvano, stomping on a couple of wooden boards, they gave me the tape so that I could write the lyrics.

I had a hard time finishing it, because at that time I was still learning how to write songs. I worked on it for about two weeks, but when I finished, I knew we'd created something special. 'Where Did Our Love Go' – the feeling was there, the mood was set, the melody was right, and Brian and Lamont had cut the rhythm track perfectly. And, considering what an amateur I was, I was able to pull it all together.

Now it was time to teach Diana the song.

When you teach an artist how to sing a song the way you envision it sounding in your own mind, it adds power. I would show them the kind of feeling I wanted the song to have, and that would help them relate to the lyrics. I would exaggerate the syncopation or the melody or the energy, little tricks like that. I would emphasise the melody – anything to make sure the artist felt it, so they really put the song over. I would keep them in the studio for hours sometimes to make sure it was correct.

But I made a big mistake when I was working with Diana on 'Where Did Our Love Go'. I started singing the song, and I added some riffs, vocal gymnastics, little tricks to emphasise the melody. I was not showing her how she should interpret the song. But Diana was impressed. She *liked* the riffs. She said, "I'm gonna sing it like you did."

"No, no, no, I don't want you to sing it like that. I want you to sing it very soft and innocent. Don't do all those riffs. Make it sexy, make it sensuous and seductive."

"No," she replied. "I don't want that."

I told her, "Diana, that's how you have to sing the song." I wanted her to sound seductive but also a little lost, and she was firmly against that. She wanted to give it a big performance, whereas I wanted the complete opposite.

Round and round we went, with Diana becoming more and more upset. Finally, she'd had enough. "Look, I'm calling Berry."

Okay, then. I said, "I'll tell you what. There's the phone over there. You can pick up the phone and call Berry. But when you do, you tell him to come to the studio so he can dub you in."

I looked at her. She looked at me. I could see her weighing up the odds in her mind. How serious was I? How seriously would Berry take it? Who had the most clout in the studio – the artist? Or the songwriters and producers, without whom the artist would have nothing to sing?

She made the correct decision. "Okay, we'll do it your way."

We left the office, went downstairs to the studio and began recording. She started singing. By now, however, she had a bad attitude. In fact, she was really pissed with me. She was singing the song but her voice was completely expressionless. So was her face. Deadpan. She was deliberately singing the song as unemotionally as she could. It was nothing like anybody had ever heard from Diana before.

Brian, who was engineering, glanced over at me. He didn't need to speak, I could read what he was thinking from the expression on his face. "Should I stop it now?"

No. I signalled to him to continue. She looked bored but she sounded incredible. "Let it go," I whispered to Brian. "Don't stop. Don't stop."

So Diana carried on, finished the song and then she fixed me with her most withering expression. "Is that what you want?" she asked sarcastically.

I sat back, beaming. "Thank you. That's exactly what I want." It was perfect. She did it in one take, nailed the sultry sound I was looking for. That was the take we went with, that's what is on the record and that is the only time I have ever had friction with Diana. Because to me, she was a jewel, always vivacious, always inspirational, even when she was disgruntled with me.

We finished recording and The Supremes went on the road with the Dick Clark tour. We were still awaiting the single's release, and the band was way down low on the bill. Diana walked into my office, and I knew when she laid her head down on my desk, something was wrong. I had never seen her looking so unhappy.

She asked me, "Eddie, do you think we will ever make it?" I guess she had so many records that weren't successful, it made her spirit weary. Although we had already given her one hit with 'Lovelight...', it was not the really big hit she needed.

I was caught off guard but I knew it was important to be positive. This was not the time to tease her like I so often did – Mary Wells was Motown's biggest star at the time, three Top 10 hits in a row, so I loved to torment Diana by saying things like, "The Queen is in town, you have to make room for the Queen. She'll be here soon." It would drive Diana crazy.

On this occasion, though, I'm glad I had enough sense to realise the delicacy of the moment. I said in my most convincing voice, "Sure you will, Diana, you most surely will." She left feeling much better. I said to myself, "Man, I pray you're right."

And I was.

'Where Did Our Love Go' was released on schedule, and Mary Wilson later told us about the night when, as they were being introduced on stage, the crowd erupted. Caught completely unawares, Mary was looking around to see if someone else had walked onto the stage. She couldn't believe they were getting such a response – none of them could.

No, the applause was for them. 'Where Did Our Love Go' had exploded on the radio. Now it was racing up the charts and, from being just another name on the lower reaches of the bill, suddenly The Supremes were the hottest act out there, the stars of the show.

'Where Did Our Love Go' was number one for two weeks in America, and its success didn't stop there. It shot to number three in the UK, a market Motown hadn't really paid too much attention to. Now they would.

Eddie: Overnight, The Supremes had become Motown's flagship. Barney Ales told Berry, "This group is taking us to places we've never been before; it's like getting a worldwide hit and national acceptance." Before 'Where Did Our Love Go', Motown was successful but it was just another label. After, Motown became a sound, and a lifestyle. Barney said, "You have to keep this group going," and Berry walked out of his office, saw me standing on the porch at Motown, and told me what Barney said. The Supremes were already a worldwide success. Now Holland–Dozier–Holland had to come up with a follow-up hit to keep them there.

Mary Wilson gave a speech when HDH received a star on the Hollywood Walk of Fame. © Paul Archuleta/FilmMagic/Getty.

I immediately rushed to our office and repeated this to Brian and Lamont. The Supremes were now our priority, and we had to come up with the next single, ASAP.

We worked feverishly for the next five evenings. We came up with three songs that we immediately cut in one studio session. All three would become number one hits – 'Baby Love', 'Come See About Me' and 'Stop! In The Name Of Love'.

Brian: 'Stop! In The Name Of Love' was another of Lamont's titles. He was dating a girl who had something of a temper, but he was also seeing someone else at the time, and the first girl caught them together.

Lamont tried to brazen it out. "Oh baby, please believe me, there's nobody here. Stop! Stop, in the name of love will you!"

"I don't think that's funny," she replied, but Lamont wasn't listening.

"Wait a minute, did you hear what I said? 'Stop! In the name of love.' Did you hear that cash register?"

He came running back to the studio – I was sitting at the piano, probably thinking about Diana, and he burst in, "Man, I've got something."

I started playing something, and Lamont was saying, "Faster, faster! Pick up the tempo," and then he started singing "Stop! In the name of love."

Lamont, however, was not the only member of the team whose love life was reflected in that song.

Eddie: Once I started writing songs, and having hits on other people, my career as a recording artist slowed down and finally stopped, which meant I was no longer performing live, either. That was a relief, but I also lost something that had become very important to me. My freedom.

I'd become aware of it very early on. Every time I left Detroit, when I was playing a theatre in Chicago, say, it was like a brick wall had been lifted off of me. I kept asking myself, "Why do I feel so light, so free?"

Then I realised it was because I was away from that so-called marriage thing I hadn't wanted in the first place. The handcuffs had been taken off, and I said to myself, "Man, you have to do something, you're not happy and she can't be happy, either."

But still it took me an age to talk Almetta into giving me a divorce. I told her, "Listen, I'm not going to change. You always expect me to but I'm not. I know myself." And I also told her there was no point in making herself unhappy. She was still young enough that she could let this thing go and find someone else.

I told her she could keep the apartment on La Salle and, because I'd soon be receiving royalties from The Vandellas, I promised I would buy her another house, give her x amount of dollars, and all she had to do was take care of our son.

But it took her a long time to agree, and things were complicated further by my mother, who kept telling her *not* to give me the divorce – "He's exactly the same as his father but he'll calm down," she'd say. Which, in our father's case, was true. After he remarried, he did calm down.

Even Almetta didn't believe that, though. It was very difficult to actually get a divorce in those days, there were a lot of hoops to jump through. But she agreed to do it and I was so grateful to her. I wanted to be free.

And I had seen somebody else I wanted.

The divorce proceedings were just getting underway when I wrote the lyrics to 'Stop! In The Name Of Love'. I was also seeing another girl. In fact, I was seeing two – one named Jamie and the other was Vernelle.

Vernelle worked for my attorney. I went down to his office to discuss how to approach the divorce, and that's when I saw Vernelle for the first time. She was so unique, so different, so charismatic. There was something special about her. An aspiring songwriter (she would write under the name Edythe Wayne), she had such an amazing personality – she was a completely different kind of person, unlike anybody I've ever met in my life.

We started seeing one another but, meanwhile, there was another girl, a friend of Almetta's, who also liked me. I wasn't interested in her but she'd seen me with Vernelle and, although she didn't know what the relationship was, she told Almetta about Vernelle, probably hoping that Almetta would break it up so that she could move in.

It didn't work out like that. Almetta and I got our divorce and, many years later, Vernelle and I would marry.

But that earlier situation was definitely on my mind when I wrote the lyrics for 'Stop! In The Name Of Love', because that's how I worked. I would use what was happening in my personal life to influence my lyrics.

Eddie also had his eyes on a new home. A few months earlier, shortly before Christmas, somebody he knew – a disc jockey or a promo guy – took him to a record hop, but detoured first through an area Eddie had never visited before.

Eddie: It was called Palmer Woods, this very rich-looking area, the most beautiful I had ever seen. I knew it wasn't far from where I lived on Lumpkin but it was new to me and, because it was coming up to Christmas, all the houses were lit up in the most magnificent way.

The guy I was with said, "Man, wouldn't you love to live in a neighbourhood like this?" I didn't say anything. I could never imagine being there. But not too long after that, I was.

It was a huge house, laid out so beautifully. We had a piano, a pool table, everything, and everybody loved the place. Lamont bought a house in the same neighbourhood a year later, and so did Norman Whitfield. Brian bought one in Sherwood Forest, which was right next door.

I suppose the tragedy was, I didn't truly appreciate it until after I moved out to California, and three or four years later I came back and realised California had never had a place like that. It was woodsy and you could walk through that, there weren't that many cars running through it, all you had to do was enjoy the sheer peace and serenity of the place.

The other sad thing is, I never properly lived in the house. I used it as a meeting place. I liked places that were very private, so I'd have business meetings there, rehearsals, things like that, and because I didn't like living and working in the same place, I bought another place, a two-bedroom apartment on Oakland Avenue, and that was where I'd sleep and write songs.

It was perfect. I had complete privacy. If anybody came to the door, I'd never answer it. I didn't even have a telephone. Berry hated that. If he wanted to reach me in a hurry… well, he couldn't. In the end I did get a phone, but he and Brian were the only people who had the number for a long time. And that's where I wrote almost all of the lyrics that followed.

Brian: It was such a creative time. All of a sudden we were coming up with great songs for everybody but especially for The Supremes. We had the melodies, we had the ideas. People loved the songs, they loved The Supremes and they loved Diana. They adored her.

Eddie: I cannot overemphasise how crucial Barney Ales was when it came to breaking The Supremes, or anything else we did for that matter. I've already explained how difficult it was to get white radio to play our records, because they looked at it as black product, and if you couldn't make it through the R&B market, you weren't going to make it to the pop.

But the kind of music we were making was pop first – we almost always went pop before R&B, and we were far more successful in the so-called white market than we were in the R&B market. The Temptations were great in the R&B market. So was Smokey, so was Marvin. But our product was not accepted that quickly, it was *too* pop.

Barney called it 'Oreo music' – like the Oreo cookie, black on the outside, white on the inside – and it was true. It wasn't R&B because we didn't particularly like R&B, and that became Barney's position as well. So while Berry continued to handle the R&B market, Barney dealt with the pop. It was a smart decision – both knew Motown would sell many more records on the pop market if only we could break into it. As Barney said, "These records are great, Holland–Dozier–Holland are great, and when this stuff hits, the black stations are going to have to play it anyway, so I don't need to talk to them."

Brian: Another important factor in the success of those early Supremes songs was the fact that Diana and I were deeply in love, and it must have come through in the music I was writing for the group – because I was writing it for her. We had continued seeing one another and, without ever intending to, I had fallen in love with her, and she with me.

All I wanted was to marry her. She was so likeable, really lovable, a really great person, and she was an emotional woman who watched for what you needed and paid close attention. She was the kind of person I needed in my life, so peaceful and kind, and not resentful about things. A very passionate person.

But, of course, I was already married with a couple of children when I met her – Letitia, my second daughter, had recently been born – and I couldn't leave. I did talk about it, but when I raised it with the lawyers at Motown, all they said was, "Do you know what kind of money it'll cost you to leave? You'd better go back home."

Of course, things got complicated. Sharon somehow found out about my relationship with Diana, and turned up at the studio one time, threatening to "kick her butt".

Another time, Sharon and her sister, Saundra, followed me to the 20 Grand, where The Supremes were performing. They waited outside and, as Diana and I were leaving, they came over. There was an argument and suddenly Sharon lashed out and hit Diana in the face. I jumped between them and managed to break them up. Diana was finally able to leap into her car and leave. But of course she told Berry about it, and he told her to sue Sharon. I remember him asking me, "Whose side are you gonna be on?" I said, "Well, I'm gonna be on Diana's side." It was wrong what Sharon did. It was ugly, but Sharon's entire family was like that, very highly strung, very volatile.

Diana, on the other hand, was one of the most gentle, beautiful people I had ever met.

The success of 'Where Did Our Love Go' took a lot of people by surprise. Even at Motown. The pressing plant was so busy they had to cut down on other records, and go all out to meet the demand for The Supremes.

A lot of artists were upset about that, although they understood the situation. They knew Berry would have done the same thing if it had been their record selling like that.

But there was more to it than simply having a hit record. In 1964, you couldn't move without seeing or hearing The Beatles. For six months, they were the only group anyone talked about, and suddenly these three African-American girls from Detroit, on this little black-owned record label, were challenging them, not only with a great hit record but also with a sound as distinctive as The Beatles' own. It was a genuine sensation.

Not for us it wasn't. In fact, we were probably the only people who weren't thinking in those terms. To us, there was no competition at all; there was room for everybody, and besides – there could never be too much great music. It didn't matter who was making it.

Not even during that week in April when the *Billboard* Top Five was made up solely of Beatles records. We knew that might happen, but we also knew that a record didn't stay in any position for long – perhaps a week or two – and that the next record behind it would slot right in. We just had to make sure that the next record was one of ours.

It was true, though; the whole country had gone Beatle crazy. We even wrote a song about them with R. Dean Taylor, called

'Ladybug, Stay Away From That Beatle'. It was a piece of fun but it was also our way of saying hello, showing them we were pleased they were doing so well.

Later in the year, Berry would have The Supremes make an album, *A Little Bit Of Liverpool*, which included five Beatles songs, together with some other recent UK hits. It sold close to a million copies but Berry did it for the same reason: he knew how much The Beatles loved Motown. He wanted to show them the feeling was mutual.

The only thing that ever concerned us, in terms of the pop marketplace, was making sure we maintained quality. If we wrote a song and we were excited about it, we were convinced it would be a hit and usually we were right.

Maybe once or twice we picked a song that wasn't as successful as we thought it would be, but we were in our own world. We didn't think there was anybody like us, and there wasn't. So we never competed with anything else. We gave our best and let the company compete with people. It was marketing's problem, not ours.

Brian: I liked The Beatles, and The Beatles liked us. I loved the way they wrote songs, plus they recorded a version of 'Please Mr. Postman' (on 1964's *With The Beatles* album) and that became one of my biggest songs ever. *With The Beatles* was number one on the album chart, and I made a lot of money with that song. But we never saw ourselves as competing with them. I loved the songs. Especially John's, because his were so earthy.

My feeling is, if you've got a good song, whether it's The Beatles or Otis Redding or whoever, it's a good song. And it was a mutual thing, an understanding about who's who, because I know they loved music as much as I did. They cut a lot of Motown songs.

One Sweet Moment

(Music by Brian Holland; lyrics by Eddie Holland)

I never thought you'd ever leave me,
I never thought there would be me without you.
Didn't you know you were my best friend?
Didn't you know how much I depended on you?

You said, "Forever"
Love would be forever
But I never knew forever
Would last just, just one moment
One sweet moment
My heart looked around
And you were gone…

Never once did I imagine
Reaching out in the dark
And not finding you
Warmly, touching, playfully
Brushing against my body
Feeling love rushing in

You said forever
I believed in forever
But I never knew forever
Would last
Just one moment
One sweet moment
My whole world looked around
Then you were gone…

I must fix it
But where do I start?
The first three months
Were the hardest part
Waking in the night
Waking up with fears
Fighting back the tears
Thinking of the years
You said forever
I believe in forever!

But I never knew forever
Would last just one moment
One sweet moment
Then my heart looked around
My whole world looked around

And you were gone
And you were gone
And you were gone…

Chapter Thirteen

A Baby Love Story

'Where Did Our Love Go' was huge, but the label had had a pop number one before, back when The Marvelettes and 'Please Mr. Postman' topped the chart. On that occasion, they were never able to follow it up with another number one. We were determined that the same thing was not going to happen again.

Brian: Diana was all I could think about. Of course, I still provided for my family, took care of Sharon and the kids. But when I was daydreaming, sitting around, I was thinking about Diana, and when I was writing, I was thinking about her as well.

Usually, I can't say who was on my mind when I wrote. But throughout this period, I knew. I felt so much for her, and it came pouring out. That's when I wrote 'Baby Love'. That song captured everything I felt for her. It was the essence of why I loved her.

It was just something that came to me. Songwriters are like movie people; they come up with an idea, they write it, they stick to it, that's what happens. I was sitting at the piano, came up with a little melody and started singing "Baby love, oh baby love…"

I didn't come up with many titles for songs, or if I did they were never as good as Edward's or Lamont's. We did have a few battles, though, and 'Baby Love' was one of them. I took it into the office,

I started singing and everybody was cringing around me. "'Baby Love'? That's horrible, that's so trite!" I don't think anybody liked that title! Maybe that's why I usually left it up to Edward or Lamont.

Eddie: I thought 'Baby Love' was the stupidest title I ever heard. It took me two weeks to even agree to write that song because it was the dumbest title – "I can't write this!"

But then I started looking at the melody, getting a feel for it and I realised. What is the principle you taught yourself? It's the *feel* that's important, and the ideas that carry the feel. And when they coincide with the melody and the sentiment, that's what you go by, the mood that it creates.

That's what I used for 'Baby Love'. I'm not going to pretend I hadn't thought of other titles for the song – in fact, I had three. But suddenly 'Baby Love' fit better than any of the others, and the reason for that was, it's what Brian had intended all along.

Brian: I agree, it was the worst title. Even I didn't want to use it because it was so corny. But I had developed a principle. Don't go with the title that is the most sophisticated, or interesting sounding. Go with the one that has the most appeal, and of all the songs that we wrote for The Supremes, it's still my favourite.

It was Berry Gordy who finally gave 'Baby Love' the seal of approval. Listening to it at the next Quality Control meeting, he simply mused, "This is kinda different. I think it could be Top 20."

In fact, it turned out to be one of the few times his prediction was wrong. 'Baby Love' followed 'Where Did Our Love Go' to number one in the United States and also topped the chart in the UK.

And we were only at the start.

It's like Diana wrote in her 1993 memoir, *Secrets of a Sparrow*: "Together [Holland–Dozier–Holland] made an incredible triangle, just as the three of us [Supremes] did. [They] became our main

HDH discussing our next hit with Berry in his office.

songwriters, and it was yet another great blend, another example of synergy that was a piece of the magic that was Motown at the time."

At the same time as 'Where Did Our Love Go' was inching down the charts and 'Baby Love' was hurtling up, a song we'd written and all but forgotten about two years earlier was suddenly in demand, and we had a second group that was considered 'one of ours'.

That group was The Four Tops.

As so frequently happened with Motown acts, The Four Tops had been around for a few years before they arrived at Hitsville – their first single came out way back in 1956. You could usually find them singing jazz and bebop in supper clubs around Detroit, and Berry was already a long-time fan by the time he got them. He'd tried to sign the group several times before but it never worked out.

It was head of A&R Mickey Stevenson who finally lured them over. He'd known the group since they were first starting out as

The Four Aims – in fact, the way Mickey told it, it was The Four Aims who set him out on his musical career in the first place. He caught them at the Warfield Theater on Hastings Street during one of the regular amateur nights, in sharp mohair suits with waves in their hair. Mickey had recently joined the Air Force, but immediately after his encounter with The Four Aims, he marched back to the base and told his commanding officer he was quitting, to pursue a career in the music business.

The original plan was for The Four Tops to record an album of jazz standards, to be released on Berry's Workshop Jazz label in 1964. That didn't happen; instead, Berry and Mickey convinced them to work with us.

Brian: Mickey asked if we had any songs that might be suitable for the group. I immediately thought of 'Baby I Need Your Loving', the song I'd written that night when I was feeling especially low because of the way things were at home, but which had been sitting on the shelf ever since. Not much of our work went unreleased but that one did.

Eddie: There are a lot of songs we wrote that I really didn't think much of, which then became huge hits. 'Baby I Need Your Loving' was one of them. I liked it a little better than some, but I really wasn't that knocked out about it. Anyway, Brian and I were in our office when Mickey happened to come in and ask, "Have you guys got anything on The Four Tops?"

I'd wanted to meet them for years. I'd been hearing about this great singer Levi Stubbs for a long time, but I'd never heard him sing. I knew about the talent contests where he used to go up against Little Willie John, though, so I kept asking people, "Is he as good?" They always said yes. "Is he as good as Jackie Wilson?" Yes.

Time went by and I still hadn't heard Levi. But then he came to Motown and we went into the studio to record 'Baby I Need Your Loving'. I was really looking forward to hearing what Levi could do with the song. Unfortunately, his first run-through didn't come out that good.

He was embarrassed about it, and I tried to put his mind at rest. I told him he needed to practise the number. I had to be as diplomatic as I could, but he said, "No, I think Lawrence Payton should sing this kind of song."

"No, I want you to sing it," I replied, but he insisted, "It's not really my kind of song."

I knew what the problem was. "Levi, this is what you did. You didn't learn the song; you listened to it but you didn't *learn* it." I told him to take it home that weekend and learn it.

I think he knew that, as well. It was the same with a lot of our songs; if all you did was listen to them and get a first-time

HDH, The Four Tops and Berry celebrating their latest bestseller, 'Baby I Need Your Loving'. © Motown Archives/Avalon Photoshot

impression, you wouldn't be able to sing them as they needed to be sung. But if you learned them, and allowed me to show you the approach, you could do it. The song sounded simple but it wasn't, so I told him that, and when he came back a few days later, man, did he sing the hell out of that song.

'Baby I Need Your Loving' got to number 11 and was soon covered by Marvin and Tammi Terrell. And, of course, we went on to have even bigger successes on The Four Tops. But, apparently, that song has had more radio plays than any other record Motown ever released, and when people talk about 'the Motown Sound', 'Baby I Need Your Loving' is often the record they use to illustrate it.

The Motown Sound was Berry's creation. Not all of it – everybody who worked at Motown, on the creative side, anyway, threw a lot into it as well. But the basics were Berry.

Motown itself was a lot of different records, songwriters, producers, and none of those records sound alike. But the one thing they all had in common, which nobody else was doing at that time, was that the bass and the backbeat were always dominant. If you listen to something like 'You Can't Hurry Love', you'll hear the way the bottom end drives it along. And that was Berry.

Back when Berry was first starting out, and he'd bought that mastering and recording equipment from this guy on a radio station, what he did was this: he was trying to learn to mix himself, and the first thing he did was push the bottom end up.

The foundation of all his mixes was the backbeat, and we all followed that blueprint. It meant the records all had that heavy bottom you hear on The Supremes, The Four Tops and other artists we recorded. That was 'the Motown Sound'. Besides, the musicians were so great you'd want to bring them up anyway. You played other pop records, they didn't mix that way, not even the ones that tried to copy us.

Brian: What I would do when I mastered a record was this. First, I'd put it through the big speakers – boom, boom, boom – and then I'd bring it down to small speakers, the size of a transistor radio. If it still sounded right coming out of the little speakers, I'd know we'd done a good job. Because the people who bought the records, they didn't have state-of-the-art studio equipment, they had tiny little speakers, so that's where you needed to focus. I could never understand bands who made vast pieces of music that probably sounded fantastic in the studio but the moment you got the record home, it sounded terrible.

I learned that from Berry. He used to do a lot of mixing and he'd let me sit in, and then take over. He was the one who said, "Play it on the car radio, home speakers, a transistor radio." We wanted our records to sound as good on the radio as they sounded in the studio.

Eddie: It also helped that we recorded everything so quickly. There was only one studio at Hitsville, and everyone was allotted that three hours' time to record the tracks because there were so many artists.

In our case, I produced the lead vocals, Lamont was a master when it came to background voices, and Brian and Lamont produced the music. But we had to be quick. We couldn't mess around trying things out. We had to know what we were doing before we went in there, and it was the same for everybody else. And I think that also brought a certain consistency to the way everybody made music.

Smokey, Norman Whitfield, Mickey Stevenson, Lawrence Horn, everybody had their own individual sound, those things that made their records sound different to everybody else's. But the one thing they had in common… they all used the same studio, the same musicians, the same mixing desk, the same engineers and, ultimately, we all took the same approach.

Where Holland–Dozier–Holland streaked ahead was, we had Brian.

I still remember someone asking Norman Whitfield about Brian and I. "One is great," he replied, "and one is good." Brian was the great one, and that was an understatement.

I always knew my brother was something special but the more I worked with him, the more amazed I was. I never understood how he could hear the type of chords he heard. He was doing those arrangements off the top of his head, in the studio!

Other producers would often go to the piano and watch what he was doing, and say that the way they were taught was different. But they also acknowledged that what Brian was playing was still correct and, even more importantly, what he did gave the chord a *better sound*.

Brian: Of all the instruments I tried to master when I was a kid – apart from the piano, which I couldn't play that well anyway – the drums was the one I could make the most noise on, and that's significant because that was our sound, the backbeat.

I could utilise what I knew about drums when I was writing the music. Even though I did most of my composing on piano, I knew what the rhythm was, and what I needed from the backbeat.

The way music was going in those days, the backbeat was *the* thing. People were dancing a lot at the time, and that beat was so important. I remember Phil Spector, the way he did his drums. He had a whole bunch of them and those kinds of things stick with you. So when we started, I thought back to, "Yeah, the Spector sound."

Phil Spector was one interesting guy, though. I met him at a BMI dinner and he was the strangest guy ever. I watched him – he would sit down, he would get up, he would walk around, look around, and he wouldn't say anything to too many people. Just walking and staring, a very strange character, and of course he got involved in all kinds of creepy stuff.

But his music! 'Be My Baby'! I loved that song, it is one of my favourite songs of all time.

By the end of 1964, we'd placed 14 songs on the Top 100, seven of them in the Top 40. With The Supremes' 'Come See About Me' to round off the year, we'd also had three number ones, and we really only had three groups we were working with regularly – The Vandellas, who were beginning to slow down now, The Four Tops and The Supremes.

The others were what you might call one-offs, when we happened to have a song that was suitable for someone else and they cut it.

Marvin Gaye, for instance, had Norman Whitfield writing for him, so he usually didn't need anybody else. But 'Baby Don't You Do It', 'You're A Wonderful One' and 'How Sweet It Is (To Be Loved By You)' (another of Eddie's songs about Vernelle) were all big records for him. And Marvin himself was a dream. He was the greatest.

Marvin could sing anything you wanted him to sing. He'd do jazz, he'd do gospel, pop music, he was that good. You give him a song to sing, you didn't have to tell him what you wanted, he knew, and he would do it. That guy was the most brilliant singer of them all.

Eddie: When we were getting those big hit records, Berry's kids were really excited. They were treating us like celebrities and Berry would tell them, "Wait a minute, *they* work for *me*! I'm the owner!"

And his kids would tell him, "Yeah, yeah, yeah, Daddy, but they're the ones who write the songs." So what Berry wanted to do was have his kids look at him in the same way, and because we were doing so well, he was, "I wanna get into that."

One time he walked past our office and heard Brian working on a song he was calling 'Wonderful One'. Those were the lyrics he had, and was singing aloud.

Berry listened for a while, then said, "You should make that the chorus." Brian agreed, and when I came in a little later, he said to me, "I just gave Berry a part of 'Wonderful One'."

"Why?" I asked.

"Because he said that was the chorus," Brian answered.

"Obviously it's the chorus!" I shot back. "You've got to be kidding!" I told him, "No, you can't do that! Brian, look; the man owns the copyright, he owns the company. We can't give him the song as well, especially for no reason."

What was so great about this period was how everybody was pulling together for a common cause. Of course, we all had our own egos and ambitions, but the main thing for all of us was, we were working together for Motown. We were Motown.

That's why there really wasn't much infighting. At least among the creatives, we were in complete harmony. Of course there were the people on the business end, and all they could think about was efficiency, productivity, economy. The rest of us, though, we relished the freedom Berry gave us. The fact that we had the time and space in which to try new things, spread our wings, without feeling there was someone constantly looking over our shoulders, that created such a happy atmosphere.

There was competition between us, of course, but it was healthy, always a love of the music first and foremost. It might seem incredible but we all enjoyed helping one other. Norman used to come and help us, Mickey Stevenson, we'd all help each other out. A lot of places aren't like that, but Berry's big thing was, we all work together and love one other.

Eddie: Brian was seeing Diana now, and Lamont was dating Mary, so I suppose there must have been a lot of people wondering whether anything would happen between Florence and I. Including Florence herself.

I liked all the girls. I didn't get familiar with them, but early on, after 'Where Did Our Love Go', they came home from Europe and they thought it'd be nice to buy us little gifts. I noticed the gift Florence gave me was more than a token – a tiny, battery-operated portable television she'd found in London.

I'd never seen one like that before and, my mind being the way it was, I wondered why she was giving me a nicer gift than the others were giving Brian and Lamont. But there was shyness about it when I asked her why.

The others all left, and Florence mentioned she didn't have any way of getting home, and would I mind dropping her off? So I said I would, but when we got to her house, she started telling me what a nice person I was and how she was attracted to me.

I said, "Flo, I think you're very nice too, but I'm not the kind of person who would be good for you, because I have several people in my life, girlfriends I'm already involved with…" And she looked at me, thanked me for telling her, and we never talked about it again. But there was always a closeness there.

Brian: Work got me through some really difficult times in my private life. Diana's lawsuit against Sharon was eventually called off, but not long after that, I broke things off with her.

I'd been to talk with Mama, to tell her I was considering leaving Sharon, and she told me that it was my life, my happiness, and I should do what I thought was best. But I should never forget I was a father and had young children, and that was what decided it for me. I could have left Sharon in a heartbeat, but I couldn't walk out on my children. Our father had left us when we were kids and I couldn't do that to mine.

Then I talked to Berry, and he said the same thing, so I thought about it and I finally decided that they were right. I broke up with Diana, and of course we continued to work together on a professional basis. But she was so distraught.

I'd called her to tell her; I wanted her to know that of course I'd prefer to be with her but I couldn't do it to the children. She started crying. I was begging her to stop, please stop, but she couldn't. Finally I put the phone down and called Berry. I told him what was happening and asked if he could maybe calm her down.

He agreed. "All right, man, I understand, let me go and talk to her." But she didn't really calm down, not for a few weeks. She would still call me up, saying, "Brian I still love you"… Oh man, I didn't want to do anything to hurt her, but it couldn't happen. So I called Berry again, and he was, "Man, don't worry, I'll talk to her again."

But Diana would talk to Gwen Gordy all the time and she would tell Gwen about us, and she would tell her what she liked about me. Diana even called me from Europe, where the group was touring. She was crying again, "I don't want to break up."

So Sharon had me all to herself again, and we even had another daughter, Holly. But things didn't improve, and in the end I couldn't take it any more, not even for the children's sake. It broke my heart, not just because of the kids but also because the reason I broke up with Diana was so I could stay with the children, but Sharon had made that impossible.

I really couldn't take it any longer. I couldn't understand Sharon. She would do things that made absolutely no sense to me. For example, there was the day our sister, Carole, came over – I think she wanted to borrow some money or something – and she and Sharon got into an argument in the kitchen.

Suddenly Sharon punched her in the face and bloodied her nose. How can you up and do that for no reason?

Another time, Sharon hit me on the top of my head with a shoe, bam, bam, bam. Again, no reason. Once, twice, three times.

I had never raised a hand to a woman before, but I said, "If you hit me again, I'm gonna hit you back." What did she do? She hit me again. BAM. So I punched her. I couldn't help it. I blacked her eye and she ran to her mother's. I remember Dorothy Pierce calling me, saying, "Why did you hit my daughter?" But she knew what Sharon was like. She was smart, and when I told her what happened, she didn't exactly say she'd have done the same thing, but close.

That was when I knew I had to get out.

Chapter Fourteen

No Stopping Us Now

Eddie: The key thing was, we wrote teenage songs. That's what I always said. "We're writing teenage songs in an adult situation. The kids are too young to feel like the songs say they felt, but they could identify with those feelings."

I listened to Top 40 radio and my favourite groups were The Shirelles and The Drifters. Even today, when I want to listen to that kind of music, that's what I play. I loved those songs, and I'm sure they were an influence.

At the same time, though, I was writing in a vacuum, my own world. I was writing about myself. Most of those songs are personal to me; they're my own life stories. And I deliberately chose themes that were not your standard pop song subjects.

The other trick was they appeared so simple. Berry once said something about me finishing a song, and I said, "It'll take me two or three weeks."

He looked at me and said, "Those ditties? I can see Smokey taking two or three weeks, but those little ditties you write?" And from that day on, I had the nickname of King Ditty.

But he obviously thought about it because, two or three weeks later, he said, "You know what? Now I know how you put those songs together. You're a psychological writer," and that was the first time I heard someone say that.

He was right. That is what I was. I was interested in the psychology behind emotions and feelings. But I was surprised he picked up on that. I always knew he was brilliant, but now I knew he was even smarter than I thought. Especially coming from a man who said, "Those little ditties?"

"Those little ditties" continued to do well. 'Stop! In The Name of Love' and 'Back In Your Arms Again' were both huge for The Supremes, and when The Four Tops' 'I Can't Help Myself (Sugar Pie Honey Bunch)' followed, we were feeling invincible.

In fact, we were.

'I Can't Help Myself…' was beginning to slip down the charts when one of the group's former labels, Columbia, announced they were reissuing 'Ain't That Love', an old Four Tops single that had been unsuccessful, presumably in hopes of people thinking it was the official follow-up.

Berry was livid. No way was he going to be beaten to the punch by a four-year-old flop. Immediately, he had us in the studio with no idea of what we would record.

Brian: Lamont came up with a melody – basically, it was the same chord structure as 'I Can't Help Myself…' but with a few new variations. So we worked on that for a while and, by 3 o'clock, we were in the studio rehearsing the musicians with Lamont still working on the melody, and Eddie sat in the corner, scribbling lyrics.

By 3.30 we were ready for a take. By 5, we had a finished mix. By 6, we had a master stamper, which could be raced the 90 miles to the pressing plant, American, in Ottawa, Michigan. Less than 24 hours after we heard what Columbia was planning, a new Four Tops Motown single was in the hands of disc jockeys all over the country.

Our song, 'It's The Same Old Song', got to number five. 'Ain't That Love' barely bruised the Top 100.

We had another hit with Kim Weston, who'd been with Motown almost as long as we had. In fact, it was one of our cousins, Johnny Thornton, who recommended her to the label in the first place.

Kim really was a very good singer, and it seems criminal that her career didn't take off like it should have. Mention her name today, and she's best remembered as one of Marvin Gaye's regular duetting partners, and the fact she followed Mary Wells into the role proves how great she was.

She was also involved with Mickey Stevenson, which you would have hoped would work to her advantage. Instead, her biggest and best-loved solo record was with us.

We'd written 'Take Me In Your Arms (Rock Me A Little While)' the year before, and while The Isley Brothers would wind up having an even bigger hit with it a couple of years later, Kim's version remains a lot of people's favourite – even if it did come about via a somewhat unorthodox route.

Mickey Stevenson tells the story in his book *The A&R Man*. He and Kim had invited us over for dinner, and we didn't need to be asked twice. Kim was a terrific cook, and she laid on a magnificent feast – southern fried chicken, smothered pork chops, candied yams, mac and cheese, collard greens and peach cobbler to follow. Of course we wanted to repay her, so we asked if there was anything she needed.

"She needs a hit record," said Mickey.

"You got it."

At the same time we were having so many successes, though, we were also our toughest critics. No matter how hurried its creation had been, when 'It's The Same Old Song' only got to number five, it really did feel like failure, something we needed to apologise for.

It wasn't arrogance, either. If anything, we had set ourselves such impossible standards that if a record didn't reach the top, obviously we had not given it the best we could. It didn't matter what other records ours had been competing with – and there were a lot of very strong singles being released that year, by all manner of people. We would never think of that as an excuse – "Ah, we'd have done it if The Beatles hadn't released a new one." No, our conviction was, we'd have done it if we'd tried harder. Which meant that next time, we would.

Which makes it especially ironic that one of our biggest hits of the year, and our fourth number one, came very close to not even being written.

Eddie: I was working on a song for Junior Walker & The All Stars, 'Road Runner'. It's not at all a 'typical' Holland–Dozier–Holland song, but we could write in anybody's style and we wanted to get records released. A little later we wrote 'Love's Gone Bad' for The Underdogs, the house band at the Underdog, a rock club off 8 Mile Road. They needed a song, so we wrote one in their style. That's how we worked.

But while I was working on 'Road Runner', Brian was writing the melody to 'I Hear A Symphony'. Berry heard it, loved it and told Brian to see if I could finish the song for the next Supremes single, which he wanted to get out as quickly as possible.

Our last one on them, 'Nothing But Heartaches', had disappointed everybody. It didn't even get into the Top 10, so it was imperative that the group bounce back with something extra special.

I wasn't at the studio at all that day. I was at home writing, and then I went to bed around 9 or 10 o'clock. Suddenly the phone rang. It was Brian, telling me he'd cut this track called 'I Hear A Symphony', and I had to have it finished the next day.

"Are you serious?" I asked, and he was. Apparently The Supremes were about to fly out for London, so he had one day in which to cut it. So I got up, put the track on – Brian had it couriered over to me – and I was up all night working on it, and into the next day as well.

I loved the melody but trying to write it was awful. I don't like staying up late, and I especially don't like staying up all night. Several times I went to the phone to call my brother and tell him I couldn't do it – I was tired, I was burned out, it was too much for me. And every time, I didn't have the heart to call and tell him.

I kept working. Through breakfast, through the morning. I finally finished the lyric while I was rehearsing Diana the next day, at 11 or 12 o'clock. That's the first time I ever did that and I said to myself, never again. Even now, thinking about it brings me out in a cold sweat. But I did it, and one of our biggest ever hits was written because I couldn't bring myself to ring Brian and tell him no, because he was so passionate about the song. I wanted to please him so badly, I didn't have the heart to do that to him.

Brian: Berry was in London with The Supremes by the time we finished cutting and mixing the record, which meant that not only would I be presenting the finished 'I Hear A Symphony' to the next Quality Control meeting, I would also be in charge of the meeting, because whenever Berry wasn't around, I took over.

This time, though, he called while we were having the meeting to ask whether we'd got the record ready yet. I told him yes, and he asked me to play it down the telephone to him. We had a special device that let him hear the music properly, so that it didn't sound as though it was coming down a phone line at all, and the first thing Berry said was, "Oh man, you've got the voice out too far."

"No we haven't," I told him. "We've got it right."

But he wouldn't have it. We went back and forth, and finally he said, "Okay, if you think so, release the record like it is." Meaning, he trusted our judgement but, if anything at all went wrong, he'd know who to blame. But then he came home, heard it properly, and the first thing he said was, "You were right. It wasn't out too far."

*   *   *

That little device for the telephone apparently became something of a legend in the UK. Years later, we heard it said that EMI Records in London, who were responsible for manufacturing and marketing Motown in the UK, would actually cut their masters from recordings they made down the telephone!

More likely, what happened was, Berry made that call, or one like it, from a desk at EMI; told somebody what he was doing, that he was listening to the next Supremes single, and the truth got garbled from there. After all, we may have been good, but we weren't that good.

Brian: Fairly recently, I was working out at the gym. I came back to the car and heard 'I Hear A Symphony' on the radio. It caught me completely off guard. And I suddenly realised how great the lyrics were. That's what got me. I pulled over to the side of the street, and I called Edward and told him how much I loved the lyric. He said it took me 40 years to compliment him on this song!

Eddie: Lamont did the same thing to me. Not too long ago he said he liked my lyric for 'My World Is Empty Without You'. I said, "I can't believe you guys. After all these years, you're finally saying you liked the lyrics." Because I remember when I was first writing these songs, I wanted their feedback so desperately, and they wouldn't say anything. I guess I was doing a good job, because at least they weren't complaining about how they didn't like it. But it took them decades before they finally mentioned they liked the lyrics.

Berry Gordy did it, too. Thirty years later he said, "You're a genius!" All I could do was laugh. Brian is a genius and, together, Holland–Dozier–Holland created genius work. But I could never describe myself as a genius.

As before, The Supremes, The Four Tops and The Vandellas were the acts that brought us the biggest hits during 1965, and those were the artists we focused on. But we were always on the lookout

Our first BMI dinner. HDH with Edythe Vernelle Craighead Holland –
aka Edith Wayne.

for the right songs for other people, or even the right people for other songs, and that's how we came to discover The Elgins.

In fact, to be completely truthful, we didn't even discover them, because Johnny Dawson, whose group it was, was our driver.

Whenever we needed to go someplace, Johnny was the one we'd call. He would also chauffeur our mother around; she had never learned to drive, so whenever she needed to go somewhere, Johnny would take her.

A couple of the other guys in the group ran the barbershop where Brian used to have his hair cut. So we knew they had this little group – in fact, they'd already recorded for Motown as The Downbeats – and every so often, almost as a joke, Johnny would ask, "When are you guys going to write a song for us?"

Eddie: Finally, I said, "Well, okay," and of course that was it. He kept after me and after me for months, and then I remembered this song, 'Darling Baby'.

It was another one of those songs that was okay, but I didn't really like it. However, I wanted to fulfil my promise to Johnny, so I gave him that one. We used the same band track that we cut for The Supremes, and recorded the vocals in 15 minutes, including a retake.

Saundra Edwards, who'd recorded as a solo act for Motown in the past, had joined the group, and they were still The Downbeats at the time. In fact, some of the early pressings of 'Darling Baby' came out as The Downbeats. But they changed their name to The Elgins, and suddenly they had this big hit, number four on the R&B charts. I couldn't believe it.

Of course, that meant there had to be a follow-up single, which was 'Heaven Must Have Sent You', which I also didn't think much of. As far as I was concerned, it was a lot like 'Darling Baby', nothing but a B-side for Diana & The Supremes, which was shelved because we thought we had something better.

But this one was even more successful for the group, and we did an album on them as well, although it was so rushed we had to put one of Saundra's old solo singles on it to fill space.

But 'Heaven Must Have Sent You' became one of those songs that took on a life of its own. The Elgins' version was a huge hit in the UK about five years later, while Bonnie Pointer came out with a disco version that was even bigger.

'Darling Baby' and 'Heaven Must Have Sent You' weren't the only songs that surprised us around this time. Early into 1966, 'This Old Heart Of Mine (Is Weak For You)' did it as well.

Brian: That was another of Lamont's titles – he used to wake up every morning at 9 a.m. with that line "This old heart of mine's been broke a thousand times" stuck in his head, so one day we decided to put it to good use. Again, it was one of those songs we cut and then didn't use. But The Isley Brothers, who had recently signed with Motown, wanted a song, so we gave 'This Old Heart Of Mine' to them.

Eddie: I told them, "I don't think it's a smash but it's a hit," so I said I'd finish it off – the track was cut but the lyrics were still patchy. It was one of those periods when I was even busier than usual, though, so I called Sylvia Moy in to help.

Sylvia is probably best known for writing with Stevie Wonder ('Uptight', 'I Was Made To Love Her', 'My Cherie Amour'), and I liked her style, so she came over to my house on La Salle and we worked on it for three or four hours.

I was still with Almetta at the time, and it was funny because she was so jealous! Sylvia was a very pretty girl, and we were laughing and having a good time. I'm sure it really didn't look as though we were working. But we were.

The only problem was, Sylvia couldn't get a feel for the song, so I finished it off myself. But what I did, because she put a lot of time in, I put her name on it as one of the writers, and that sort of thing happened a lot. Another writer would come in and maybe they would contribute, maybe they wouldn't. But if they were involved in the process, we'd credit them because they deserved it.

I finished the song, the Isleys cut a tremendous version of it and at first I thought I was right. It was a hit, but it wasn't a smash. A couple of years later, though, 'This Old Heart Of Mine' was released in the UK and made the Top Three, and after that, it became one of our most popular songs ever. The Zombies recorded it; Rod Stewart has recorded it a couple of times, including one version with Ronald Isley, and that was really big; Randy Crawford, Boyzone… Tammi Terrell, too. We only did that one song with her, right at the end of our time with Motown, but she was one of the most beautiful people I've ever met.

'This Old Heart Of Mine' also made money for us in other ways. Curtis Mayfield's group, The Impressions, had a song called 'Can't Satisfy', which sounded sufficiently like 'This Old Heart Of Mine' that our names were added to the credits for Curtis's song.

That sort of thing happened – and has continued to happen – a lot. After 'Please Mr. Postman' hit, Dee Dee Sharp came out with

'Mashed Potato Time', which also sounded very similar. We're on the credits for that song also. Another one was '1-2-3' by Len Barry, which sufficiently resembled 'Ask Any Girl' (The Supremes) that we own part of that song, too. And, years later, there was Aerosmith's 'The Other Side', which reminded so many people of 'Standing In The Shadows of Love'.

In the midst of all this success, however, Brian's personal life was becoming increasingly embattled.

Brian: I left Sharon and I went to stay at Edward's house in Palmer Woods while I sorted myself out. A few nights later, Sharon called and asked me to come by to talk. So I went over there, and what did I do that for? Fool that I was, because we got to arguing and suddenly she pulled a gun on me.

She had it in the pocket of her housecoat. I said, "What are you doing?" and tried to grab it, and she fired, bam bam. I felt the bullet go past my ear, I heard the ringing.

I was, "Damn, what is this? You're the craziest woman." I pulled the gun away from her, went home and called her mother. I told her, "Listen, Sharon had this gun and she tried to shoot me."

I intended turning it over to the police but it turned out that it belonged to Sharon's brother, Skipper, and she'd taken it without his permission, so I handed it over.

Another time, Sharon came around and shot out Eddie's windows while I was staying there.

Eddie: At first, nobody knew who did it. A car pulled up, shots were fired, and then it drove away again. But my cousin Willie Davis was staying at the house as well, and the moment he heard the shots, he picked up a gun, ran downstairs and started firing back! He didn't hit them, but a few days later Sharon called him up and said, "Willie, you were shooting at me!" That's how we knew it was Sharon who did it.

★   ★   ★

Brian: She was so crazy, and yet, for some unknown reason, back I went to talk to her again. I felt I had to try and normalise things, if only for the kids' sake. But once again we got to arguing. She'd bellow at me, I'd bellow back at her, and all of a sudden she picked up a knife and lunged to cut me.

I grabbed her hand, but she was a strong woman. I couldn't hold it, and the blade scraped my stomach. Finally, I got the knife away from her, ran out of the house – and she got into her car and drove after me, followed me and tried to run me over. I was dodging between trees and into gardens to get out of the way, and suddenly a school bus full of kids appeared, coming along the road.

The driver stopped. "Do you need to get in? Get out of here?" Because he'd seen this mad woman trying to run me down. And I was so tempted, but I could also imagine Sharon driving into the back of the bus or something, and I didn't want anything to happen to the kids. So, I said no, and kept going. I must have run a marathon before I finally got away from her.

Eventually, we got the divorce. I didn't ever go back to the house, I didn't even want to know what she was going to attack me with next. And about 10 years later, Sharon committed suicide.

I'd seen her try to take her own life once, back when we were first married. She took an overdose of pills. Even her mother, who was very intuitive, as well as intelligent, predicted that Sharon would one day kill herself, and that's what happened. Sharon shot herself in the head with a pistol. Our youngest daughter, Holly, was sixteen at the time, and was there with her. She saw it happen. She hasn't been right since.

Chapter Fifteen

With The Beatles

It was early 1966 and Barney Ales called us together to deliver some astonishing news.

Nothing had been confirmed, but it looked like we were going to England. Somebody from Brian Epstein's office had been in touch, enquiring whether or not Holland–Dozier–Holland would be interested in recording some sessions with The Beatles.

Motown was already negotiating with them over the terms. We were, after all, under contract to the label as writers and producers, but Barney appeared confident it would happen.

It was exciting news. Two years on from their American breakthrough, The Beatles were still the biggest group in the world. Even more interestingly, it would mark the first time they had ever recorded away from producer George Martin.

Later, we heard that around the same time the band had made enquiries with Stax Studios in Memphis about maybe recording something there and having Steve Cropper produce. This, however, was different. The Beatles would not be flying to us. We would be flying to them, to record at the fabled Abbey Road Studios in London.

There was a little trepidation. Lamont aside, we weren't the most enthusiastic travellers. In fact, aside from occasional visits to Las

Vegas or Los Angeles, neither of us had really ventured outside of Detroit and its environs since 1963 or 1964. But this was *The Beatles* – even the most reluctant passenger could overcome his fears for a crack at them.

We waited and waited. We were sure something would happen. It never did. In fact, we never heard another word about it, and we never got to the bottom of why it didn't.

Who knows what would have happened had it gone ahead? Maybe we'd have liked England so much we'd have stayed, and begun a whole new career working with British bands? We knew that the British loved Motown and loved us – as big as we were in the United States, we were as big over there and, in a lot of ways, bigger.

When the Motown Revue travelled to the UK in 1965, *Ready, Steady, Go!*, one of the UK's top music TV programmes, devoted two entire shows to nothing but Motown acts.

Records that weren't that big in America became huge hits in the UK, and because there was only the one broadcaster for the entire country – the BBC – our music was being heard everywhere, whereas in the United States, different local markets had different priorities. A song that was big in Detroit might not be as big in Chicago. But a song that was big in London would be no less popular in Leeds and Liverpool.

We didn't ask a lot of questions about why the offer fell through. But it was definitely a disappointment.

That aside, 1966 was shaping up to be another really good year for Holland–Dozier–Holland.

We had another (minor) hit on The Isley Brothers, and we had more on both Marvin Gaye and The Miracles. The Supremes gave us two more number ones with 'You Can't Hurry Love', another title based on things our grandparents used to say – "You can't hurry love," meaning don't always be in such a rush – and 'You Keep Me Hangin' On'. Those tracks marked the beginning of another of those runs when everything The Supremes touched turned to gold.

Hitsville at the height of its glory. Three members of the house band
emerge from the Snakepit to join Berry, the Supremes and HDH.
© Barney Ales

Eddie: 'You Keep Me Hangin' On' was another of those songs
that I drew from my personal experiences.

I was still seeing Vernelle at the time, but I was also seeing
another girl who had recently become pregnant.

I went to Vernelle to tell her, and she was so upset. She started
crying, then sobbing heavily. "I can't deal with this," she said.
"You don't really love me, you just keep me hangin' on." And
then she started screaming, "Go on, get out of my life, just get
out of my life."

I felt so badly about what I was putting her through, realising
what I had done. I started thinking about what she was saying,
but, at the same time, the songwriter in me couldn't help but
take a mental note, about how her words could be set to music.
And, of course, we would get back together, thanks to Vernelle's
mother, Lena.

Vernelle told me that Lena liked me, thought I was "mannerable"
and down-to-earth. She also understood me, how I was young
and successful, had a lot of money, how I looked.

I've already mentioned how women would come to Detroit, come to Motown, specifically to meet me because my lyrics touched something inside them, and it was very hard to turn them all away. "He does not have to chase women," Lena said. "They chase him in ways he knows and in ways he doesn't know. You shouldn't expect a young man to behave like a mature adult."

And then she asked, "Do you love him?"

Vernelle said yes.

"Does he treat you well?"

Yes, again.

"In that case, you're not going to find anyone better than him. So deal with it." And that's what Vernelle did. We reconciled and we would eventually marry.

Meanwhile, The Four Tops were preparing to deliver another chart topper of their own, 'Reach Out I'll Be There'.

Eddie: I happened to be in the room when Brian and Lamont wrote 'Reach Out I'll Be There'. We were in the office upstairs. Brian was sitting at the piano, playing around, and Lamont and I both liked what he was doing. It sounded different.

All of a sudden, like a bat out of hell, Lamont jumped onto the piano stool next to Brian, pushed him out of the way, and started playing the chords to what would become the verse – "And if it feels like you can't go on…"

I thought he'd flipped out, because he came out of nowhere! But what happened was, Lamont got an idea in his head and he didn't want to lose it. So he jumped to the piano and started playing it. He didn't bother asking Brian to move, he pushed him out of the way. And he really started banging that piano.

Brian: 'Reach Out…' was a strange one. When we took the finished record into Quality Control, almost everybody said, "Whoa… wait a minute. That sounds strange." Smokey, especially. "That's too strange. That ain't gonna sell."

Eddie: Even Lawrence from The Four Tops, when he heard it. I played it to him and asked, "What do you think?" He said, "Kinda strange."

Brian: The chords were different, the arrangement was different, everything. But Berry said, "Wait a minute… let me hear that again." So we played it again, and he thought about it for a moment, then said, "That sounds good. It's different enough to sell." He decided it would be The Four Tops' next single, and it went to number one.

Meanwhile, things were changing at Hitsville.

Mickey Stevenson had been Motown's head of A&R since the post was created. A couple of years older than Eddie, Mickey admitted that he barely knew what A&R meant (for those who don't know, it stands for Artist and Repertoire) when he was first offered the role. Indeed, when Berry first asked him to come by the office, Mickey was expecting to be handed a recording contract. He'd already had a hit of sorts with 'If Only The Sky Was A Mirror' as a member of the doo-wop group The Classics; he'd sung with Lionel Hampton's backup group, and he was a great songwriter as well. Instead, Berry told him, "Your voice is for shit," and gave him his own office.

Over the next six years, Mickey was an integral part of the glue that held Motown together. He was responsible for introducing almost every significant act to the Motown family. He'd written some of the greatest songs. The idea of Motown without Mickey was unthinkable. Except to Berry.

Berry was one of the most open, honest, loyal people you could ever hope to meet. But he played his cards very close to his chest. You never really knew exactly what was going through that shrewd head of his, even when he was telling you everything you needed to know.

So when he told Mickey that he was promoting him to president of the company, with a new office, a new secretary, a generous pay raise and a whole new area to explore – breaking Motown onto Broadway – he probably expected Mickey to be the happiest man in the world.

Instead, Mickey asked why he was no longer the head of A&R.

"I've given it to Eddie Holland," is how Mickey remembered the conversation concluding. But that's not the way it happened.

Eddie: As far as I was concerned, Mickey leaving came completely out of the blue. Of course, I was never around the office enough to know whether or not there had been mutterings or rumours beforehand, but to me, one day he was there, and the next day he wasn't.

The first I heard about it was when Berry stopped me and said he'd noticed how well I worked with Brian and Lamont, that I knew how to deal with them and get the best out of them, and that I was the same with all the artists we worked with. He told me that through my direction, everybody became a lot more prolific. He then said he'd let Mickey Stevenson go, and that Harvey Fuqua had been recommended as his replacement. One or two others as well, I think.

But he didn't think they were right for the job. I don't know why – Harvey was probably second only to Berry and Mickey when it came to spotting new talent, and he was already heading up the Artist Development Division. Maybe that was Berry's reasoning; he didn't want to move Harvey out of a position designed especially for his talents. No! Berry said he was going to recommend me.

He had a fight on his hands, particularly among the lawyers and accountants. I think the big objection was, "Eddie's not a company man, he's too independently minded." But Berry took the position of he'll be a company man if you pay him.

Those other voices were right, though. I didn't come around a lot. I functioned mostly as the writing hand of Holland–Dozier. I didn't go to parties, and I rarely socialised.

Brian was always there, especially after Berry made him vice president of Creative Evaluation. Lamont was often around, as well. So, they looked at me as being somehow separate from Motown itself, not a part of the team. And those kind of people have long memories. They remembered that for all that time before I started writing with Brian and Lamont, I was never there.

But Berry held out for me because he understood me, and he knew me. He didn't always agree with me, but he understood me. And I understood him. Don't forget, I met him when I was still a teenager; he was one of my oldest friends but he was more than that. He was a mentor, no question about it.

He asked me how much did I want to take over A&R. I told him, "Let me do the job for a while. Don't pay me anything. If you like what I'm doing, we'll talk about it, but if you don't like what I'm doing, then you owe me nothing."

I knew I could do the job, but I also knew I had to prove I could do it, and I didn't want a wage obscuring people seeing that.

The other thing that decided me was, my ultimate goal was to become the president of Motown, which is something I never told anybody. I said to myself, "You know what? I could run this company." Berry was dealing with business on a higher level – finance, distributors, whatever. He needed somebody to handle the day-to-day running of the company and I knew I could do it. That was my goal.

I didn't think it would happen soon. I was estimating five years, maybe a little more. After all, I'd had the best teacher and I think I was his best pupil. So five years, but maybe less once I proved what I could do in A&R.

I told Berry I'd take the job, even though I knew I would have to learn it from scratch. I knew what Mickey Stevenson did but I didn't know how he did it; all the hundreds and hundreds of little things that had to be put into place before he had something he could show people.

It was like songwriting, in a way. We would walk in, teach the musicians the number and as far as they were concerned, Holland–Dozier–Holland had written a new song. They didn't think about everything that went into writing it, the hundreds of notes and bars discarded along the way, the words piled up on countless scraps of paper before the lyric was finished.

A&R is the same. When Mickey presented a new singer, all the rest of us knew was that he'd reached into his magic bag and pulled them out. But there's a lot more to it than that; following leads, listening to suggestions, untangling other relationships, and making certain not only that the artist was right for Motown but that Motown was right for the artist. In fact, the same questions certain people were asking about me, I'd later have to answer about other people as head of A&R.

I had to learn office politics. Again, as a comparative outsider, only around the offices when I needed to be, I was oblivious to the undercurrents that swirl around any workplace, the little power plays and jealousies that are part and parcel of the environment.

We've already established that Motown was, for the most part, a very happy place. But there were always those petty things that rankle, particularly when the business side got one of those occasional bees in its bonnet and tried to infringe on the artistic side. In fact, one such situation was currently looming, and I wonder whether this was also a part of Berry's thinking when he offered me the job. Completely unbeknown to me, Ralph Seltzer, Motown's so-efficient administrator, was also interested in the A&R job.

I don't know what he thought when he learned I'd been hired, but he was smart. He knew I'd be trying to find my way for a time so, generously and selflessly, he volunteered to have regular meetings with me, to help ease my way into the position. He would say things like, "Let me handle the administrative work," or "Let me do this and that." Friendly gestures and favours, helping me to find my way.

I'll be honest and say yes, I did need somebody to do that for me, at least at the start. So I went to those meetings and I listened to him. All the time, though, I was watching his secretary, Bette Ocha, and I could see that she, too, wanted to work in A&R

very badly. And shortly after I told Ralph I was ready to run A&R myself, Bette contacted me and asked if we could have a private meeting.

Of course, I said yes, and it was during that meeting she told me she wanted to come and work for me, as I knew she would.

I asked her, "What about Ralph?" and she said, "I don't want to do that any more." I asked if she'd spoken to him, and she said not yet, she wanted to see what I said. But she would handle it, and we left it at that. If Ralph agreed, and Berry agreed, the job was hers.

Ralph was furious. He stormed into my office: "I don't appreciate you taking my secretary. I was trying to assist you and you end up taking my secretary." I didn't say a word until he'd finished, and then replied quietly, "Well, I didn't ask her to do it."

He walked out and slammed the door. But Bette came over regardless and started her job. And she was very, very good. She organised things, she handled the administration, and she allowed me to get on with what I wanted to do. But about two weeks later, Berry came up to me and said, "I should never have let you take Ralph's secretary."

That's all he said, and I didn't answer. But I think he sensed that, somewhere down the road, it was going to create problems. Nothing had happened yet, but Berry knew it wasn't far away.

Even with Eddie now sitting behind a desk, rather than writing his songs at home, we were probably creating some of the best songs we'd ever come up with. As the annual BMI Awards came around, the three of us were supremely confident that this was the year we would make history.

BMI itself is one of the premiere performing rights organisations in the United States; Brian joined it in 1960, Lamont in 1961 and Eddie in 1963, and twice before, in 1964 and 1965, we had won the Songwriter of the Year award. We were confident that 1966 would see us make it three in a row.

It was not to be, and here's why.

Of all the groups in the Motown stable, the one that had most completely eluded us was The Temptations. Everybody wanted The Temptations – we wanted them, Norman Whitfield really wanted them. But they were Smokey's, and although the group did keep asking if we had anything for them, we didn't want to get involved, stepping on anybody's toes.

We had a couple of songs that they recorded, 'One Look', which went on to one of their albums, and 'A Tear From A Woman's Eye', which was actually in the running to be their next single, at least until Smokey came up with 'The Way You Do The Things You Do'.

So we never did get to do anything on them, at least while Lamont was alongside us. But in 1978, we would finally write and produce an album with the group, *Bare Back*. Ironically, it was for Atlantic Records, not Motown.

Eddie: Smokey dominated The Temptations, but Norman wanted that group so bad. He felt them. Sometimes, you hear a group and you think, "This is the kind of group I need" – it's almost like when you see somebody across a crowded room and you know you want to be with them. It's the same kind of feeling. It hits you in the gut.

He wasn't excluded. He wrote a bunch of songs that The Temptations recorded, including some I was involved with, like '(Talkin' 'Bout) Nobody But My Baby', 'He Who Picks A Rose', 'The Girl's Alright With Me', 'Girl (Why You Wanna Make Me Blue)', a bunch of numbers. None of them were big; they were album tracks and B-sides, but Norman wouldn't give up.

I used to tell him, "Man, why don't you leave them alone? You know that's Smokey's group, and you know Smokey's going to win out, because all he has to do is write their next hit. Why keep whacking your head against the wall?"

He said, "Eddie, I want this group. I have to come up with the right thing," and one day he came into my office and said, "Listen, I did a track on The Temptations that I know is a smash. All I need is for you to write the lyrics."

I said no. I never liked writing to Norman's tracks because I liked the big melodic tracks that Brian did, whereas Norman's thing was a little raunchy. Even back when we were writing together a lot, they were good but they weren't my kind of thing. But he was so keen, kept on and on at me, so finally I said, "Okay, let me hear it."

I listened to the track and I listened to the bits of lyric he had, and I said, "Norman, there's nothing here." There was no melody, I seriously couldn't even find the melody line. At least Brian and Lamont always inserted chords so you could hear the melody.

I looked at his face and I could see he was so disappointed, so I said, "Listen. There's one line in the third verse, 'Ain't too proud to beg'. That's the only line in the song that makes sense to me, and I could take that and make a song out of it."

He said, "Well, do it." I knew I'd be messing with his lyrics, throwing almost all of them away, so I asked again. "Are you sure you don't have a problem?" He said, "No, do it." So I took the track and I started listening to it and I realised that, once I found the heart of the song, it started to make sense.

I listened and listened, and I ad-libbed through the chords. I created a melody based on how the track was going, and then I took David Ruffin into the studio and dubbed him in. After that, I did the same thing two other times with the other Temptations, and little did I know, but 'Ain't Too Proud To Beg' was destined to become a hit.

It wasn't the kind of hit that Brian, Lamont and I were accustomed to, but it was still a hit. The Rolling Stones went on to record it, and everybody else, and the only thing that I felt bad about was…

I never paid that much attention to the record. It came out, it got to wherever it got to in the chart, it slipped out. I didn't think about it. Until BMI was giving the awards out, and we had won twice in a row and we wanted to make it three times. And we would have, if it had not been for 'Ain't Too Proud To Beg'.

Brian and Lamont came in second, I came in first. Songwriter of the Year. And Brian was so angry. For the first time, he was so irritated about me working with someone else.

At the BMI Awards. (L-r) Lamont, Brian, Janie Bradford, someone from BMI, Rae, Clarence Paul, his escort, songwriter Hank Cosby and Rae's sister.

"I wish you'd spend more time concentrating on our tracks, instead of other people's stuff," he said, and that's the first time he ever said something like that.

I didn't say anything, but I did ease out of working with Norman. We would write a few others together, including another couple of Temptations numbers, 'Beauty Is Only Skin Deep' and '(I Know) I'm Losing You', which would go all the way to the top.

I felt so bad, though. I felt like I'd sort of jilted Brian and Lamont. I'd wronged them. I'd taken something from them, because three times in a row would have been an amazing achievement. And it still haunts me to this day.

But that song has never gone away. A play about The Temptations came out in 2017, and it has done so well. Its title? *Ain't Too Proud*. I don't understand how these songs take on other lives, I really don't. But I'm grateful they do.

Chapter Sixteen

Big Decisions

1967 was a strange year, not solely for Motown but across the music industry. New bands were rising up, a great wave of so-called psychedelic acts, for whom 'pop' was suddenly a dirty word. They were 'rock' performers.

It wasn't a new stance. A lot of R&B acts felt the same way, almost as if they were embarrassed when one of their records 'crossed over' from the R&B stations to the pop ones, and now we were seeing the same thing, as FM radio began turning its programming over almost exclusively to white rock LP tracks, rather than 'pop' singles.

To a lot of people, it was as though an entire new mood had swept through the music industry, but to us it was business as usual. A song was a song, a hit was a hit. We'd bridged such a gap before, when the divide was between R&B and pop; we'd do it again.

In fact, we already had. Vanilla Fudge was a band out of Long Island, New York, who specialised in extended instrumental jams around both their own songs and other people's. We'd never heard of them, but one time somebody asked if we'd heard their single – it was their first ever release. And when we said no, they laughed and said, "You should."

Brian: I always felt so proud when somebody covered one of our songs. I still do. There have been so many great cover recordings.

I really liked Johnny Rivers' version of 'Baby I Need Your Loving'*. I also loved The Band singing 'Baby Don't You Do It'. I was in Las Vegas when I first heard their version; I said to myself, "That song sounds familiar! Oh yeah, I wrote it." I hadn't heard that song in so long.

But the one that really got me was Vanilla Fudge's version of 'You Keep Me Hangin' On'. The Supremes' version was only about six months old at the time, so it was still relatively fresh, but what Vanilla Fudge did owed nothing to how we did it.

It was phenomenal, it was eight minutes long, they slowed it right down, they completely rebuilt it. The first time I heard it, I said, "Oh, man, that's great…"

Motown itself was slow to react to the changing times. Later, Norman Whitfield would make some fabulous records with The Temptations, things like 'Cloud Nine' and 'Ball Of Confusion', which were totally in tune with the political mood of the day. Later still, Berry would launch the Rare Earth label and start signing up rock bands.

Before that, though, he wasn't interested in following trends. He was still building Motown.

Eddie: Berry was not the kind of person who was a 'boss boss'. He wouldn't order people around. He'd give you his opinion but he wasn't hanging over your shoulder, watching all the time. All he cared about was getting product that could pass through Quality Control, and then he might get involved, saying if it was an A-side, a B-side, or whatever.

Once or twice, he might come into the studio to listen to a session, but not often. I saw him do it a couple of times, and if he heard something he didn't like, or didn't think was eloquent,

---

* Released as 'Baby I Need Your Lovin'' in 1967.

he would gently let you know. He wouldn't force you to respond, but if you didn't make the correction, then once it got to Quality Control he would still have the same position, and that would cause you to lose the release.

I found him extremely intelligent. He understood product and the quality of the product better than anybody I had ever talked to, and everything he did at that time, he did it for Motown.

In my new role as head of A&R, I'd go into the office every day and have meetings twice a week, to get reports on what was being done.

One of the first things Berry did was place me in charge of looking at everybody's lyrics except for Smokey's. He liked my ability to examine a song and make a fair judgement – how well it was put together and whether or not it was complete – so I had to approve every lyric before it could be cut.

I agreed; it needed to be done. A lot of times, people would write and, although they could be very eloquent, it wasn't a Smokey lyric or an Eddie lyric (again, I always looked at Smokey as the best, not only at Motown but everywhere). And the writers were usually happy with what I suggested. There were some situations that might have caused conflict, but generally, they were content and so was I.

There was another area in which I differed from Mickey as head of A&R. I wasn't interested in people sending me tapes; rather, I was interested in auditioning people. I wasn't bringing in new talent, for instance, unless they were someone brought to my attention as exceptional, which Jeffrey Bowen (another of the writer/producers at Motown) would do sometimes, or Berry once or twice, and I would obviously do what he wanted, even though I could say no if I felt especially strongly about it.

I wasn't in the A&R post for long, but while I was there, I suppose the biggest name I signed was Ashford & Simpson, whom I went to New York City to meet with.

Husband-and-wife team Nickolas Ashford and Valerie Simpson would become an integral part of the Motown set-up later on, writing and producing some of the biggest names of the 1970s, but they were writing great songs from the moment they arrived, things like 'Ain't No Mountain High Enough' and 'Ain't Nothing Like The Real Thing', and all those great sides that Lamont and Brian produced on Rita Wright.

In fact, I signed Rita as well, although she was Syreeta at the time. But Brian thought 'Syreeta' would be a difficult name for the DJs to handle, so he had her shorten it. Of course, a few years later, she started having hits under her original name.

But signing new talent was another thing that brought me into conflict with Ralph Seltzer, because he didn't like us signing people unless they really, really wanted to be on Motown. He didn't like any arm-twisting stuff to get the person to come to us. Berry felt the same way, so Ralph was doing no more than following his lead. But Berry would also understand if an artist was worth it. Ralph did not make that exception. I'm not certain whether Ashford & Simpson fell into that category, but I know Jeffrey Bowen had spent some time talking them into it, before then talking me into flying to New York to seek out Nick. Again, Ralph wasn't happy with me, but I was getting used to that.

I also brought in one of Motown's biggest ever hit records. Barrett Strong had been a part of Motown all the way back before there was a Motown, but he had been gone for a few years by now. I was in the office one day when he came in with a song he wanted me to hear, called 'I Heard It Through The Grapevine'. I listened to it and approved the song on the spot.

I knew the song was going to be a big hit. I couldn't wait to play it to everybody else. I think Norman Whitfield was the first person who heard it, while Barrett was still in the building. Norman had some ideas for the song, and decided to record it with Marvin Gaye.

Shortly after that he recorded it again with Gladys Knight & The Pips, and that version was released first, because they needed an immediate release. The song sold a million copies for Gladys Knight & The Pips but it sold millions more for Marvin.

A short time later, I was driving somewhere when this big, pretty green Cadillac pulled up alongside me. The window rolled down and it was Barrett Strong. All he said was, "Thank you, Eddie."

Speaking of Gladys, though…

Eddie: I always thought Gladys was a great singer. I remember the first time I heard her, we were both teenagers and she'd just made her first records… even then I thought she was an exceptional singer. I couldn't believe how young she was, either, no more than seventeen or eighteen when they cut those first things for Vee Jay. When she came to Motown in 1966, I was really looking forward to working with her but unfortunately I never got the chance.

At this point, singles were still Motown's bread and butter because they drove the market. However, there were even greater profits to be made from album sales, and it wouldn't be long before LPs outsold singles in the United States for the very first time.

Before that, however, Berry wasn't especially interested in LPs, and neither were we. Singles were where our hits were, whereas we put albums together by sweeping up everything we'd recorded since the last one – A-sides, B-sides and anything else that was there.

Which isn't to say they weren't very good. Every song Motown released had to go through Quality Control to ensure it was up to standard, and they did so before anybody knew their ultimate fate – A-side, B-side, a B-side that the DJs decided they liked better than the A-side, so they flipped it over and played that instead. Nothing was released that somebody didn't feel very strongly about.

But LPs were growing increasingly important, and Barney Ales knew it. So, now, did Berry.

Eddie: I was preparing to hold my first ever meeting as head of A&R and it so happened that Berry was in California at the time.

Instead, he instructed one of his staffers, press officer Al Abrams, to oversee things.

I called in all the executives and company people, everyone who was dealing with the creatives, and laid out the problem for them – which was that nobody was coordinating album production. Bands were coming in and out of town all the time, but nobody was keeping track of their schedule or their availability, so they could be taken into the studio for any amount of time. That's one of the first things I insisted on; schedule the time for the artists to record an album.

As a writer I hadn't previously had much to do with LPs. That was more Brian and Lamont's department, because they were the producers, and they decided what went on the albums. But I did enjoy the way they were making little concept albums, years before people like The Beatles and The Who did it. Things like *The Supremes A' Go-Go*, which was the greatest pop party you had ever been to, great versions of all those big hit singles, bang, bang, bang one after another, as though they were stacked up on a little record player. That was such a great idea.

So the other thing I insisted upon was, if an album didn't feel strong enough, bring in some outside tunes. Not every song we recorded had to be written by Motown people. Don't worry about who wrote it; concentrate on what the artist could do with it.

The room murmured its agreement, but then somebody asked why we'd not done that before, outside of The Supremes and maybe one or two others. I told them it was Berry's fault, and I could see Al writing something on a piece of paper. The meeting ended shortly after that; I barely had enough time to walk downstairs before the phone started ringing.

It was Berry.

I picked it up. "I know what you're going to ask me," I said, but he asked me regardless.

"Eddie, I understand you had an A&R meeting, scheduling the artists and discussing the problems that A&R had?"

"That's right."

"I also understand that you said I was the problem."

"Yes I did."

There was a pause and then he said, "Okay." Which meant he got it. "You do what you want to do."

Most people were so afraid of Berry they'd never have said something like that. But he respected me for saying it. It was an uncomfortable position for me to be in when he asked, though!

Brian: It's true, you do make more money with albums, but I didn't find that out until later. The albums were my territory, though; the sales department would suggest we come up with an album's worth of material, so that's what we did.

Lamont and I would have the concept if there was one – an album of Sam Cooke songs, an album of Broadway songs. We'd written so many songs ourselves, it struck us as a good idea to cut a bunch of our favourite show tunes and put them on an album.

It may have been my idea, it may have been Lamont's, but we were all in agreement about it. It was our tribute to the kind of music that all three of us grew up listening to, and to the people who played it to us, our Uncle James, and Lamont's father.

The most audacious idea, however, was an album we cut on The Supremes, called *The Supremes Sing Holland–Dozier–Holland*, because that was exactly what it was – a dozen of our songs, some recorded at different points in the past, some brand new, some covers of numbers we'd cut on other artists. Twelve of the songs we considered among our best.

Berry didn't want to do it. He thought it was a terrible idea. Smokey might have got away with it because he was Smokey. But could you imagine Norman, or Harvey, or any of the other non-performing songwriters trying to do something like that? Berry let it go out simply to appease us, and when the album wasn't especially successful, he said, "See what I mean?"

But really, we were ahead of our time. We figured we had established ourselves as what you would now call a 'brand'. Even though we didn't actually sing or dance or make records in our own right, it felt as though Holland–Dozier–Holland had become an entity in its own right. Particularly overseas, for some reason. Years later, we heard that people would go into their local record store and they wouldn't ask for the latest Supremes single, or even the latest Motown release. They'd ask for the new Holland–Dozier–Holland.

The Supremes Sing Holland–Dozier–Holland was a way of testing those waters, and also introducing ourselves as individuals to the world. Lots of people had heard of Holland–Dozier–Holland, after all. But how many knew what our full names were?

In truth, the record really didn't do too badly, and certainly not as badly as Berry liked to say. It got to number six in the United States, and somewhere in the teens in the UK, which wasn't that different to a lot of other Motown releases. It was number one on the R&B chart, and it also included The Supremes' two most recent chart toppers, 'You Keep Me Hangin' On' and 'Love Is Here And Now You're Gone'.

Beyond that, too, 1967 was looking like another vintage year.

First, The Vandellas bounced back with their biggest hit in a long time, 'Jimmy Mack'. It was actually an older number – you'll remember that we recorded it in 1964, only for Quality Control to turn it down in case it was misconstrued as a Vietnam protest song.

Now, with the war a major bone of social discontent, and the battle lines between the pro-war and anti-war factions becoming thicker with every passing death, we knew Motown needed to make it clear which side we stood on. 'Jimmy Mack' was retrieved from the archive and became one of The Vandellas' biggest ever hits.

The Four Tops, Motown's biggest act outside of The Supremes, maintained their dominance, and 'Standing In The Shadows of Love' should have given them their third number one. We could never believe that it didn't. But 'Bernadette' was the one that truly blew us all away, first when we recorded it, and later, whenever we heard it on the radio.

Eddie: "A gift from Diana."

Eddie: We were in the studio one day and Brian was sitting at the piano playing some chords, and he kept singing 'Bernadette'. I turned to Lamont and said, "I really hope Brian doesn't want me to write lyrics for that song." I didn't like the name, not at all.

But Brian was insistent. That was what the song was called and, as we discussed the title, we realised that each of us had a relationship with someone named Bernadette! Lamont was dating a girl named Bernadette – in fact, she had also inspired the title 'I Hear A Symphony', as it's something he used to say when they were together. I had gone out with a girl named Bernadette, and Brian was dating a girl whose middle name was… Bernadette. It was one of those crazy coincidences, and that's probably why I was able to write it. It was one of those things that was meant to be.

Brian: After Sharon and I broke up, I probably played the field a little more than I should have. I did a whole lot of crazy things, and some I do feel bad about if I look back. Terrible, in fact.

But I'd come out of what was basically a sexless, loveless marriage that went on for far too many years. I had a lot of catching up to do. Maybe I'd have done better going into a monastery and becoming a choir boy, but in a way, that's what I felt like I was escaping from. At one point, I had about seven girlfriends on the go at the same time. It got real crazy.

Then I met up with one of my old school girlfriends, a lady named Miriam Bernadette Martin, and somehow I got involved with her again. She was a lawyer now, and when I wrote 'Bernadette', Eddie and Lamont were listening and they kept asking, "What are you calling it?" and Eddie said, "How am I going to write that?"

But finally he relented, "Oh man, okay", went away and wrote such a fantastic lyric. It was so good; he wrote a heck of a thing and it didn't even matter that nothing rhymes with the title. I loved it. I played it for Berry, and even he was bowled over. It was that strong.

As for the three Bernadettes, each was individually convinced that the song was about them. But The Four Tops' Duke Fakir knew the truth, and one night at a show, he looked out and saw Miriam in the crowd, and he said, "This is for you, Bernadette!"

Eddie: I wrote the song about my relationship. But I didn't want to use that title. I was saying, "Bernadette, is that someone you know? It's kind of difficult for me to write with; I don't know what I can do," and Brian didn't respond. I looked at his face and I knew he was dealing with the melody, so I made up my mind. I wrote about the girl I knew, because that's all I could do.

I struggled with that song for hours and hours in my apartment, into the wee hours of the morning. Most of it was already done, but there was something missing – sometimes, you need just that one line.

By this time I'd had a phone for a while, and I'd now given the number to about five people, and one girl called me while I was working on the song. I'd not talked to her in a few weeks and she was whispering these sweet nothings to me, and I was saying, "I've got to go, I'm working on this song," but she ignored me and kept on talking, and suddenly she said this one line, about how people can go their whole lives without finding the kind of relationship we had.

I heard her say that and I said, "That's it!" That was the line! I said, "I gotta go," and hung up.

Recording the song also proved a little fraught.

Eddie: 'Bernadette' was a hard song to record. We had a tendency to have a high note in our songs, and it didn't worry me because my voice was very rangey. I could hit it.

It was Brian who did it. There were certain songs – 'Standing In The Shadows Of Love', 'Bernadette', 'Can't Help Myself' – Brian had to hear in certain keys because he felt that the fidelity would otherwise not come through. He could hear certain things, all these instruments, but if they weren't in the right key, it didn't work for him. So Brian had to have them in certain keys.

Now, high C was easy for me; I could sing high C all day long. Levi Stubbs wasn't so comfortable with it and, for some reason, he assumed it was me putting those songs into those keys, and they challenged the hell out of Levi, in a way he'd never been challenged before. In fact, he developed a bit of an attitude towards me. Nothing was said but I could sense it.

So there was a certain part of 'Bernadette' that Levi was really having trouble reaching. We tried and tried and he couldn't do it, and I could see him getting more and more frustrated.

Suddenly, I had an idea. I could hear some girls outside the studio – it backed onto the street, and there were often fans standing around, listening to what we were doing or waiting for autographs, and I thought to myself, "I wonder?"

Because Levi's a performer. And what does a performer do? He performs. I opened the door and asked the girls to step inside. I told the engineer to start the tape at the particular spot we'd been having problems with, and the moment they came into the room, Levi hit the note like I knew he would. He had a lot of pride in his abilities. And after four bars I told the girls, "Thank you very much," and opened the door so they could leave.

Later, I was downstairs playing cards and Levi walked in after the session, and a guy he knew, someone he grew up with, said, "I heard that song, man, you did a helluva job." Levi walked past me, glanced down and said, "I had a good teacher." And that was the first and only time he ever acknowledged me regarding a song. Then he walked out of the room.

Chapter Seventeen

Storm Clouds Forming

It was around this same time that we cut what could be (and often is) described as our first psychedelic record, although we didn't look at it like that.

The Supremes were going through a difficult patch, personalities wise. Diana and Florence were at constant loggerheads, and while Mary did her best to stay out of things, she couldn't help but get caught in the middle. People even said that's how she managed to miss the car accident that hospitalised Diana and Florence while they were in Florida at the beginning of 1967. They were on their way to go fishing, but Mary chose to remain at the hotel.

The problems were elemental. The girls' work schedule would have punished the most road-hardened veteran; they had no time off, no time to themselves. The pettiest squabble could develop into a full-scale battle, some of which even spilled over onto the stage. It didn't help, either, that Florence had started drinking heavily.

In April 1967, Berry replaced Florence with Cindy Birdsong, around the same time as he decided to restyle the band as Diana Ross & The Supremes. So that became another bone of contention, a sense that anybody else in the group was there to back up Diana, and was completely disposable too.

Like Mary, we worked to avoid getting involved by doing what we did best – making music that made you feel good, and with that in mind, we had a new song for the group, 'Reflections'. We even tried to ignore the fact that there would be only one Supreme on the record, since both Mary and Cindy were replaced for the occasion by session singers.

Eddie: 'Reflections' was another song where I didn't quite get the lyric as it should hve been. The line "*the hurt that* you have caused", I thought about it and thought about it, and what I really wanted to say was "*that loving you* had caused". But I didn't, because I was trying not to use as many words as I usually did.

Then I was talking with Ron Miller, who was a songwriter whom Berry had discovered, and who struck gold with songs like 'For Once In My Life' and 'Yester-Me, Yester-You, Yester-day'. In other words, he was one of our greatest songwriters, and he loved to tease me by criticising our songs. He said, "Edward, I love the song, but you should have said…" and he was correct, because that was the thing that bothered me. I have to confess, though, that I felt a lot better about my progression as a writer when Ron heard 'Falling In And Out Of Love'. "Edward," he said, "I listened to that song and I was impressed. I didn't know you could write that way." I knew then that I had arrived, because he was a very tough critic.

We booked Lawrence Horn as our engineer for the occasion. We liked him – he always had really good ideas in the studio. Not all of them were practical but they were usually interesting.

Eddie: Lawrence had got hold of a synthesiser, at a time when they were still very, very new on the market, and he was playing with it, making all these strange noises, and he wanted to add them to 'Reflections'.

Brian didn't like it at all. He said it sounded artificial, but I listened to it on the demo and I liked it. Yes, it was different, but it also sounded really new, really fresh.

I'm not usually a big fan of 'technology' in the studio because so many people use it in the wrong way. They hear a new drum effect, for instance, on somebody else's record, and decide to do it themselves, not because it works with the song but because it makes them sound 'up to date'. And synthesisers would go that way. But not yet.

The more I listened, though, the more the sounds tied into the lyric. It was one of the few songs I wrote really fast – it flowed straight out, and the synthesiser sounds flowed with it. Plus, I really couldn't think of a single hit record where the synthesiser was an integral part of the song, and I loved the way it made the record sound. It was spacey, it was mysterious, it was euphoric.

I said to Brian, "Keep it on. You really should use that," and he still wasn't sure, but finally he agreed, and we were all glad that he did because when it started turning up on the radio, you could see people react with surprise as they stared at the radio. They'd say, "This is The Supremes?" That's how 'out there' that record sounded.

It was a Saturday night, July 22, 1967. A friend of ours, a doctor, had invited us over to his house for an all-night poker game. Naturally, we said yes. We were both keen players, and we were good as well – you cannot grow up playing cards with Berry Gordy and not pick up a few tricks!

Brian: My happiest memories of Motown – well, I should say I have very fond memories of the whole place. From the day we started working there, we'd have great times, there are so many great memories. But the best? We used to gamble a lot; we used to meet at Berry's house once a week, usually at the weekend, and we'd play poker: myself, Edward, Berry, Mickey Stevenson, Harvey Fuqua and a couple of other guys.

The winner was usually Berry, but I won a lot, Edward did. There'd be a bunch of $100 bills stacked up there, thousands of dollars riding on a game, especially when Smokey came along.

He was the worst poker player in the world, but he hated to be left out, even though he always lost. In the end, Berry had to ban him from coming to any more games.

Eddie: Mickey used to have poker parties too, although I only went to one. The guys were going for several years because there would always be a lot of women dancing and doing whatever, and the guys loved them. I went to one, just to see what it was about, and I only stayed for about an hour before leaving. Maybe an hour and a half. It was a wild party… a real wild party.

We also had a lot of poker games in the offices – in fact, Ralph actually sent a message round one time, "No poker in the office." We'd still do it though; we just stationed a lookout on the door. Three or four times a week, Brian, myself, The Four Tops, Hank Cosby, Mickey Stevenson and Clarence Paul would take a break from the studio or whatever, and play. Some games lasted a few hours, one went on all night.

Brian left around midnight and went home. When he returned the following morning at 10.30, we were still at it. "Are you guys still here?" he asked.

"Yep."

He sat down, rejoined the game and within an hour, he had won all the money.

But the most memorable game was when I played with Berry and lost $30,000 in one night. I kept raising him and he kept calling me. He had nothing even close to my cards yet he kept calling. I kept raising, he kept calling.

It was five-card stud and when we got down to the last card, he made a huge bet, then paused, hesitated and looked down at his card.

It so happened that I'd borrowed some money from him earlier that day. "Let's just wipe that debt away," he said, and he called.

All of a sudden, it was as if I'd lost my hearing. There were a lot of office people there, Billie Jean and people like that, and they were loving it. The game had been so exciting. But I looked around at the faces and all I saw was their mouths moving and their hands going up in the air, and I heard no sound for about 10 seconds. It was like something you see in a movie. Then, I said, "Okay, you win," and I left.

I was on my way to Tennessee that evening. I was there about three days and Berry called me… he said, "Eddie, you know you owe me $30,000?" I said, "I know, you'll get it."

He said, "I want to tell you this. I know how you are, you'll pay me, but it'll cost me more in the end because the next thing I know, you'll be wanting to renegotiate a contract or something, so instead, I'll advance you $50,000 and you repay it whenever you want."

On this particular Saturday evening, we played through the night and nobody disturbed us. We didn't have the television on and there was no radio. The phone was switched off. We played. And the following afternoon, following a few hours' sleep, we left the house, got into our cars and drove home.

Eddie: I was on my way to visit a friend in Cleveland, Ohio, and at first I couldn't believe it. The streets were burning. Entire neighbourhoods. There were roadblocks everywhere, and the Near West Side around 12th Street was completely impassable.

But the radio was silent. Nobody was reporting anything. We drove through what felt like an apocalyptic wasteland. There were people on the street, shouting. Windows shattering. Cops everywhere. It was the most surreal thing I had ever witnessed in my life.

It took days to piece together what had happened. An early-morning police raid on a blind pig bar – an illicit speakeasy – turned ugly when they found it crammed with revellers, celebrating the return home from Vietnam of a couple of GIs. The law had expected the place to be deserted.

Rather than back off, the police proceeded to arrest everybody in the place, more than 80 people. A crowd gathered outside to watch and, in the same way these things often develop, a handful of minor flashpoints got out of hand. By the time the police departed with their prisoners, it was clear the protestors were not going to disperse willingly. Instead, a handful started looting and vandalising.

Again the police miscalculated. Instead of moving in quickly to clamp down on the disturbance, they decided to wait, believing that the unrest would burn itself out. They even asked the local news channels not to report on what was unfolding, in hopes of keeping a lid on things.

It didn't work. Instead, the trouble grew worse, spreading from street to street. Fires broke out. Fights, too. Windows shattered, stores were emptied. Finally, the police told the media to go ahead and report the events, by which time the riot was out of control.

It would take five days for the trouble to be quelled, during which time anybody with any sense did their best to stay indoors. But the scenes that appeared on local television news were never to be forgotten, images of the National Guard parking its tanks on Detroit streets, snipers hanging from rooftops taking shots at passers-by.

Forty-three people died, hundreds more were injured. Over at the Algiers Motel on Woodward Avenue, The Dramatics – a local band that once auditioned for Motown, and who were playing a label showcase at the Fox Theatre on the night the riots broke out – were caught up in a police raid of such brutality that two of their members were severely beaten, and three of their associates were killed.

Finally it was safe to go back outside, although we didn't even attempt to go to the office until the rioting was over. When we did, we found the place in turmoil. Everybody, ourselves included, knew of at least one friend or relative who had been caught up in the trouble. Martha Reeves was actually onstage at the Fox Theatre, headlining the same event at which The Dramatics performed, when the trouble started. They were told to stop the show and evacuate.

We had no time to process the damage done to the city we grew up in. For, no sooner had we returned to work than we found ourselves embroiled in a firestorm of our own.

Eddie: Another of my A&R responsibilities was to monitor how the songs performed after release, and how well they did on the charts. That was the most important barometer at Motown – even more important, in some ways, than the quality of the song. You could write and record the greatest song in the world but if it didn't sell any copies, all you had done was spend money.

Even though we had our own studio at Hitsville, it was still expensive to produce music. The musicians needed to be paid, the arranger, the producers, the engineers, the cleaners. Tape costs money, electricity costs money, coffee costs money, the shelves in the tape library cost money. Even the luxury of cutting when you wanted to, mixing when you wanted to… all the things we took for granted, and which taught us our trade through trial and error, cost money. It just wasn't us who had to pay for it.

Expenses that never even occurred to us piled up, and I know this for a fact because I remember my shock when I saw the royalty statement for my hit song 'Jamie'.

It quickly became apparent to me that Motown was underperforming. Not by some labels' standards – companies like Capitol or Columbia, the so-called major labels, could get by on a very different level to us because they also had albums sales to sustain them. But, as we've already explained, Motown didn't work like that; we were in the business of hit singles and the fact was, we weren't getting enough of them.

Berry was already aware of the issue, which is why he sent out a memo that said, "We will release nothing but Top 10 product on any artist." The next line was addressed directly towards Brian, Lamont and myself: "Because The Supremes' worldwide acceptance is greater than other artists, on them we will release only number one records."

So far, the latter had not really been a problem. As Berry said when he passed Brian in the hallway one time, "We dangerous." But we were definitely falling down in other areas.

I had somebody, probably Bette, prepare some reports. Who spent the most time and money in the studio? I already knew the answer to that one, but it was good to see it in black and white. Of those hours (and dollars), who then had the most hits? And, on the other side of the coin, who had the most non-hits, by which I mean records that didn't touch the Top 40? I had my suspicions about that as well, but again I wanted to see it on paper.

I don't have the exact figures to hand. But I remember looking at the numbers for Brian, Lamont and I, and they made for fascinating reading.

In 1965, Brian and Lamont produced something in the region of 70 sessions. I then factored in how many of those sessions involved songs I'd had a hand in as lyricist. Nine were Top 40 hits in the United States that same year, which meant one out of every eight sessions we oversaw was a success.

Add B-sides to the equation, because we usually had both sides of the single, and you're close to one in four. Add songs that didn't do so well in the States, but were major hits in the UK – things like 'Take Me In Your Arms (Rock Me A Little While)' by Kim Weston, or 'Love (Makes Me Do Foolish Things)' by Martha & The Vandellas – and don't forget the songs we recorded in 1965 that became hits in 1966, and the numbers were impressive. And they only got better.

In 1965, we were running close to one hit record for every three sessions we recorded. Given the amount of work we were doing, I doubt whether anybody could improve on that. Except us.

The following year, 1966, we handled somewhere around 90 sessions. Using the same formula, 15 of those sessions produced Top 40 hits on one side of the Atlantic or the other, 30 when you count the B-sides. More when you include the handful that were held over for the new year. Now we were looking at close to a 40 per cent hit ratio.

But what about 1967? For one reason or another – and my A&R duties certainly played a part in it – we'd spent a lot less time in the studio – 22 sessions between January and July. And how many of those sessions produced Top 20 singles? Five – 'Bernadette', 'The Happening' (written for the 1967 movie of the same name, starring Anthony Quinn and Faye Dunaway), 'Seven Rooms Of Gloom', 'Reflections' and Marvin's 'Your Unchanging Love'.

It wasn't only Holland–Dozier–Holland who were falling down. It was the same across the entire label, and I couldn't pinpoint the cause. Were writers and producers not pulling their own weight? Was Quality Control growing complacent? Were the sales and promotion teams not doing everything they should? Did it go even deeper than that, to Motown's distributors?

I didn't know, but I resolved to find out. And, in the meantime, I needed to start making cuts and arrest the decline. Beginning with Holland–Dozier–Holland. After all, if I wasn't willing to follow the rules myself, how could I expect anybody else to do so?

I called a meeting between Brian, Lamont and myself, and I laid everything out for them. Holland–Dozier–Holland were not doing their best work.

Some of the responsibility was definitely mine. With a regular nine-to-five job, I couldn't sit around thinking about lyrics like I used to, and that was something I had to work out for myself. And I would.

I pointed to the latest Supremes single, 'Falling In And Out Of Love'. We'd recorded it at the end of July, and the single came out in October, as the follow-up to 'Reflections'. The latter had reached number two, with only the immovable 'Ode To Billy Joe' preventing us from making it five Supremes chart toppers in a row. 'Falling In And Out Of Love', on the other hand, climbed no higher than number nine.

I didn't understand it. It was a nice song, and we liked it a lot. I knew we were still writing great songs, and they would prove their worth in years to come – 'Gotta See Jane' and 'There's A Ghost In My House', which we wrote with R. Dean Taylor, for instance, are as beloved today as they ever were. But the product we were doing on The Supremes – and you have to understand, The Supremes were key – was fading. We were always looking to go to number one, and we loved the records, but the public didn't.

I looked at Brian and Lamont. "Until we come up with better product," I told them, "we're not going into the studio. We're not going to waste any more money." And once we had set the example, I was going to call in all of the other producers and tell them the same thing. We had the best team in the world at Motown. Now it was time to prove it.

Except I was never given the opportunity.

Chapter Eighteen

When Good Friends Fight

Eddie: It was around now that I approached Berry with what I thought was a very fair idea.

Brian, Lamont and I were still on the same deals we had agreed to back in 1961, 1962, when we were first starting out, and I felt that Brian, more than anybody, deserved some kind of renegotiation. In terms of hits, and despite the recent shortfall, he had been Motown's dominant producer for three years now. He was also responsible for more hits than anybody else.

I knew Brian would never say anything himself. That's not how his mind worked. He got on with his job. But I also knew when somebody deserved greater recognition, and I knew what Brian was worth. I decided to go to Berry myself.

Brian: I knew Edward was trying to get me a better royalty rate, but all I really wanted to do was write songs and produce. I felt so much passion and enjoyment doing that, the other stuff was immaterial.

But when Edward looked at the overall scheme of things, when he saw that other people were getting the same amount of money as I was getting, regardless of how many hits they had, he thought that was a little unfair. So he said, "Let me find out if we can get a better deal," and, from a business point of view, he was probably right.

Eddie: You could say that it goes back to when we were kids, when our mother and Ola and Uncle James used to tell me that I was the big brother, and it was up to me to look out for Brian. And you'd be right. All my life, I'd been watching out for him – not because he needed it but because that's what big brothers do. This was one more example.

I arranged a meeting with Berry to tell him what I was thinking. He demurred, as I had expected him to. Motown was doing well, but the fact of the matter was, he also had a lot of expenses.

"You guys make a lot of money," he explained. "But you don't understand how much you're making. You don't pay for the lights. You don't pay secretaries, you don't pay gas bills, you pay nothing. All you have to do is pay your taxes. Everything that I'm getting through Motown, I have to pay everybody here. I have to handle all the expenses, the distributors, all the legal things. The lot. There is nothing in this building that I didn't have to buy myself."

Our earnings were net. It was all profit. But for some reason, that argument didn't impress me too much. I still felt Brian was worth more. Motown literally lived from hit single to hit single, and there was no way Berry was going to pay out more in royalties when his priority was always Motown's overheads. I didn't understand that at the time, but years later, when I had to run my own operations, it made perfect sense.

Besides, if he increased Brian's royalty, then somebody else would be knocking on his door the next day, demanding that theirs, too, be increased. Then someone else, and someone else. He had to control the costs.

Instead, Berry suggested that he give Brian a million dollars worth of stock in the company, and I was okay with that. Except Berry still had doubts. He wanted to do it but he wasn't sure how to do it or when to do it, whereas my feeling was, he should just get it done.

I kept pressuring him, he kept pushing back, and one thing led to another led to another, until finally I said to Brian, "You know what? Rather than get into an argument about this stock thing, I'll talk to Berry about Holland–Dozier–Holland having our own label, as part of Motown."

It didn't feel like an impossible request. Motown had never been one label. There was Motown, there was Tamla, we had Gordy, Soul and VIP. Back in the early days, there was Checkmate, Miracle and Mel-o-dy. There was Workshop Jazz for jazz and Divinity for gospel. Some labels didn't last long, but others were a part of the furniture.

The way I saw it, it wouldn't cost much to set up a new imprint, design a label around our initials (the label had to be called Holland–Dozier–Holland, of course) and give us a modest operating budget. We'd start with three artists, and the deal would be, if they were successful, we could expand.

Where would we get those artists? We would discover them ourselves. We wouldn't poach anybody from elsewhere in the Motown family. And it wouldn't detract from our work with The Supremes, The Four Tops or anybody else Berry wanted us to be with because, if nothing else, Brian and Lamont would not allow it to. In fact, I could imagine the chorus of disapproval if I'd even suggested such a thing – "What, give up the acts we've worked all these years to establish, to work with artists who nobody's ever heard of? You're out of your mind."

I had it all mapped out, but again Berry said no.

I understand his reservations. He knew how aggressive I could be if I was pursuing something I wanted; he translated it into the belief that, the moment I smelled success with my own label, all our best songs would end up with our artists. And it didn't matter how much I sought to reassure him on that, he didn't want to take the chance.

Stalemate. I felt awful being in this conflict with him, he felt bad about being in conflict with me. We'd always had a very close relationship and he'd always been very tolerant of me. I knew I would get away with things that nobody else would, and he was always very patient in dealing with me. But we had reached an impasse and it was wearing on him. Berry stepped back – and others stepped forward, pointing out for example how little session work we were doing. Suggesting that perhaps Holland–Dozier–Holland had gone on strike.

Strikes were big news in Detroit that year. The auto industry had suffered major stoppages as workers demanded better conditions, higher pay, greater security. According to some interpretations, weren't those the same demands I was making?

In fact, going on strike was the furthest thing from my mind; it had never even entered my thoughts. I would never have done that and, besides, how could it even be true? I'd just signed Barrett Strong and 'I Heard It Through The Grapevine'. That wouldn't have happened if I'd been on strike.

This was turning nasty.

In the event, I only had one meeting with Seltzer. After that, it was turned over to a lawyer, George Schiffer.

George and I got on well. He understood my position, in the same way he understood Berry's. He agreed that, because of our long-standing friendship, this was difficult for both of us; that it was almost like having a dispute with a family member. He also remarked, during one of our lunchtime meetings, that if Berry was ever going to give a record label to somebody, it would be Holland–Dozier–Holland.

"So why don't you tell him that?" I asked.

He laughed. "Nobody's going to tell him that."

"Well, maybe you should." I pushed, and I kept pushing, and that's when George got irritated with me as well. Until finally he snapped.

"Eddie? Look. We have contracts on you, we have contracts on your brother and we have contracts on Lamont. We don't have to give you anything."

I was astonished. Contracts? Yeah, you've got them but so what? How long was it since anybody had even looked at them?

We signed them, they were put in a folder and they had been gathering dust ever since.

I could not count, and I doubted whether Berry could either, how many times one or other of us had gone beyond the terms of the contract in order to get things done. The contracts were a legal nicety – one of the lawyers even told me that they were "a matter of fun", a pile of papers that had nothing to do with the reality of our life with Motown.

There had always been room for compromise – so much, in fact, that we didn't even think of it as compromise. If something needed to be done, it would be done. It was common sense.

Clearly, that had all gone out of the window.

This was it. Prior to that moment, I'd been negotiating. But now, the gloves were off. I was going to fight. It takes a lot to push me to that point, but I have never been the kind of person you could push around and control. My entire philosophy is based around my ability to reason things out, to discuss them and find common ground. I have never reacted well to ultimatums. George was saying those options were off the table. And why? Because they had the power.

I was accused of failing to carry out my functions as the A&R director. In exactly the same way I had gathered documents to show how much work we were doing, others gathered documents that showed how little we were suddenly cutting. "Holland," Berry was told, "is not doing his job."

And Berry seemed to believe it. He was so disillusioned, and so frustrated, that he didn't even ask me for my side of the story. We were having a meeting and I could see, from the expression on his face, the pain he felt, the disappointment. He was heartbroken. He genuinely believed what he'd been told, and it bothered him deeply.

A piece of paper was handed to me. It was my letter of resignation.

"Sign this," Berry said sadly. "You've quit. You're no longer head of A&R."

I was so angry. He hadn't even asked me if any of the accusations were true. He never asked me why we weren't recording. He didn't even question what my intent was. He just assumed the worst, and this was where we had ended up.

I signed it. I was so furious, with him, with Ralph, with Motown, with the entire stupid situation, that I picked up my pen, scrawled my name across the page and walked out of Hitsville. I was still under contract, I was still a songwriter. But I was not going back.

Big surprise. Ralph was appointed to replace me as head of A&R. Bigger surprise. He didn't last. Bette Ocha – who I believe was the only one of the three of us who had ever genuinely wanted the job for all the right reasons – moved up to replace him.

Time passed. Berry called. He wanted to arrange a meeting, just me and him. Okay.

"Eddie," he said. "We have to straighten this problem out, and this is what I'm going to do. I'll make a deal with you, right now."

I listened as he outlined the numbers. They sounded impressive. "What do you say?" he asked.

"I don't know." The fact of the matter was, this wasn't about money. It truly wasn't. I know some people probably portrayed it like that, because that was the world in which they lived, one where money was the prime motivator for all. They might even have believed that, when the financial pressure was on, I would cave; that I didn't have the stamina, or the finances, to sustain a long, drawn-out battle.

But that wasn't the case. Just as I had my entire life, I saved my money. Yes, I lived well, and if I wanted something I bought it – my house in Palmer Woods, for example. My Cadillac. Whatever. But I didn't waste money, I didn't throw it around. In fact, as far as that whole subject is concerned, there are two points I would like to make.

Although I always felt it was a necessity to have, and to make, money, it was not because I wanted to be rich. My belief has always been that people who live their lives for the sole reason of becoming rich are wasteful and vacuous, and I wasn't interested in being those things. All I wanted was to be comfortable and to enjoy my independence. I felt the same way as I did when I was a kid, watching the neighbours trudging home after a day at the factory, so tired from work they couldn't even begin to enjoy their free time. I didn't want to waste my life like that.

Instead, I wanted to do what I felt comfortable with, and enjoyed, and I hoped it would help other people along the way. All I wanted was 'fuck-you money', which meant I didn't have to do anything I didn't want to. I wanted money so I could live my life as freely as I desired, without harming or depending upon anybody else. Enjoying my life on my terms.

The second point is, I had achieved all that and more. So had a lot of other people. At the same time people were thinking I couldn't afford to fight, I was sitting on something like half a million dollars in the bank.

So, when Berry made that offer, it really didn't appeal to me.

"Let me think about it," I said. "And let me talk to some other record companies, and find out what we're worth to them. If their offers are the same as yours', you have my word, we'll take it."

I could see the disappointment in his eyes. "Look, I can tell you this right now. You're worth more to me and to Motown than you ever would be to them."

"Maybe that's true," I replied. "But let me find out, and I'll get back to you as soon as I can."

I left the meeting, left the building. Lamont was sitting on the bannister of the porch. I'd never discussed any of this with him – it was between Berry and me alone. But of course he'd heard the whisperings.

"I understand that you're leaving Motown," he said.

I didn't reply. I just looked at him, and he said, "Well look, if you're going, I want to go with you."

I still didn't say anything. It was too early to be having this conversation. In my heart, we were nowhere near that position. I smiled, nodded and walked away.

Brian: It was getting really uncomfortable. Edward went back to Berry to negotiate, and that's when he mentioned talking to other labels. Of course, Smokey got wind of all this, and told me I should let Edward and Lamont go if they wanted to but that I should stay. I told him, "We aren't going anywhere."

Eddie: I started talking to other labels, a little negotiation here, a little there. A week went by, and then another. I know I'd promised I'd get back to Berry, and I fully intended to do that.

I didn't feel as though there was any kind of rush, though. I was certain Berry wasn't spending his every day sitting by the phone, waiting for me to accept his offer. However, at some point during this period, somebody got Berry's ear.

I know they were not attacking me directly. They were trying to protect Berry, to relieve him of the misery and anguish the situation was causing. And the easiest way they could see of doing that was to cut off the source of his pain. Something along the lines of, "Berry? Why are you getting so upset about these guys? You're spending all this time talking to Eddie Holland but you know how stubborn he is. You need to show him you mean business. Fire his brother."

Brian: I'd done my best to keep out of everything that was going on. I got on with my job, and Berry let me do that. But one time I went into Motown to pick up my pay cheque for being head of Quality Control, and they said, "We don't have a cheque for you."

That scared me. I believed it meant that they weren't serious about working it out with us. So, I turned around and walked away. I left the building and went home, and I never went back.

Eddie: Up to this point, in the back of my mind, I'd always believed we'd work things out. I'd talked to labels, I'd heard some numbers and they were attractive. More than Berry had offered.

But I never doubted that, at the end of the day, I'd be back at Hitsville, with Brian and Lamont, The Supremes and The Four

Tops, making great records until the end of time. Now I wasn't so sure. I still hadn't written it off, but I wasn't quite so confident.

Then the other boot came down.

I was still having conversations with Motown, George Schiffer and Barney Ales, but things felt deadlocked. I was still involved in music – I was spending a lot of time with Jeffrey Bowen, talking about artists we liked, records I'd like to make. Keeping myself active, mulling things over. And Brian and I were keeping busy; we'd got into horse racing and we now owned six or seven horses. We loved racing them; it was relaxing and fun.

One time I was at the racetrack with Brian. It was a warm day, our horses were doing well, I was feeling bubbly. My mind was off the stress.

Suddenly the telephone in my Cadillac rang. It was my attorney, Fred Patmon. "Gordy is suing you for breach of contract."

I was shocked. For a moment, my entire body went numb. Fear. Horror. The umbilical cord that connected me to Motown and to Berry, the one thing I believed would cause all this mess to go away, hadn't been cut. It had been slashed.

It was like, if you're a kid, saying, "I'm gonna leave home if I can't get what I want!" Then all of a sudden, the parents say, "You know what? Here's your bags, they're packed. Now get the hell out. Go ahead and leave." That's how I felt… for about three seconds.

Then my brain kicked back in and I started to process the words. "Let's get it on!" Because basically by nature, I'm a fighter. But, during those seconds, I suddenly saw things with a clarity I had never experienced before.

Hitsville was my home and Berry was my friend, somebody I'd known since I was seventeen years old, my entire adult life. Everything I'd experienced over the last 10 years, I'd shared with him. I probably knew him better than I knew anybody apart from Brian.

I knew people had talked him into this. He'd been so despondent with the situation, I knew he'd simply listened to what they insisted was the easiest way of solving things. I believed, and still believe, that people saw him in this state and they played on it. "Stop trying to talk to him, just sue him. He'll soon come running back."

I wasn't running. My lawyer drew up our response and, because I was so angry and disappointed, I didn't even read it. It was lawyer's talk and I didn't care. It would be years before I finally sat down and read what was written there, and I was astonished at the ferocity of the language and the nature of the allegations. The document went on for 32 pages.

It could have been solved with one phone call.

Again, the dispute with Motown was never about money. Nor was it about copyright or royalties, or any of the material items that the lawyers made it appear we were fighting over. In fact, all the rumours about Motown not paying the artists what they were due, they were absolutely false. Berry paid better than anybody else in the business, and the reason for this, as he would often say, is because when he was having all those hits on Jackie Wilson, he *wasn't* paid. He was adamant he would never treat anybody the way he'd been treated, and he didn't.

The end result was, Motown produced so many black multimillionaires, probably more than any other company in the world; and, even more significantly, it was set up to help us achieve that. For the most part, we were young people starting with nothing, with no experience whatsoever. Everything we did, we learned how to do it there, in the back of Motown. We contributed, absolutely, of course we did. But it was Berry who opened the doors for us to learn and flourish, and that situation did not exist anywhere else in the world.

It doesn't matter what it said on paper. The lawsuit had nothing whatsoever to do with the business. It was a personal conflict between Berry and I, a fight in which, yes, we both lashed out, but only and always in the heat of the moment. We were reacting emotionally, not thinking about what we said, or meaning it either.

Left on our own to figure things out together, Berry and I would have sat down and talked it through. And at the end of it all, we would have reached an agreement and we would have lived up to it, in word and deed. Berry put it so well, years later, when he took the podium to induct Holland–Dozier–Holland into the Songwriters Hall of Fame. Punning furiously, he told the audience, "When [they] left Motown I was devastated. I said 'Stop! In the name of love. You've got nowhere to run and where did our love go? My world is empty without you and I can't help myself.' Then I gave up and said, 'Well, if you ever need me, reach out and I'll be there.'"

I believe him, because I felt the same way. But sometimes, feelings get swept away by other factors. Instead of sorting it out ourselves, we allowed other people to get involved, other people to have their say. Suddenly, what had once been the greatest friendship of my life was torn asunder by anger and disappointment. And sheer stubbornness on both of our parts. As Barney Ales once put it, the mountain wouldn't go to Mohammed and Mohammed wouldn't go to the mountain.

Consequently, the lawsuit took on a life of its own.

There were private detectives following me around. I knew it wasn't Berry who sent them, and I don't know what they hoped to discover, or catch me doing. In fact, I don't think they did either. We even used to wave to one another.

Everywhere I turned, every time the telephone rang, there were attorneys and advisers and experts in every field you could think of, constantly pushing me to ever more absurd extremes. It was the most nonsensical lawsuit that ever existed in the music business, and the most unnecessary.

Two people who cared for and respected one another immensely, and who still feel that way today, pushed and pulled by an army of outsiders, until suddenly I was on one side of the bridge, Berry was on the other side, and there were all these people who we barely knew standing in between us, setting fire to the middle of it.

Whirlpool Of Emotions
(Music by Brian Holland; lyrics by Eddie Holland)

Oh my God, Help Me!
I just want to die! I gave up 25 years of my life!
I just want to scream
I believed in you!
I trusted you with my Heart and my Life.

25 years of believing in us!
I kept our home clean,
Washed the dishes,
Cooked the food, put it on the table,
Paid the bills, did the laundry, took your clothes to the cleaners,
Picked them up from the cleaners!
And I work a full time Job!

What about our Child!
I took her to voice lessons
Piano lessons, Dance classes
Even her Soccer games.

Right now my mind is going through
A whirlpool of Emotions
How did I go wrong?
Where did I go wrong?

My Emotions are swirling around
In my Head
I'm caught in a whirlpool of Emotions
The fear of facing uncertainty
Doubting myself
Being let down and momentarily lost
Being pushed to the edge.

How could I have been so Stupid!
I tried so hard to do
Everything to please you
trying to be what you wanted me to be.

I'm trapped in a nightmare
And there's no open door
I've never felt so afraid
I've never felt so alone.

Right now I hate you
I never believed I would
I hate your face
I hate your name
I would just like to smash your face in.

I want you to hurt just as much as
I hurt right now!
I find the both of you despicable
I hope you and that damn Shrink
Burn in Hell!

Screw you! Screw you! Screw you!!

Chapter Nineteen

Invictus Rising

Eddie: I still believed that we would sort this all out. Deep down, no matter how angry I was, I remained convinced that, sooner or later, Berry and I would put all the fighting behind us and march on together, even stronger than ever.

But I also knew that I needed a Plan B. Just in case.

The time I spent with Jeffrey Bowen saw us scheme any number of things. I wasn't going to get caught up in the doom and gloom; I was looking to the future all the time.

My first step was to register some company names. Invictus and Hot Wax were reserved for any record company I might form; Gold Forever Music, named for one of our racehorses, would become our publishing company; and the Creative Corporation was the body that would oversee it all. I didn't think they would ever be needed, but they were there. Just in case.

I was on my own. As both producers and writers, Brian and Lamont were still bound by the terms of their exclusive contracts with Motown, and legally could not lift a finger to help. I, too, was constrained, at least as a writer. As a producer and an A&R man, however, I was a free agent.

I knew what I was worth. So did the rest of the music industry. Even Motown's lawsuit painted me as some kind of superman – the head of A&R, the most successful American lyricist of the decade, and so on. Unequivocally, I was portrayed as one of the powers behind the rise of Motown and, if you look at the charts for those last few years, you'll see that nobody was having more hits than Eddie Holland, and nobody was coming through to displace me, either.

In fact, the competition was suddenly looking thinner than ever. The Beatles were publicly fraying; if matters continued as they appeared to be (and they did – The Beatles broke up in early 1970), we'd have the field entirely to ourselves.

Suddenly, the phone started ringing. The moment other labels heard that I could soon be available, of course they were interested. They knew how much energy I had created around Motown. They wanted to have it for themselves.

Capitol Records quickly established themselves as the frontrunners. Of all the labels with whom I spoke, Capitol were the most enthusiastic and, in a way, the most desperate. They had been The Beatles' US label since 1964 and, while their deal with the four musicians would see them continue to distribute their music until 1975, nobody at the company knew whether four solo Beatles would have even a fraction of the impact of the full band. They needed a replacement, and they needed it now.

The first time I met anyone from the label, I was in the lobby at Motown. This guy introduced himself and said, simply, "I understand you have a problem here." I didn't comment, but he carried on, "If you ever think about leaving, give me a call."

I asked him what kind of royalties the label offered; he mentioned one number, I asked for another. But the guy simply looked at me. "We can put whatever we want into the contract," he said, "but we both know it will always be what I said." We left it there. A while later, though, I received another call. Would I be interested in meeting with Stan Gortikov, the head of Capitol?

It was a gentleman named Clarence Avant who set the wheels in motion.

Clarence was known as the Godfather of Black Music. If a black person was having problems in the music industry, he was the man they would go to, and he would sort them out. He was a rugged man, but a smooth and foxy individual, very good at what he did and the best at what he was doing. He created a niche for himself, and it takes a lot of work to operate like that in the pop market if you're of African descent.

I didn't deal with him directly. My attorney, Fred Patmon, made the initial contact, and the next thing I knew, Clarence had put us in touch with Stan Gortikov and was setting up the meetings.

I said I was interested. Stan wanted to make a deal with me – my own record company going through the distribution arm of Capitol. There was just one drawback.

Capitol was looking for an exclusive deal, and that was the one thing I didn't want. I had come out of an exclusive deal with Motown, and Brian and Lamont were still bound by one. I was a little gun shy.

So I continued listening to other offers, and two days before I was due to go back to California to meet Capitol again, Neil Bogart flew into town. He was head of Buddah Records, an independent like Motown, but one that had done very well out of so-called bubblegum music. They also distributed, or were in talks with, Curtis Mayfield's label Curtom, The Isley Brothers' T-Neck Records and, coincidentally, Clarence Avant's own Sussex Records – an impressive roster.

I liked Bogart, too. A very straightforward man, more or less the first words out of his mouth when we met were, "Man, I'd like to make a deal with you."

"Great."

He asked how much money I wanted. "What do you have?"

He told me what he could afford and I accepted. In terms of payment upfront, it was probably the smallest deal we'd been offered, but I wasn't concerned with the money itself.

I wanted a bargaining chip and, when Neil and I shook hands on the deal, I had it. It meant that when I sat down again with Stan Gortikov, and we started negotiating over the exclusivity clause that Capitol required, I could tell him in all truthfulness that it was no longer a possibility.

Stan was shocked. "Hey, did you sign with someone?"

"No, I haven't signed the papers yet. But I gave my word…"

"You gave your word?"

"Yes, and that's the end of it."

He looked at me as though I'd gone mad. "You're going to sacrifice $1.5 million in cash for $50,000 because you gave him your word?"

I looked at him. "It's my word."

Now I knew that Stan was the kind of gentlemen who would never tell you to break your word. That's the sort of person he was, old-fashioned and honourable. Besides, my attorney backed me up. "If Mr Holland gave his word, he'll never go back on it," and, as he was saying that, I began easing myself out of the chair, as if I was going to walk away, all the time saying to myself, "Please let him stop me, please let him stop me, because I'm bluffing like hell."

Stan didn't say a word. Finally I stood up and there was a moment of silence. Then Stan broke into a big grin.

"Okay Holland, okay, okay. You've been reading me and I've been reading you too, and I like what I see. I'll make the deal. Under this condition. You can only have three artists at Buddah to begin with. But for every artist you have a hit on with Capitol, you can sign one more at Buddah."

And I said deal, because I only had three artists for Buddha anyway: Honey Cone (it was my favourite ice cream flavour) and 100 Proof Aged In Soul – neither of which were actually bands at the time, merely more names I had come up with and registered – and a rock band called The Flaming Ember.

But here's the downside of the Capitol conversation. I found out that other people at Capitol were so afraid of the financial enormity of the deal that they were worried Stan would lose his job if anything went awry. Nobody doubted that the deal was worth the money. But they also knew something I'd never considered, and that was, Capitol did not understand black product at all.

In fact, their attitude was very strange, almost as if they'd looked at Motown, and how easy the label made it look, and had assumed that things would carry on in the same way. They didn't even consider the vast apparatus operating behind the scenes – promotion, marketing, sales, all of that. They saw me writing smash after smash, not only with Brian and Lamont but also Norman Whitfield and R. Dean Taylor, and decided that was it. They believed I'd release one record on Invictus and the hits would be self-perpetuating.

Of course it doesn't work like that, and I soon realised what I had gotten myself into. Capitol didn't know how to market the music and they didn't know how to promote it. They didn't understand that the mom and pop stores are the heartbeat of black product. They didn't know that you need to build a relationship with the market. People would go in to buy a record, and they couldn't, because Capitol weren't putting it in the stores that needed it. They probably hadn't even heard of the stores.

I caught on quickly, of course, and hired my own national promotions man – two of them, in fact – and a sales person, to try to give our product a chance.

Buddah Records, I was less concerned about. They were small, but they were tenacious. They knew what they were doing. I didn't think they'd make us much money, but I knew they wouldn't cost us much, either.

Brian: When Eddie got the deal with Capitol, I was very depressed about it because I was so close to Motown, so close to Berry. I had very mixed emotions, because I didn't think we should ever have got into that situation. At the same time, though, it was exciting for him to be starting a new label, because it's something we had talked about in the past.

Eddie: I established our headquarters in the 40-storey Cadillac Tower, on the corner of Cadillac Square and Bates in downtown Detroit, and set about marshalling our resources.

The company's creative staff was second to none. From the outset, I surrounded myself with people who could do all those things I needed – writers, arrangers, producers, everything.

I had Angelo Bond, who struck up such a great partnership with my old friend William Weatherspoon, and Greg Perry, all of whom were terrific writers; I had my future wife Vernelle, writing under the name of Edythe Wayne; and I also had Ronald Dunbar, who I came to rely on for so many songs. Not as many as he was credited for, though.

Ron was someone else I'd known for years, since he used to drop by Motown every day when his shift at Chrysler ended, and try to push songs he'd written. He rarely got very far – he helped with 'Greetings (This Is Uncle Sam)', an anti-draft song by The Valadiers, in the very early days (1961), and Shorty Long recorded another of his songs, 'Sing What You Wanna'.

Brian: I liked Ron's songs. There was another one, 'Your Love Controls Me', which he wrote for Marvin, and I did my best to get it to him, although the opportunity never arose. Ron was another one with a good ear – I remember playing him a couple of mixes I'd done for The Four Tops' 'I Can't Help Myself', and asking him which he preferred. He picked the same one I'd already decided to use – a discerning man!

We used to go to the racetrack together as well, the two of us, or three if Eddie wanted to come along.

Eddie: Another key person was Jeffrey Bowen, whose contract was up at Motown, so he came over to me. I could not have done any of it without Jeffrey – he was the best I'd ever seen at finding and persuading acts – he was that good, that talented.

Very, very temperamental, too. He was the kind of guy who, if he didn't think you were talented, he wouldn't want to deal with you. He wouldn't even talk to you. As a matter of fact, he'd be mean to you. He loved talent, but if there wasn't any, he'd say, "The hell with it, we don't need him."

But he did all the groundwork for me, getting things set up and moving, so I asked him if there was anything he wanted in return… of course, I was paying him a salary, but what else did he need? He said he wanted an artist of his own to manage, and that would be an English girl named Ruth Copeland, who he later married; and he wanted a Rolls Royce Silver Cloud. So I bought him one.

Musically, too, the labels were in good shape.

The Flaming Ember were already off and running. They'd been around the Detroit scene for years – in terms of local popularity, they were second only to Mitch Ryder, when his was one of the biggest rock bands the city had ever seen.

They were also a Motown reject. Around the same time I left the company, Berry bought up Ed Wingate's Ric Tic label, with an eye for the company's soul catalogue.

They got The Flaming Ember too, but Berry wasn't quite ready to move into rock yet, so the band was dropped. We picked them up, and it's ironic because their first single for Hot Wax – the label I'd assigned to Buddah – was 'Mind Body And Soul', which Ron Dunbar wrote with Edythe Wayne. No fewer than three Motown artists – Rita Wright, Suzee Ikeda and the post-Diana Supremes – would record covers of that song.

The other two bands on Hot Wax I put together myself. I'd recently seen the group singing behind Burt Bacharach on his television show. Edna Wright was Darlene Love's sister, Shelly Clark had been one of Ike & Tina Turner's Ikettes, and Carolyn Willis was a session singer. I don't think they had a name at the time, and when I offered them the chance to become Honey Cone, they weren't keen on that one, either. But they agreed, and Hot Wax had its next act.

As for 100 Proof Aged In Soul, Joe Stubbs was Levi's brother, and used to be in both The Contours and The Originals; Clyde Wilson had run up a bunch of local hits under the name of Steve

Mancha; and Eddie Anderson was one of his bandmates in a group called The Holidays.

All three groups hit immediately. Across its first year of operation, Hot Wax had a 100 per cent success rate – seven singles, seven hits. 100 Proof's first single, 'Too Many Cooks (Spoil The Broth)' was Top 30 on the R&B chart, and their second, 'Somebody's Been Sleeping', sold a million. Honey Cone had three R&B hits, The Flaming Ember had two in the pop Top 30.

Maybe they weren't the kind of monster smashes I was accustomed to, but I never expected them to be. I was starting from scratch – a new label, new writers, new bands, a new distributor. But still, it was a good start.

Over at Capitol, meanwhile, things were looking even better. Invictus was the label I pinned most of my ambitions on – you could tell that from the logo, based on Rodin's Thinker, the famous statue that welcomes visitors to the Detroit Institute of Arts. Not even Capitol's lack of expertise could slow us down.

The first release on Invictus was by Chairmen Of The Board, another band that Jeffrey Bowen and I formed from scratch.

I wanted to sign General Johnson to the label. I'd loved his voice since he was in The Showmen, back when I was first starting out. It was so unique. I'd never had the chance to work with him before, and I'd never met him. But Jeffrey did whatever he did to try and get him, and when we got together I played him a song called 'Give Me Just A Little More Time'.

General was singing it but it wasn't right. I said to Jeffrey, "Are you sure this is the guy?" And I listened some more, and I said, "This is *not* the guy." But Jeffrey kept telling me it was, so finally I said to General, "Man, I don't know… could you try singing it like this?"

I showed him how I wanted it, in the same style as the guy from The Showmen, this bouncing rhythm and this cracking in his voice; I said, "Sing it like this," and behold! The voice came out.

Jeffrey wanted to put together a soul supergroup, so I contacted General and told him about it – it would be a four piece: General

Johnson; Danny Wood, who loved to sing Jackie Wilson songs and had a big voice and a lot of range; Eddie Custis, who was a handsome guy with the Johnny Mathis style; and a guy from Canada named Harrison Kennedy, who was completely different to anyone I'd ever heard.

I said we should call them Chairmen Of The Board, because all four guys were lead singers. Between them, they could handle any material we threw at them. They were a lot like The Four Tops or The Temptations in that respect, every one of them a great singer.

The first record we did on them – which was also the first actual release on Invictus – was 'Give Me Just A Little More Time'. There was something about that song; it was so strong, there was nothing else like it out there. And it was huge. It sold a million. Pop radio took to it immediately, with or without promotion. Number three in America, number three in the UK, a hit everywhere else. And Chairmen Of The Board went on to be our most consistent band, in terms of hits.

Immediately after that came Freda Payne's 'Band Of Gold'.

Brian and I had known Freda since we were teenagers – we were all at Central High School together, and I had been longing to work with her for years. But 'Band Of Gold' was very different to the usual pop fare, and open to all manner of interpretation – was the husband impotent? Gay? Disinterested? The song doesn't say and maybe that's why it struck such a chord.

Freda herself was very unsure about recording the song. She felt she was too old to carry off a lyric in which the protagonist is clearly an inexperienced virgin, and when Ron Dunbar tried to persuade her to at least learn the words, she told him, "I can't! It makes no sense."

"You don't have to like it," he told her. "Sing it."

Recording the record was such a laborious session. It required a lot of editing, and something like 30 overdubs – so many that I actually turned the session over to Ron at one point, I needed a break that badly.

But it was worth it. A couple of years later, I was negotiating a new distribution deal for Invictus with Columbia, and Clive Davis admitted that one of the reasons he wanted me was because I'd had a number one hit with a jazz-singing actress! He told me, "You must be a miracle man to have done that!"

'Band Of Gold' was a number one in Britain, number two in Canada, number three in the United States and number five in Australia. It was a big hit all around the world. In fact, the only record that outsold 'Band Of Gold' at that time was The Beatles' 'Let It Be', which of course was their last big hit. We sold over 300,000 copies in New York City alone.

Those weren't our only hits, though. There was 'The Music Box' by a group called The New Play – Ruth Copeland was their singer; and there was 'Crumbs Off The Table' by Glass House, with Ty Hunter, someone else we'd known forever*. Freda's sister, Scherrie, was in the group as well and, of course, we knew her too – she was dating Lamont at one point.

I didn't know how well Scherrie sang, though, until I was talking with Freda on the phone one day and I could hear somebody singing in the background. I asked Freda who it was, and she was, "Oh, that's my sister," and she was about to tell her to be quiet but I said, "No, let her keep singing."

Brian: I was so proud when Eddie started having hits on those labels. I'll never forget Smokey Robinson telling me how he opened up *Billboard* magazine and read that Eddie's publishing company, Gold Forever Music, had more hits than Berry's Jobete Music. I felt really good about what he did with those labels.

Eddie: For a while, everything went smoothly. Freda Payne followed up 'Band Of Gold' with 'Bring The Boys Back Home', a song about the Vietnam War. Honey Cone, The Flaming Ember

---

* Ty Hunter was a member of The Voice Masters along with Lamont when they recorded for Anna Records.

HDH with Smokey Robinson in Los Angeles, 2019. © Shirley Washington

and 100 Proof continued having hits, and Chairmen Of The Board were doing incredibly well.

But I was growing increasingly uneasy about Capitol Records.

Around the same time as I signed with them, they also set up a deal with Rick Hall's Fame label. It wasn't a big operation, and I didn't give it any thought at the time.

But a very strange thing happened. Ron Dunbar and General Johnson wrote 'Patches' for the first Chairmen Of The Board album, and a lot of people fell in love with that song. And somebody at Capitol, rather than telling us that Fame was planning to release a cover of it as a single, by Clarence Carter, instead told Fame that Invictus *wouldn't* be releasing it. Clarence Carter went to number one.

Even Berry called me about that one. "Eddie," he asked, "how did you allow that to happen?"

Yet, the bands and hits kept coming.

I signed George Clinton, who was somebody else I knew from Motown – he even helped us out on a song once, 'Baby That's A Groove', which Roy Handy cut. George's band, The Parliaments, never signed to Motown, but Jeffrey and I did so much work with them. They're the band playing on the two albums we did with Ruth Copeland, after she left New Play, and they were also around for Chairmen Of The Board's *The Skin I'm In* album. At one point, we were even planning a George Clinton solo album, *Black Dracula*.

There was The Barrino Brothers, who were discovered by Dave Hamilton, who was one of the guitarists at Motown for a while, and the 8th Day, which was actually the same band as 100 Proof Aged In Soul, who I'd signed to Hot Wax but I thought could do better on Invictus. I was right, too – 'She's Not Another Woman' was another hit.

I even picked up another rock band, Lucifer, a Canadian group led by one of the guys from Ronnie Hawkins' Hawks, Eugene Smith.

By the end of 1971, there were eight separate acts on Invictus, plus solo releases by Ruth Copeland and General Johnson, and a couple of licensing deals. I had my own studio up and running, too.

Engineer Lawrence Horn was another one who came over from Motown. He and Brian had become especially close after working together on 'The Happening' for the 1967 movie of the same name, so I was keen for him to join us at Invictus, and so was Jeffrey Bowen.

We were supposed to be building a studio, and Jeffrey wanted Lawrence to be a part of that. Lamont's brother, Reggie, was learning engineering, but Jeffrey needed somebody who was already experienced, so he asked Lawrence to come and do some sessions for us.

At first, Lawrence said he couldn't do it because he was still at Motown. But Jeffrey managed to persuade him to do one session and when he heard the music, he got so excited. He said, "Man,

I've been missing this for so long, I think I wanna stay with you. This is what I've been missing since you left Motown."

So we met to discuss terms – he asked how much I could pay him, I asked what he wanted, we fixed that. And after that, we'd go to New York, do sessions there and meet people, cut demos. We did that a few times, and then we started talking about setting up our own studio, back in Detroit.

We had our eye on this old theatre, the Town Theater on Meyers and Grand River. I originally intended to tear it down and then rebuild it but we ended up not doing that. Lawrence put the studio together, we fixed it up and started recording there, and some amazing records came out of that place before we sold it. We brought in a bunch of the old Snake Pit veterans, and we also hired the house band from the 20 Grand, McKinley Jackson & The Politicians. They played on a lot of our sides.

I think my favourite memory of Lawrence from this time, though, is the time Capitol Records sent over a few cases of very expensive Burgundy wine.

I was not a drinker, and I never have been. The odd glass of wine every so often, but that was all. I opened a bottle of this stuff, took a taste and, "Whooah! This is horrible!"

Lawrence looked at me and asked, "Well, what kind of wine do you drink?" I really couldn't remember what it was, but it was a sweet wine, so he said, "Is that what you like?"

I told him, "I can drink it. I don't like wine, but I can drink it. This stuff is nasty."

So Lawrence said, "If I get you a case of the wine that you like, will you give me the case Capitol gave you?"

I said yes, so he went off, bought the wine, came back and we traded. And as he was walking out of the door he burst out laughing. He couldn't wait to get out, he was laughing so hard. I knew then that we'd been had.

Everything was going well. True, the hits-to-misses ratio was not what it had been during our first year, but we were releasing more records now, and taking more chances. We were having fun.

At the same time, however, there was always a sense that Invictus and Hot Wax suffered from a lack of identity, and that came down to the lawsuit with Motown. When the labels were at their hottest, our hands were completely tied.

I was in charge of A&R at Invictus, but it was hard to keep my mind on things. My office was right next to the people who were listening to product – things we were going to release, artists we were thinking of signing, all of that. So I'd be sitting there dealing with lawsuits and meeting with lawyers, accountants and administrators, at the same time as I was listening to the music coming out of that room.

If I heard something that excited me, I'd have to say, "Excuse me for a moment," then I'd get up, go into the other room and find out who it was. It was very distracting.

But there was always a light at the end of the tunnel. Late 1971 would see my songwriting contract with Motown come to an end, and Brian and Lamont's deals as well. And when that day arrived, and the pair of them were finally able to join me at Invictus, we got straight to work.

Songs like Honey Cone's 'Who's It Gonna Be' and Chairmen Of The Board's 'Working On A Building Of Love' flew from our pens. But the most appropriately titled of them all was a song we cut on the 8th Day. It was called 'It's Instrumental To Be Free'.

Chapter Twenty

The End of the Beginning

Unfortunately, just as Holland–Dozier–Holland finally shook off the handcuffs, dealings with Capitol had gone from bad to worse.

It had felt like a struggle to get attention from the marketing department, and once Invictus had established its own, Capitol took even less notice. Stan Gortikov had left (he went on to become president of the Recording Industry Association of America [RIAA]), and while the new regime did try to keep things going, all they could offer were promises about future promotion, but with nothing to back it up.

We even started a new label, separate from either Invictus or Hot Wax, called Music Merchant. The idea was to try and stockpile new, potentially successful artists and songs away from any other label, but it really didn't get off the ground despite us having some great acts: Brenda Holloway, who had been at Motown in the early years – in fact, she recorded one of Eddie and Janie Bradford's earliest collaborations with Lamont, 'Don't Compare Me With Her'; Eloise Laws; and The Jones Girls, who went on to considerable success with Philadelphia International later in the decade.

The hits had dried up. We had one Top 40 US hit in 1972, on Honey Cone, and a few more in the UK. We were still doing okay on the R&B chart, but it was like 1967 all over again, spending a lot of money on music that we believed in but never bringing enough in.

Which is when Clive Davis at Columbia Records began courting us.

Eddie: Clive invited me to one of Columbia's functions, and that's where I first saw Meatloaf. I was sitting with Clive and everybody was looking over at me: "Wow, he's important, he's at Clive's table."

We had a meeting shortly after, and Clive came out with it. "I want to make a deal with you. You've got the right artists, we've got the promotional muscle." So he worked out the relationship, and Columbia bought us out of the Capitol Records contract.

We settled, and then my lawyer and I went into the meeting with Columbia to work out our own contract. We negotiated all that Friday evening, into Saturday, straight through, and all we were eating were jelly beans. Nobody went out to get lunch or anything; we sat and ate jelly beans until we had a deal. Clive wanted this thing done, and finally it was.

Columbia cut the cheque on Saturday afternoon, we caught the plane back to Detroit that night, and made arrangements with the bank to come in Monday morning to cash that cheque. And that's what we did. We were now signed to Columbia.

Clive himself had one condition. We were in another meeting and he turned to me and said, "Eddie, I've noticed that when you have meetings, you usually have somebody representing you. That's not going to work with me. All I want you to do is, when I call you, you answer my calls. This is the way I deal with my people. I don't want to go through an in-between person."

I agreed. Talking to Clive, I knew he was as straightforward as I was. I also knew he was a fan. But the other thing that swayed me was a report that Columbia had commissioned from Harvard University on the state of the black music market at the time, and which essentially shaped the label's marketing strategy.

Like every other white major label, Columbia had been frightened by Motown's success in dominating the black music field for so long. Unlike those other labels, it did its research. The ensuing report was long, about 70 pages, but the key to success lies in the opening statement.

"A market of approximately $60 million at manufacturers' prices exists for Soul music recordings. CRG [the Columbia Record Group]'s previous efforts have been hampered by an organisation staffed by personnel oriented to the popular music field, which differs fundamentally from Soul music in the critical factors required for success."

In order to change that, CRG "must establish an internal Soul music group *and* [my italics] improve the quality of Soul music product released on recordings."

They already had Gamble and Huff, whose Philadelphia International label had been set up a few months earlier as a direct challenger to Motown. Now they had Holland–Dozier–Holland as well.

For the first time since those first months of Invictus, everything was looking great again. About five minutes later, Clive left Columbia.

Clive's ousting, in 1973, effectively left us friendless at the label. As so often happens when there is a major change at a record company (or any other business, for that matter), we were seen as one of his signings, and in the fallout that accompanied his departure, we were left to fend for ourselves.

We wound down Hot Wax and tried to consolidate, but it was difficult to concentrate after that, let alone recuperate. In fact, simply being a part of Columbia opened us up for even more problems.

Eddie: I got a call from the government, saying they wanted to come in and audit me because I was affiliated with Columbia. I knew we had nothing to worry about, because we'd done nothing wrong, but then my attorney said we were being hit with seven counts of payola – making illegal payments in return for having our music played on the radio. There was a Grand Jury investigation looming and they wanted all of our documents. I simply looked at him. Later, my lawyer said he thought I had ice in my veins, I showed so little response.

Payola had always been a problem in the music industry, all the way back to the beginning. But we had never been involved, Barney Ales made sure of that. One time, one of the big Detroit DJs, a white guy at a pop station, was moving to a new house and he asked Barney for some "big black bucks" to help pay for it. On moving day, Barney sent the three of us over to his house to help carry things.

We never got another request like that, and we wouldn't have been interested if we had. What was the point of achieving anything, whether it's a hit record or a win at cards, if the only way you can do it is by cheating? It might look good to other people, but you'd always know that your accomplishments were meaningless.

Besides, how could Invictus be wrapped up in a payola scandal? We weren't being played on the radio.

Eddie: Of course we had to fight it. This was a felony offence, and my lawyer admitted he couldn't handle it. So he recommended I cross the street and visit this other lawyer – in fact, he was Freda Payne's attorney. He said, "Go and see him, and I can tell you right now, he's going to want $10,000. But he'll want to interview you first, before he'll agree to take your case."

I went across the street, and sat down alone in the lobby. The attorney was in his office across the way, talking to somebody, and every so often he'd glance over at me. This went on for a while – he'd be talking, he'd glance over, then go back to talking.

Finally, after 20, maybe 30 minutes, someone said I could go in, and it was the strangest thing. He said, "Okay," and I was thinking, "He's not interviewing me at all." He'd been sizing me up that whole time, and when I went into his office he didn't have anything to talk to me about. He knew all he needed to know.

I went back across the street, got the $10,000 for the guy, had all the books and records ready for the auditor, and you know what? I never got a call. Not from the government, not from anybody. They never showed up. The lawyer I talked to took care of it all.

That worked out. But we were still tied to a label that didn't know who we were; still struggling for hits that should have been effortless. Financially, things were not looking good. And in the midst of all this, Lamont left the partnership.

Emotionally, it was a replay of our break with Berry and Motown. Like Berry, Lamont had been with us our entire adult lives; like Berry, he had shared in both our triumphs and tragedies.

But of course he was more than that. Lamont was a part of the team. Forget legal definitions and contractual obligations. From the moment the three of us sat down to write together for the first time, and for all the years since then, Lamont was our right arm, as we were his. Yes, we all had our personal ambitions, and we all had free rein to pursue them as often as we wanted. The Holland–Dozier singles Invictus released were effectively Lamont solo projects, and so were the albums he released.

But when it came to Holland–Dozier–Holland, we were one – or so the Holland–Holland part of the equation believed, because the three of us had a very compatible relationship for a long time.

Eddie: Relations with Lamont were never less than cordial, but in recent times they had rarely been much more than that, either. We were still a team, we were still Holland–Dozier–Holland. But the enthusiasm that had once bound the three of us to both our work, and to one another, had faded.

Part of it was financial. Back when we first formed the partnership, it was agreed that, while Brian and Lamont would each collect 25 per cent of our proceeds, I would receive 50 per cent, in recognition not only of my contributions to the songs themselves but also the other tasks that had fallen to me.

Although I took no formal production credit, I was effectively producing (not to mention schooling) the singers in the studio. I was also active from an administrative angle. Whenever there was a decision to be made, or a problem to be solved, I was the one to whom both Brian and Lamont, and everybody else, turned.

That was especially true now, as I poured more money into Invictus than anybody was taking out of it, in efforts to stay afloat. Indeed, it was fast reaching the point where maybe some would have thought about stopping. Not me. I already had our future planned. Holland–Dozier–Holland had never known failure in the past. I was adamant they never would.

Lamont no longer seemed so sure.

It was little things at first. He wouldn't attend meetings like he used to. He seemed less interested in projects that were not directly his own, and when he was in the studio, even Brian – who is one of the most forgiving, tolerant people I have ever known – had to admit that Lamont was no longer pulling his weight. As time passed, however, his disgruntlement became increasingly apparent.

But it was about more than money. A lot more.

I knew Lamont wasn't happy about being forever sandwiched between the Holland brothers. He was tired of hearing the words "Holland–Dozier–Holland". It frustrated him. Even at Motown at the height of our powers, when Brian was in charge of Quality Control and I was head of A&R, Lamont felt like a second wheel, less important to the company. That wasn't the case at all, and deep down I believe he knew it. I hope he did, anyway. Unfortunately, it wasn't something we ever talked about; it just hung there, unspoken and unacknowledged.

His ego, however, would not let him rest.

The fact of the matter is, Lamont was a great writer, a great producer. Maybe his ear wasn't as intuitive as Brian's, but whose is? Not mine, not Smokey's, not Berry's, nobody's.

Not even Lennon and McCartney's. He hears the things that nobody else would.

But it appeared Lamont still felt he was second fiddle, and all through that period, the last years at Motown and the first years of Invictus/Hot Wax, it was on his mind. He saw himself as an individual, with a magic of his own, and he believed he wasn't getting the credit he felt he deserved.

It shouldn't have bothered him; in my eyes and Brian's, we were equal partners, and in the wider world as well. It was Holland–Dozier–Holland all the way.

Unfortunately, Lamont didn't share that belief. He became so focused on how "unfair" things were, and how "unappreciated" he was, he didn't see that it was what he did that made it possible for us to do what we did.

As is so often the case, Lamont's actual departure was precipitated by a whole different set of circumstances, after an employee of mine got upset with me. He was angry because he thought I betrayed him, and I see his point. It was another instance of me making a decision without necessarily thinking it through from the point of view of the people it affected, until it was too late.

We had a sales guy named Otis Smith, who oversaw both Invictus and Hot Wax, at a time when Hot Wax really wasn't doing very well. I decided to separate the two jobs. Otis kept Invictus, because that was our main money-spinner, and he was very good at his job. But I gave Hot Wax to this other guy and my mistake was, I didn't talk it over with Otis first.

I should have, I realised that very quickly. But I made a business decision and that's all I thought it was, a business decision.

Otis was very wounded and, naturally, I suppose, he wanted to get back at me. He convinced Lamont to leave us and sign with ABC Records. Which he did, moving to California and taking with him some of the people I had hired at the label.

Lamont wasn't stepping out completely on his own. He would still team up and collaborate with other writers and producers, but that was fine with him. He wanted to say, "I can do it without the Holland brothers." In his mind, as long as it wasn't with the Hollands, he retained his individuality.

I believe he did, as well. 'Two Hearts', the song he wrote with Phil Collins in 1988, would receive an Academy Award nomination, a Golden Globe and a Grammy for Best Song Written Specifically for a Motion Picture or Television. Brian and I were so excited for him. Lamont later told us that he had based the melody on Brian's old Four Tops melody 'I'm In A Different World', and it was a beautiful piece of work.

We could have sued Lamont, but we didn't. We had been through so much together, for so many years. We simply couldn't bring ourselves to do it. I felt almost as bad about what had happened with Lamont as I did about Motown. It wasn't worth it to me to fight. And the end result was, the Holland–Dozier–Holland partnership was dissolved.

The final agreement was simple. Anything we had done together in the past remained our joint property. But going forward, whatever was ours was ours, and whatever was his, anything he took with him to ABC or came up with afterwards, that was his.

Eddie: Lamont left us, and even today, he only deals with Brian and me when he has to. I believe that's because, throughout those first few years after he went out on his own, people were constantly asking for the three of us. He was always having to explain that he could do it himself and he didn't need us. I don't think he understood that the three of us really were much stronger together than apart.

It was a team in every way, and he could never get that into his head. He would always fight it. He had the thirst for it to be D without the HH. And now it was.

But I remember telling him, "You could do whatever you wanted on your own, and Brian and I could do whatever we wanted on our own. But we could never be bigger than Holland–Dozier–Holland. Never."

And he looked at me and said, "You believe that, don't you?"

"Absolutely," I answered.

Brian: I did enjoy the Invictus years; it was a very, very happy period. But all the time, in the back of my mind, there was that conflict, first losing Motown and Berry, and then at the end, losing Lamont too.

But I carried on. I did what I felt I had to do, which was to keep Invictus going, and when that became a mess at the end, I ignored it. All I worried about was the creative side. All the other nonsense, the high blood pressure, I had no interest in that.

Chapter Twenty-One

Return to Motown

Eddie: The lawsuit with Motown dragged on for four years and, even at the end, I don't look upon myself as winning. Berry thought we won, but I didn't see anybody winning.

We settled out of court. The agreement itself is not important. The vital thing was, we resolved it.

The timing could scarcely have been more opportune. Invictus was over, and we were looking for new challenges. We knew they would come along, too. It was simply a matter of answering the right phone call, meeting the right person, having the right conversation. And that is exactly what happened.

Only the right person wasn't a stranger. It was Jeffrey Bowen.

Eddie: I was in Los Angeles trying to sort out the dispute with Lamont and ABC Records, and I happened to meet up with Jeffrey, who had recently returned to Motown.

He started telling me how Suzanne de Passe, who was running Motown at that time, was always looking for talent and wanted to get the label back to the way it used to be. The way it was in the sixties, that kind of quality, that kind of spirit, because things had changed a lot since then. It was no longer the legendary Motown. It was just another record company.

The label had retained many of its biggest names – Marvin was still there, Diana, Stevie, Smokey, Ashford & Simpson. A new generation had come along, and they were equally successful, people like The Jackson 5 and The Commodores.

But the material was all over the place, and there wasn't that old sense of 'Motown' about it.

Eddie: We talked about that, and Jeffrey asked if Brian and I might be interested in coming back and putting things back on an even keel.

I admitted I was interested, so Jeffrey went to Suzanne and asked her, "How do we get Eddie and Brian back? Let's get them back."

I spent a year negotiating with Motown, and this is an example of how things had changed. In the old days, you had one person to talk with, and that was the boss, Berry. I was in LA at the time, in a hotel. They must have sent three or four different people along to talk to me. One would come, and then another, all trying to get the best arrangement, and if they couldn't get what they wanted, the next person would be brought in, and so it went, around and around until finally I said to Jeffrey, "I've had enough. I'm tired of it. I'm going home."

He came to my hotel room and asked, "What are you doing?"

I said, "I'm packing. I'm so tired of this, it's gone on way too long."

He called Suzanne and told her I was leaving. She said, "Wait a minute," and finally I was meeting with Suzanne, and not another one of her people. She said, "We want to make a deal. You deliver product, you work with x amount of artists, like you did before," and it all sounded great.

But I said to Jeffrey, "This is what you have to do for me. I have to talk to Berry. It's important. But I don't want to offend Suzanne, so handle it smoothly."

So Jeffrey talked with Suzanne, told her what I needed, and she said okay. The next thing I knew, I was having a meeting with Berry at his place in Malibu.

Now, Berry knew everything that was going on, because nothing of significance ever happened at Motown without him at least appearing to agree with it. But that was the key: he *appeared* to agree with it.

I knew from long ago that Berry was very happy to allow people to make their own mistakes; let them ignore – or not even notice – some little signal he had given them at the start of whichever process they were involved in. He'd let people make deals, let them think they could do whatever they wanted, but if he didn't like it, he'd find a way to stop it happening. I wanted to make certain that was not what was going on here, and he knew that.

"Berry," I said. "First of all, I don't care what Suzanne is saying. There will be no deal unless you approve it. You know that and I know that."

All he did was smile and say, "You got that right."

I started laughing and that was it. The ice was broken. We talked over the past, my departure, the conflict, the lawsuit, and I told him, "You know what? I blame you for that, because you were the oldest. You knew how to handle that stuff, but you sent me to this person and that person, you refused to talk to me about it and it spiralled out of control."

And he said, "Yeah, you're right. So, let's make a deal."

It was as though the lawsuit and the recent past had never happened. Berry told me to negotiate our contract with the lawyer, and then added, "What I want you to do is negotiate on my behalf as well." So that's what I did.

Brian: We went back to Motown, wrote songs, and it was such a change. The company had moved from Detroit to Hollywood, and that was different enough. But there was also a different way of doing things. It wasn't the same. I didn't have the same kind of authority I used to. People were different. There were more lawyers, more accountants, more non-music people.

We had a good time, we worked with Michael Jackson, we kept moving along. I still got the respect I needed to work, and nobody really stopped me doing what I wanted to, other than Berry.

But there were a lot more people making decisions, or not making decisions. It was very organised from a business point of view but that kills creativity. In the sixties, we could run in and record when we felt like it. You have an idea, you write it down, you call up the musicians you need, you go in and record. Out in California, though, everything was business. You had to book the studio weeks in advance. There were different people making decisions about what was going to be a hit; all these promotion guys, not really music people, sticking their personal opinions in. It wasn't about music any more, it was about what would make money, or what they thought would.

The problem was, they often thought wrong.

The label was still doing well, still having hits. But they were no longer having the hits that defined an era, and that came down to one single truth. Berry should never have left Detroit. By all means, he could have opened another office in LA, but he should have kept Hitsville.

As far as we were concerned, Detroit was still the heartbeat of American music, and it still had a lot of untapped talent, as we had proven with Invictus.

The urban cities are always more creative than the industry hubs, because there are less distractions and more inspirations. Less calculation, less desperation. In the cities, an act is able to develop its own personality. In the hubs, it does what everyone else is doing.

Gamble and Huff proved that. As much as Motown had dominated the sixties, Kenny and Leon's Philadelphia International was dominating the black market in the first half of the seventies. People like The O'Jays, Billy Paul, The Three Degrees and Harold

Melvin & The Blue Notes swept everybody else out of the way, and they did that because Gamble and Huff ran the same tight ship as Berry had. They had the artists, they had the musicians, they had their own studio, everything was self-contained and, because they were having hit after hit after hit, they could get away with things that other labels couldn't.

It was a lesson that Motown learned but did not absorb. One of Motown's biggest hits of the 1970s was Thelma Houston's version of Gamble and Huff's 'Don't Leave Me This Way'. It was a terrific record, and a deserved number one, but it would never even have been considered 10 years before. Could you even imagine if one of the biggest hits on Motown in the sixties had been a cover of a recent Stax number?

We tried to do with Invictus and Hot Wax what Gamble and Huff did in Philly, but we were unable to because we didn't have the machinery behind us. Whereas for Motown, the opposite was true – there was too much machinery behind them, but nobody who could sit everybody down and make them shut up and listen. Berry was almost completely hands-off by now, and a lot of the original team had broken up. These were the people who had taken Motown to the top because they felt invested in the concept of it.

Eddie: The problem was, people looked at Motown as a relic from the past. It didn't matter what the label did, or what we did for that matter; the records were very much overshadowed by the earlier Motown and even the Invictus stuff.

Also, I must confess I didn't care for a lot of the records that were coming out. It was the beginning of the disco era, when the production and the mix became more important than the songs, and the beat became more important than the melody.

We could do it – we made several disco records, and other people rerecorded our songs as disco. Jeffrey Bowen produced almost an entire album on Bonnie Pointer, disco versions of some of our old songs. Shalamar did the same thing for a medley.

But a lot of disco felt mechanical to me, and overrun with gimmicks, and Motown was especially guilty of that, particularly after Lawrence Horn came back to be a mixing engineer.

Lawrence had always been into technology and new sounds, but now that was all he wanted. He had all these gadgets and he'd be saying, "I want this frequency and that frequency," saying it would help the mixes sound good, and it didn't. It never sounded good. We knew what he was doing, he was using certain technical tricks he'd invented to try and create a signature sound. He was trying to create something new, but Brian and I didn't like it.

Going back to Motown started out well. We did some songs on Eddie Kendricks, The Supremes, Junior Walker and The Temptations, all of whom we knew from the past – although there were some very different line-ups! Diana had left the group to pursue her hugely successful solo career in 1970. Scherrie Payne was now singing with The Supremes, alongside Mary Wilson and Susaye Greene, and those weren't the only aspects of the group that had changed.

The Supremes had not enjoyed a big hit in the United States since 'Floy Joy', two years before, and it was our task to reverse that trend. We did, as well. We recorded two albums with them, and we got them back into the Top 40 with 'I'm Gonna Let My Heart Do The Walking'.

We did a song on Jermaine Jackson, and were disappointed when 'I'm So Glad You Chose Me' was not chosen as an A-side. We worked with Thelma Houston, and new artists like the Dynamic Superiors and G. C. Cameron. We also reunited with Diana Ross, recording three songs with her in 1978, although only one, 'We Can Never Light That Old Flame Again', would be released – and that was not until 1982.

Our biggest assignment, however, was the songs we did with Michael Jackson, across both his solo album Forever, Michael and The Jackson 5's own *Moving Violation*. Michael was still young at the time, fifteen or sixteen, and he was still performing with his brothers as The Jackson 5. *Forever, Michael* was only his fourth solo record, and Motown was still marketing him towards the same teenybopper audience he'd had when he first came along.

You could tell what a prodigious talent he was, but he wasn't yet 'the Michael Jackson'. He was still a kid, very pleasant, friendly and easy to work with, very personable and approachable.

Eddie: Neither Michael's album or The Jackson 5's did well, and that was wholly down to promotion. Motown no longer had a team that was capable of breaking records, or at least not like they used to. Barney Ales had left in 1972, and while the label would soon be bringing him back when The Jackson 5's 'Forever Came Today' was released, they couldn't get the kind of airplay it needed.

My brother was convinced that 'Forever Came Today' was a smash record, and it took a lot out of him when it didn't do as well; in fact, Barney once said he'd been talking with Elton John, who described that song as the biggest record that never made it.

Brian: I loved Michael. He was such a great little guy to work with, very shy, very modest. He was so into what we wanted to do, and Berry made sure we had complete control – meaning, we didn't have Michael's father, Joe, coming in saying this and that, which is what I heard sometimes happened.

That really impressed me because we didn't know what the dynamic would be any more. I think of the situation with Diana, when Edward wanted her to sing 'Where Did Our Love Go', and she threatened to go to Berry but backed down because she knew what his response would be.

Would the same thing have happened when we went back? Berry was saying we had control but there were other people involved and making decisions, because to them, the artist was the most important person. The artist had to be kept happy, otherwise they might leave and go to a different label and take all the hits with them.

But Berry told Michael from the start, "Brian and Eddie are in control, so pay attention," and he did. He was so good to work with.

Eddie: I think the funniest thing was, Michael was so in awe of us. He used to run and make us coffee all the time, and ask us questions about what we did with our free time, how we wrote all the old songs. He was overjoyed to be working with us and having songs written by us. He would come in to the studio and wait on me!

Berry used to laugh at him about it. He'd say, "But Michael, you're the star," and Michael replied, "Yeah, but Berry, he wrote the songs." That's the way he was; he was a super guy and he never lost that.

Years later, we were at the BMI Awards with Lamont and Michael sent somebody over to round us up, and Berry as well, so he could take a picture with us. I couldn't believe it – "What the heck you

Eddie and Brian with Lamont collecting the BMI Icon Award, 2003.
© Jeffrey Mayer/WireImage/Getty

wanna take a picture with us for?" But the answer was simple. Michael admired anyone he thought was an exceptional talent. He felt a kinship to them, and that's what made him such a wonderful person. There was not a jealous bone in his body. So Berry came from his table, we came from ours and we all took the picture.

Another time, around 2003, I ran into him again in Las Vegas at Caesar's Palace. Michael was shopping with his children, but word had spread all over. I was with my assistant, Shirley Washington, and we heard about it from the valet who took our car: "Michael Jackson is in the mall!"

Shirley took control. I was more interested in finding the men's room.

Shirley remembers: "When I saw the huge crowd that had gathered, I pushed my way to the front where the security guards were and told them, 'Tell Michael, Eddie Holland is here and wants to say hello to him.' He went up in the glass elevator to where Michael was and came down a few minutes later and asked, 'Where is he?'

"I said, 'I'll go get him.'"

Eddie: It was the last thing I wanted to do. I didn't want to disturb him so I walked away. Of course, Shirley then had to run halfway across the mall to find me.

Shirley continues, "I returned five minutes later with Eddie and the guard escorted us through the crowd – Eddie said it was like Moses parting the Red Sea to allow us to walk through.

"I was so excited I could hardly breathe, but all Michael wanted to do was introduce us to everyone – 'This is the great Eddie Holland, the songwriter. He's a genius!'

"He introduced us to his two children, Prince and Paris, and invited us, with Brian, to visit him at Neverland. Eddie said we'd only go if he was going to be there, but Michael said sure, he'd be there and even gave us his private numbers to call him. Unfortunately, before arrangements could be made, Neverland was raided, time passed, and it never felt like the right time to call…"

Eddie: My favourite memory of Michael might be the time he called me at the office, completely out of the blue. He was thinking of buying the Jobete publishing catalogue at the time, and while he was going through the list of songs, he kept coming across our names. Over and over again.

"How could you possibly have written so many songs, so quickly, in that short period of time? It's completely unheard of."

He told me I was a genius. I said, "No, no, no, Michael. I'm not a genius."

"Well, Paul McCartney said you are," he replied. And then he said, "You know what? I want a book about you guys. There has to be a book about you."

Well, Michael, wherever you are… here it is.

Stevie Wonder drops in to the Michael Jackson session during the recording of 'Forever Came Today'.

Chapter Twenty-Two

Murder Happen

There is a tragic postscript to our reunion with Lawrence Horn, one that we still don't fully comprehend. Because it truly was the stuff of nightmares.

Eddie: Fast forward 15 or so years. One time, Lawrence turned up at the office, completely out of the blue. He and Brian still spent time together, they were still friends, but this was the first time I'd seen him in a while. I knew he had a family, two daughters and a disabled son named Trevor, and Brian kept me up to date with occasional things.

Anyway, Lawrence said, "Eddie, listen. Is there a room where I can talk and have private telephone conversations, without anybody disturbing me?"

I said yes. I thought it was a little strange, but we'd always had a good relationship, and obviously he had some kind of business deal going on, so I found a small space in our office and allowed him to use it.

It still felt odd that he was around after all this time, but I was seeing him relatively often and everything seemed normal. Then one day I arrived at the office and they told me somebody from the FBI had been in to see me, left a card and wanted me to call.

And that's when I discovered that Lawrence's ex-wife, Millie, little Trevor and his nurse, a woman named Janice Saunders, had been killed. Mildred and Janice had been shot, Trevor's air supply had been disconnected.

The FBI believed Lawrence was somehow mixed up in it.

I was completely stunned. I didn't, not for a moment, think Lawrence could have been involved, but later that night I was at a party with Brian and I asked him, "Do you believe this rumour I'm hearing about Lawrence?"

He was quiet for a moment, and then said, "You don't wanna know."

Of course, I wanted to know. I'd known Lawrence for years; I'd always liked him – even when he was playing with his gadgets at Motown. He wasn't a friend, somebody I spent a lot of time with, but I had great affection for him. I pushed Brian to tell me, but he repeated what he'd said before. "Believe me, you don't wanna know."

I asked whether he believed any of the stories and this time he didn't respond. But he knew I needed to know, because that's the kind of person I am, so finally he said, simply, "I suspect it's true."

I was incredulous. "Are you serious?" He said yes. And I felt my stomach start churning. I said, "Oh man, I've got to leave, my stomach's really playing up."

Brian looked at me and said, "I told you, you didn't want to know…"

I couldn't imagine it happening, remembering how Lawrence was and who he was. I was thinking about it all that night, and nothing made sense. But he was arrested, put on trial and found guilty.

He wasn't the killer. But he hired the killer. What happened was, Lawrence was having some kind of financial difficulties, and he and his wife had taken out a fairly large life insurance policy for Trevor. Lawrence wanted the money so he hired this guy, James Edward Perry, to kill Trevor and Mildred. He agreed to pay him $6,000.

Perry wasn't an experienced hitman. He actually went out and bought a book called *Hit Man: A Technical Manual for Independent Contractors*, and on March 3, 1993, he followed the instructions.

At first, the FBI thought it was a random killing. But Mildred's family kept on and on. They knew about Lawrence's financial problems, they knew about the insurance and they didn't give up. Finally, they got through to the local mayor and convinced him to take up their case. He was able to make the FBI look a little closer, and Lawrence was finished.

Eddie: Time passed. It was now May 1996. The trial phase of the case was over and Lawrence had been found guilty. Now they were into sentencing, and Lawrence's lawyer contacted Brian and me to ask us to testify in court on his behalf. He wanted us to help save Lawrence from the death penalty.

We said yes – of course we did. But Brian's wife at the time, Deirdre (Dee), was furious with us, really upset. I asked why… didn't she like Lawrence as well? Which is when Brian explained that his son, Brian Jr., was friends with Lawrence's daughter, Tiffani; they were at college together, and Tiffani had been planning to visit her mother on the night of the killings. She asked Brian Jr. to go with her, and he said yes.

As it turned out, something came up and she had to cancel the visit. If she hadn't done that, they would have been there when the killer arrived.

Deirdre knew this, and she was wild. "Why are you even trying to defend this guy?" She didn't want to hear my reasons – what's the point of him being executed? All she could think about was what might have happened to Brian Jr.

I met with the lawyer and he told me, "Look, all I want is for you to testify for Lawrence. I don't want you to try and say he's innocent," because he knew that I was still torn over whether he had done this, whether he could have been responsible. I was completely conflicted, off balance, and the lawyer kept telling me, "You're not talking about his innocence, the jury has already found him guilty. Don't tamper with their decision."

I said, "Listen, I have to know about this case. You can't tell me what to do and create a blind spot in my head to blot out certain facts and circumstances. You have to tell me exactly what happened."

He looked at me and he said the exact same thing my brother asked. "Do you really want to know?"

He started explaining the background. How the authorities assembled their evidence. Montgomery County police later described the case as "the most exhaustive and labor-intensive" investigation in the department's history. One that was planned "long in advance and arranged with a great deal of preparation and evil". He had, he said, never seen such a case in almost three decades working as a prosecutor. "There have been a lot of amateurish attempts, but nothing that rises to this level."

Brian: There was more. Perry wanted more money but Lawrence didn't have it. The insurance payment wasn't happening because of the questions that were now being asked. But Perry didn't believe that. He started threatening Lawrence's family, unless he got more money.

So what did Lawrence do? He came to me and asked to borrow $50,000, supposedly for a business deal. I gave it to him, and Lawrence gave $10,000 to Perry.

This all came out while I was on the stand. The prosecuting attorney asked me straight, why did I give money to Lawrence, which he promptly handed to Perry?

I told him, I didn't know anything about that, but he wouldn't relent. I had to know, he insisted. After all, it was my office that Lawrence used when he called to tell Perry he had the money!

I was stunned. I didn't know Lawrence was calling Perry from the office, Edward didn't know – and why would anyone even think about that? Why, if somebody asks to use your phone, would you ever think, "Oh, he must be calling the hitman who murdered his ex-wife?"

Lawrence Horne seated with Michael Jackson, with Eddie standing behind and an unknown observer during the 1975 sessions.

Eddie: My head was spinning, trying to take all this in, trying to process it, and I couldn't. It was information, information, information, and nothing I was hearing matched the picture of Lawrence I had in my head. He couldn't have done it. It was all a terrible mistake, a miscarriage of justice, a put-up job... I didn't know what, but none of it was Lawrence.

There was no way this guy I'd known for half my life could ever have done something like that. All I knew were the laughs and the fun and going out, New York, Motown, California, the studios... the cases of wine. I couldn't shake those images, not even when I was on the stand in the courtroom.

The prosecuting attorney knew how I felt. He asked a question and he couldn't have liked the way I responded because all of a sudden, he asked if I was telling him that Lawrence was innocent.

I remembered what Lawrence's attorney told me. "Don't cross that path, don't make it worse by saying he's innocent."

No I was not saying that. But I told him, the Lawrence Horn I knew couldn't have done it.

He asked another question, explained the things Lawrence had done, described the situation, and I said the same thing. The Lawrence Horn I knew couldn't have done it.

Again, was I contradicting the jury's decision? No! I started to repeat what I'd said, that the Lawrence Horn I knew… And I thought of the things that some of the other witnesses had said, how Lawrence was working in the prison library, teaching the other inmates how to use computers, helping them with books and reading, all the good that he was doing in there. He was writing computer manuals for them, using language free of the technical jargon you always needed another manual to even understand. He was doing so much good in there, and that's what I said.

"This is important. This is adding something back to society. You can't bring the people back but you can add something to society that can save other lives."

I finished my testimony, and the strangest thing happened. As I left the court, suddenly I was surrounded by reporters. None of the other witnesses were; they all made a beeline for me, all asking for interviews.

I asked them why and they said, "You humanised him. You talked about him in a way that we could relate to. You made him sound like a special human being."

One of them even said I made it sound as though I would never have been as successful if it wasn't for Lawrence, so I definitely put a stop to that. "No, no, no." But the rest? I could live with that.

A short time later, I was in the office and I received a call from Lawrence himself. It was the first time I'd spoken to him since his arrest, and I was surprised to hear from him, but he said much the same thing. "I didn't know you as well as I knew Brian, but you sounded like you'd known me all your life." He said I saved his life.

I said no, and reminded him that there were many people who testified on his behalf, but he replied, "You made me sound like a person, you humanised me, and after you testified, they didn't give me death, they gave me life." And then he said, "I want to thank you because the conspirator always gets the death penalty. I got life."

He said that, and cold chills went through my body as I realised – he was confessing. He was telling me that he had done the thing I was still refusing to accept, refusing to believe.

I don't think I even responded. My mind went adrift. But the last thing he said to me will always be with me. He said, "What I wouldn't give for a cold beer."

Lawrence Horn died in prison on April 13, 2018.

Chapter Twenty-Three

My Heart Wants to Try One More Time

The problem with describing something as 'the end of an era' is, you really don't realise that's what it was until later. So far as we were concerned, the work was the important aspect, and the people who made (and still make) it possible for us to continue working.

We left Motown for the second time in 1984, ironically not too long after we reunited with Lamont for a very special project. For us, then, it wasn't the end of an era. It was the beginning of a new chapter.

In 1983, The Four Tops returned to Motown after 10 years away.

It was a momentous occasion, all the more so now, because a lot of the classic acts had finally departed. First Michael and The Jacksons, then Diana in 1981, Marvin in 1982, and they were all headline departures. So, the return of The Four Tops was a rare piece of good news. They'd always been one of the label's flagship acts, their oldies were still consistent sellers, and the idea was to make a really big deal about it. And a really good album too, the very aptly titled *Back Where I Belong*.

The reunion with Lamont felt no less special.

Of course, a lot of the magic that had sparked between us had gone. But some of it returned. We worked well together, and we came up with half an album's worth of new songs, which we wrote and produced in exactly the same fashion as we did in the old days. Listening to Levi's voice after all those years was like stepping into a time machine.

The first single from the album, 'I Just Can't Walk Away', was doing really well. Radio was keen, sales were good, and the promo man was adamant that it was heading for the Top 20. But only, he said, if Motown put some money behind it.

Eddie: Berry and I went back and forth on that, and various other issues, but ultimately we could never reach an accord. And then the single started to drop down the chart, so it didn't matter anymore.

I still believe in that song, though. In fact, I was watching the video recently, and I was very pleasantly surprised by one of the pop DJs saying, "Thank God for Holland–Dozier–Holland." That song was so different to anything he'd been playing before.

Probably the best thing about our deal with Motown was, unlike the first time around, we weren't bound by an exclusivity contract, so if either of us wanted to work with another artist, on another label, we could. And when we left, we could carry on doing so.

Alongside everybody we worked with at Motown during the late 1970s and early 1980s, therefore, there were also people like Mavis Staples, The Family Affair and The Energetics. And Donny Osmond!

Brian: Our cousin Richard Davis, who runs our publishing company Gold Forever, was friends with one of the vice presidents over at Polydor. I suppose my name must have come up in conversation at some point, because all of a sudden Polydor wanted to know if I'd be interested in working with Donny on his next album.

Donny Osmond, Marie Osmond and Brian.

He was a few years away from that period when everything he and his family did was a huge hit, and I think they were looking at revamping his image a little, in much the same way as Michael started doing after he left Motown.

I was happy to help, so I flew out to Provo, Utah, where The Osmonds lived; I stayed at the family home, their mother was great, their father was great.

They gave me my own key so I could come and go as I pleased, although most of the time I didn't go any further than the studio. They had their own recording studio, so we could work whenever we wanted; I'd go in there and work and fool around with the machines.

It's funny because I'd heard so much about Provo and how prejudiced people were out there; that you couldn't have a drink, all the liquor stores closed at 6 o'clock, all that stuff. But I really enjoyed myself. I had my son Brian Jr. with me, and they adored him. I got to know the family, the brothers – we were all very friendly and it was a great relationship. And we recorded an album as well!

So our second 'departure' from Motown was neither as traumatic nor as dramatic as our first. We simply got on with our lives, helping other writers, collaborating with our friends, looking after the back catalogue, racing horses. We were doing our thing. We were living.

Money wasn't a problem, so we enjoyed ourselves. And there was never a time when we left the music industry because there was always a new project or act to occupy one or other of us – like Bonnie Pointer and Heavy Traffic.

The difference was, we could pick and choose, and we weren't driven, or allowing ourselves to be driven, to keep having hit singles.

In 1984, we launched our own label, Holland–Dozier–Holland, originally to rerelease highlights from the Invictus and Hot Wax catalogue, but inevitably we also branched out into new talent that excited us, Liquid Heat and Cassandra in the 1980s and, later, Ronnie Laws* and Rick Littleton. Yes, the music industry had changed a lot, taking the emphasis off the word 'music' and putting it on 'industry', but working in our own little corner, under our own speed, we didn't allow it to concern us.

Eddie: I suppose I stopped writing for the pop market when rap and hip hop became dominant, and I realised how much things had changed. No disrespect to the music, but the stuff that was selling out there, it didn't take my talent or Brian's talent to do it. So, we stopped competing.

We had lives to live, and that's what we concentrated on. Our families and our friends. And if the projects came a little slower than they used to, or arrived with less of a splash, that was also

---

* Ronnie was singer Eloise Laws' brother.

deliberate. We had already made our mark, working our hearts out at Hitsville in the sixties.

There was no way we could compete with that, and we knew it. We could sit down and write the greatest song in the world, and have the biggest hit in the world. But it would never overshadow the music that we made in the sixties.

Eddie: I remember talking with Lamont once, and telling him that any fame we had was nothing to do with our talent. Sixties Motown was an era, and Holland–Dozier–Holland were a vital part of that era. We were caught up in it, and we always will be. People will always remember us for being a part of Motown… being a part of this special generation. Having more hit records could never replace that.

Lamont looked at me and he sort of smiled. He didn't believe it. But I knew it was true.

It was during the early–mid 1970s when we first realised that the songs we'd written in the 1960s were showing no sign whatsoever of going away.

Lee Michaels, The Band, Donnie Elbert, James Taylor, Linda Ronstadt and Rod Stewart all scored hits with versions of our classics. On the disco scene, Gloria Gaynor took 'Reach Out I'll Be There' to new and unexpected heights.

In the UK, old recordings by The Supremes, R. Dean Taylor and The Elgins were still battling it out in the charts, and an entire new scene, northern soul, grew up around Motown and the soul music of the sixties. More than 40 years on, we still hear from people reminding us of songs that we'd forgotten even writing and recording, and telling us their own stories of how much they mean to them.

The 1980s dawned. Tracey Ullman, Kim Wilde, Soft Cell, Phil Collins, Carl Carlton, Third World, Sheena Easton, Bonnie Tyler, The Fall, the 1990s, the 2000s, the 2010s. Every new decade, every new generation, puts its own unique spin on the songs we wrote in the sixties and seventies, and it never ceases to amaze us.

Brian, Kris Kristofferson, Lamont and Eddie at the Lifetime Achievement Awards, 1987.

In fact, Phil Collins proved to be one of our greatest ever cheerleaders. In 1982, his version of 'You Can't Hurry Love' gave him his first ever British number one, and American Top 10 hit, and almost 30 years later, his version of 'Heat Wave' became the first single taken from his *Goin' Back* album, his first UK chart-topper since 1993. And in between times, of course, he wrote some great songs with Lamont.

Brian: I would be a fool if I told you I knew those songs would be so big. I felt we could be successful, but I had no idea that those songs would live as long as they have.

It's been phenomenal. I remember saying back at Motown, "Man, I would love to write classic songs, like a 'White Christmas'." As it turns out, many of our songs have become classics, too. But back during that time we were focused on writing songs for our current project.

Eddie: It was astonishing to us. I was never thinking these songs would last like that. My thing was, if every song we wrote was recorded and became a hit, we'd be doing well. If it was then rerecorded by someone else, and became a hit once again, then we'd be doing even better. But that was it. That was as big as I could even conceive.

Little did I know… It's still mind-blowing to realise how long those songs have been around. I never would have dreamed it. It's flabbergasting when I hear that someone who wasn't even born when we wrote the song has recorded something of ours. We hit a perfect chord, and we kept on hitting it.

As gratifying as all of this was, however, and how rewarding it remains, one fact is incontrovertible. We had no interest in constantly reliving the past.

Eddie: I don't play the 'what if' game. As far as I'm concerned, what's done is done and you have to make the best of it, whether you wish it had never happened or not.

It's true, I cannot help but occasionally wonder how things might have panned out, the day I walked into Berry's office to propose a royalty increase for Brian, if Berry had cut me off mid-sentence and said, "Yeah, I wanted to talk to you about that. How big of an increase should I offer him?"

If, when Berry decided to move Motown to Los Angeles, to further his interest in the movies, he had agreed to maintain a presence in Detroit, and left me there to continue running the A&R department?

If all the acts that we brought to Invictus and Hot Wax had instead become Motown artists, with all that weight of both promotional muscle and history the label could bring to bear? Because it's true; we did little at our own label that we would not gladly have done at Motown and, without the non-musical distractions that played their own role in the slow demise of Invictus, how much bigger could they all have been?

And finally, if all that had come to pass, where would we be now?

It doesn't matter. We are where we are, and we're happy with that.

We continued to move forward. Maybe we were no longer interested in writing pop hits. But writing itself was still fascinating and, as we broadened our horizons, so the opportunities came from further afield as well.

Although we had never acted upon the inclination before, theatre was an area that had fascinated us both for a long time. It is a very different discipline to pop, of course, but that was a big part of its appeal. We had grown up on show tunes, courtesy of Uncle James's record collection, and had returned to them for various projects during the Motown days. Now, we were being offered the opportunity to explore the field more deeply.

The first project to come our way was an all-black version of Charles Dickens's *Oliver Twist* – one of the stories Eddie had thrilled to in those *Classics Illustrated* comics when he was a kid. It would not be the novel's first musical outing; the English playwright Lionel Bart wrote and staged one back in the 1960s, and revivals (plus a successful movie version) had kept it alive ever since. Knowing that our work would automatically be compared to the classic songs that Bart created simply added further incentive for us to become involved.

Eddie: The deal was, they wanted us to write the songs but they wanted Lamont involved as well, and I understood that. It's like I've said before, the very name 'Holland–Dozier–Holland' has a cache that goes way beyond our individual names; it represents and, to some people, encapsulates an entire era, and that was what the show's producers wanted to recapture.

The three of us started work and, for a while, we were going great guns. But, at the same time, Lamont had been working on a play of his own, *Angel Quest*, and people were showing an interest in that too. And the more it developed, the more time he wanted to spend on it, to the detriment of *Oliver Twist*. And finally, he got a bite, and that was it.

He pulled out of *Oliver Twist* and, because that entire project was predicated on having new songs by Holland–Dozier–Holland, that was the end of it.

As it happened, Lamont's play didn't happen either, so when we were first approached about a new project, a musical version of Olivia Goldsmith's novel *The First Wives Club*, again with music by Holland–Dozier–Holland, he jumped at it.

It was Harold Beatty who first introduced us to the project. Harold had been working for us as a songwriter since we'd gone back to Motown in the 1970s and he was a great writer, and very loyal. I remember he wrote a few songs with Michael Jackson when we had that project, and at one point Motown offered him twice what I was paying him, to come and work for them.

I told him he should take it but he wouldn't. I asked him why and he said, "Because I'm more comfortable with you." Over the years, we wrote a lot of songs together. So it was Harold who introduced us to Paul Lambert, who was one of the co-producers of *First Wives Club* (alongside Jonas Neilson), and we will always be grateful to him for that. I truly believe, if Harold hadn't passed away so soon after, he would have made a major impression on the people around that show.

Harold's death came as a dreadful shock but, despite it, everything was great to begin with. The writing itself was fun, challenging – Eddie described it as becoming "a new life for us", and he was correct.

Eddie: I prefer writing for musicals than just writing pop songs, because there's so much more depth to it. Not that writing songs for the pop world isn't important, but when you are older and your mind has grown or expanded with life, there is just so much more to express, and you want to express yourself differently.

It's important to constantly have your mind and your emotions stimulated, especially when it comes to song. And in theatre, there are the characters you are writing for, with their own arcs and realisations. There is just nothing like it.

There's a lot more detail involved than there is in pop because you have to write for the character, and you have to be aware of the director and where he and the writer want to take it. It keeps your mind thinking in different ways, always moving on these different levels, wondering how the characters play out in their individual journeys. It was perfect for me, though, because I already write in a very analytical way, and I'm always considering people and relationships.

The biggest difference for me was, when you're writing a pop song, you usually think about one person singing it. You have control over the entire shape of the song, so it is almost like you can do what you want to do. When you're writing for a musical, you can't do that. You are part of a group, and the songs are part of a story, so that makes a big difference. But it also makes it more interesting, especially if you are already fascinated by people as a rule, the combination of the dynamics between people and, in this instance, the characters.

It was a lot of work but I really enjoyed the challenge. Brian later said I was writing the best songs I ever had, and the reason for that was, I was enjoying myself more than I had since the old Motown days.

In fact, the hardest part for me was putting so much time into writing a song only to find out they're not going to use that particular scene. Or you have to rewrite the song, or watch it get cut up differently to how you originally intended. It was very difficult for me to adjust to that, mentally. It took me a few years. When you're writing pop songs, once you write that song, it is what you want, and the only judge, as a rule, is going to be the public when you release it. In writing for theatre, you can work hours and hours on a particular song and scene, only for it to be changed and you think, "Wow, after all that work!"

It's okay now. I can live with that fact and make the emotional and psychological adjustment to do whatever it is I have to do for the whole, rather than one particular part of it. And the reason for that is, I became a much better songwriter than I ever was. It would never take me three weeks to write a song any more.

First Wives Club took years… literally years… to advance from the initial idea to a final production, but it was worth it. Francesca Zambello directed, we had a great cast, and the premiere at the

Promotional poster for *First Wives Club.*

Old Globe in San Diego in 2009 was a genuinely thrilling occasion. The show was a sell-out and was extended for an additional two weeks.

The play did so well, in fact, that we were headed for Broadway. An opening date sometime in 2011 was mooted. But again, Lamont was growing restless.

Eddie: If there was a single moment when I felt things going awry, it was during the writing phase. Brian and I were ploughing ahead, and we felt things were going great. But we also noticed that whenever there were 'problems' with a song, or questions about one, it almost always involved one of Lamont's contributions. Or, if there were problems with something we offered, it would be sorted out instantly, whereas the discussions over Lamont's songs seemed to drag on interminably.

The final straw for Lamont came when I introduced a song called 'My Heart Wants To Try'. It's one of two songs in the show that I thought really stood out – the other is 'Shoulder To Shoulder'. But 'My Heart Wants To Try' is the one which, when I brought it in for people to hear, it reduced everybody to tears. Even Lamont! That's the song that won everybody over; it proved that Holland–Dozier–Holland were the correct choice for the show.

And I could see it in Lamont's face. He was thinking, "Here it goes again." It didn't matter that his name would be on the song, and that so far as the rest of the world was concerned, just like in the old days, he was as much a part of its creation as Brian and I.

Neither did it matter that, when we first got back together for the show, we redesigned our old contract, a straight 33 per cent split between the three of us, regardless of how much usable material Lamont did or didn't contribute. In his own mind, all he could see was the Holland and Holland part of the equation pushing forward, and the Dozier element receding into the distance.

The situation worsened when we arrived in New York to begin fine-tuning the show for Broadway – because, the more we fine-tuned it, the more the director was finding fault with some of

Lamont's contributions. Finally he suggested that Lamont should get together with me, so we could clarify the storylines together.

That was it. All those old ghosts came flooding back, and he did what he always did when those fears assailed him. He turned against us.

In interviews, he started reminding journalists that, not only was this the first time we'd worked together in more than 20 years, it was strictly a one-off.

The producers begged him not to keep saying that, reminding him that if *First Wives Club* was successful, there was sure to be more work for the creative team behind it. But not if one of the team was already saying this was the last time it would happen.

That probably made Lamont feel even worse. Would he never be free of the Holland brothers? Would he never be able to stand out on his own?

It was the end. Everything we thought we had agreed to was thrown aside. It was already becoming apparent that the Broadway venture was not going to take off after all – mounting such a show is an incredibly expensive venture, and the finances just weren't there. Losing its musical masterminds as well was simply the final nail. Because, again in the public eye, if you take the 'Dozier' out of 'Holland–Dozier–Holland', all you're left with are Brian and Eddie.

We weren't ready to give up on *First Wives Club*. The material that we – Brian and Eddie – had contributed was strong; some of the best writing we had ever done in our lives. Few people had heard the songs, just those that caught the show in San Diego. But we heard good things from audiences and critics alike. We'd already experienced the disappointment of the *Oliver Twist* songs getting lost, and they weren't even close to the quality of our latest material. We weren't going to go through that again.

It took time, but slowly, *First Wives Club* pulled itself back into contention. A Chicago run, to commence early in 2015, was mooted, and we started looking back over the old material, working to improve it even further.

There was just one cloud. Legally, Lamont was still a part of the team.

What followed was ugly. Ugly and devastating. Of course, the producers had to break with him. But so did we, and though we knew it needed to be done, that did not make it any less heartbreaking. It was the last thing we wanted to happen.

Eddie: I can understand what Lamont was going through from a purely ego-driven point of view. What I can't understand is why his ego was like that. Lamont is part of musical history, and so what if the majority of people know him only as part of a team? They feel the same way about Brian and me.

The first major hit single that the Holland brothers had together, 'Come And Get These Memories', was written with Lamont. So was the last one, 'Back Where I Belong'. And, in between times, the vast majority of all the others were, as well.

Yes, we can look at some of the melodies… 'Baby Love', 'Where Did Our Love Go', 'Baby I Need Your Loving', 'Bernadette', 'This Old Heart Of Mine'… and say they were largely written by Brian, just as we can look at 'Heat Wave', 'I Can't Help Myself' and 'Nowhere To Run' and say they were chiefly Lamont's work. But it doesn't matter. Though it rarely took three people to write any one of those songs, history believes it did. And who are we to argue?

Lamont would not be placated. He didn't want to be involved any longer, but he didn't want to be cast adrift, either. Legal papers were served. Complaints flew, old grievances were reborn. And the end result…

Eddie: The end result is, I can't see us ever working with Lamont again.

There's no point in beating about the bush. When it became clear that there was no going back, and Lamont was no longer a part of the team, the musical's producers were terrified. The involvement of the world-famous 'Holland–Dozier–Holland' was, they believed, one of the key selling points of *First Wives Club*.

Eddie: They took a lot of convincing but I told them, very firmly, "Look, stuff can be straightened out. Not only can we do it, we can do it better." And I was correct. The songs they thought they loved before, now they loved them even more.

First Wives Club opened for a six-week run at the Oriental Theatre in Chicago on February 17, 2015. The old songs were revised, new ones were written to wipe away any last trace of Lamont's presence. And again we had – and still have – a hit on our hands. Once again, Broadway… and beyond!… is in our sights.

Chapter Twenty-Four

Back in My Arms

Time has passed, our families have grown up, and the past has become another lifetime.

It was, and it still is, bizarre when we get a call inviting us to this award ceremony or that one, up on the podium looking out at a sea of expectant faces, knowing that we wrote the songs that soundtracked their lives, but also thinking, "But it was my job!" A great job, one of the very best anybody could ask for, but ultimately, that's what it was.

What is important to us is knowing that other people value what we did. Every time we receive another award, be it the Ivor Novello International Award or our own star on the Hollywood Walk of Fame, our first reaction is always, how truly and deeply honoured we are. And while hearing that we'd been voted into the Rock and Roll Hall of Fame was one thing, actually walking into the Hall of Fame in Cleveland, seeing all those other heroes of mine, was awesome.

Eddie: I was completely overwhelmed. I'm often asked in interviews what are my happiest memories of Motown, and there's a lot of them. But being inducted into the Hall of Fame is definitely one of them.

Our cousin Richard Davis and Eddie's daughter Lauren on the day she started working at BMI. Three of her fellow coworkers share the moment.

At the time, I was in my office on Highland Avenue in Hollywood. My cousin Richard Davis told me the news. Learning that we'd been voted in was exciting enough, but when I saw my name, Brian's name and Lamont's name up there alongside all those people we loved, it was a very proud moment. And it was great to share that moment with Brian and Lamont, as it has been great to share all those other moments, going back for so many, many years, with them.

But my happiest memories aren't single events. They are the friendships and relationships that came out of Motown and which, in many cases, are still a part of my life today.

Berry, for example.

We had our ups and downs, of course. In fact, if you read the history books, you'll see that we had another legal dispute, much later on, which ground on for 12 years – and that should tell you something. A lawsuit that goes on for 12 years is not a legal matter at all. It's a personal conflict.

Even my attorney said that. We were meeting and he told me straight, "This doesn't make sense. No lawyers would want to fight like this. I couldn't settle this, no one could. This is personal. The only people who can settle this are you and Gordy," and that is what eventually happened.

Before that, though, something else occurred and I believe, if there is one incident in either of our lives that truly sums up what he and I mean to one another, the depth of love and respect and friendship that we feel for one another, this is it.

We were in the thick of the lawsuit and I had run into a problem. I was in the process of losing a $4.5 million property; I had three weeks in which to come up with a quarter of a million dollars, and the finance people I had, and the lawyers I had, couldn't get it done. They'd been working on it for three or four months, and they were in exactly the same place as they were when they started. So when they said it would only be another three weeks, I didn't trust them. I told them I'd handle it myself.

I called Berry.

He was incredulous. "Eddie, are you crazy? Man, we're in the middle of this fighting and you say you need…"

I said, "Berry, that has nothing to do with it," and he agreed.

"You're right. It doesn't."

I said, "Give me 30 days and I'll pay you back," but he was still laughing.

"You know my lawyers are going to think you need the money to fight the lawsuit," but I gave him my word; not a penny would be spent on anything other than the property. And Berry said yes. He'd loan me the money.

I told my attorneys what was happening, and they couldn't believe it. "What are you fighting for, if he's going to lend you this money?"

"One doesn't have anything to do with the other," I replied, "and Berry knows it." Meanwhile, Berry's lawyer was saying the same thing, but Berry didn't care. He took the money from his private account, I saved my property and then I paid him back.

As for the lawsuit itself, it took another couple of years but we resolved that, as well. Like Berry said, "None of this makes sense. We've only got so much time to live. Let's get rid of this thing and enjoy our lives."

It was Berry's executive assistant, Edna Anderson, who made it happen.

Edna was amazing. She was the only person who could take Berry's anger, and mine as well, and make them go away. She could go between the two of us, listen to what we each had to say, and then take it back to the other one and explain it in a way that didn't set off another explosion of rage or frustration – which is something that no lawyer could ever do. I've never met anybody who could do that, and how I've wished, over the years, that she'd been with Berry the first time we fought. She'd have fixed it long before the lawyers got involved.

Because we certainly couldn't. I'd spent two years trying to figure out a way of sorting things out, and I know Berry had as well. Neither of us were able to – we were both too proud. We were afraid of losing face.

Finally, an opportunity presented itself.

Janie Bradford was (and to this day, remains) the producer of the Heroes And Legends (HAL) awards, tirelessly raising much-needed funds for performing arts scholarships. Every year, she would host a massive fundraiser in the name of a different hero or legend. This particular year she was honouring Berry, and I thought to myself, "Aha, this is my chance to finally settle this thing."

I took out an ad congratulating Berry and I knew Edna, shrewd as she was, would see that and say, "Wait a minute. If Eddie has that kind of feeling and attitude, we can settle this thing." I knew she would read that into it.

I went to the awards and Berry looked over his shoulder, saw me standing there, and he said, "Oh, Eddie." I hugged him, gave him a kiss on the cheek and we both started laughing.

Then, a few minutes later, I heard Edna, "Where's Eddie? Where's Eddie?" I knew she was not going to let that opportunity pass; she tracked me down in that place, and said, "We gotta talk."

We made arrangements to meet at her hotel, before her next meeting with Berry, and we discussed everything. In fact, we talked so long that she was late for her meeting with Berry.

Of course, the first thing he asked her was, "Where were you?" And the same thing happened before her next meeting with him as well. He'd say, "Why are you late?" and she'd tell him, "I was talking to Eddie." And finally he told her, "You like Eddie more than you like me!"

Much later, I asked him, "Did you really say that?"

He answered, "Yes, I said that. She really did love you."

And I loved her. What I had with Edna was one of the best personal relationships, business-wise, I've ever had.

After Edna died on June 13, 2015, Berry told me that she talked to him like she was his mother, and all I could say was, "You, too?" Because Edna could say anything she wanted to me, and I took it. It was almost like Ola was talking to me. I accepted it. She was rational, she was reasonable.

Occasionally Berry would come back with a piece of negotiation I didn't like, and she would say, "Eddie, calm yourself down. The two of you have this thing about who's right and who's wrong, and I'm telling you now, I don't care. This has gone on far and long enough, and if you don't settle this thing, I'm going to be one mad, angry bitch."

I don't think anybody alive could have got us to settle that thing, other than Edna. We had five or six different meetings and I remember at the very first one, we were having lunch at the Bel Air Hotel, and Berry started fussing over something. I was so angry that I started to get up to walk out. Suddenly, I glanced at Edna's face and she looked so hurt that I eased back down in my chair and let Berry go on, say what he had to say. I couldn't disappoint this woman. I let him finish, and then I said, "Berry, let me tell you something. You're not all right and I'm not all right. You're

Celebration of Life

Edna Anderson-Owens

1938 ~ 2015

The front page of the brochure issued for Edna's celebration.

not all wrong and I'm not all wrong, so what we have to do is get together and finish this thing."

He looked at me and said, "Yeah, okay." And that's what we did.

Edna never allowed our friendship to fail. In fact, she was forever trying to do things that she thought would bring us even closer. She knew we had a genuinely strong relationship and love, but she was also aware that it was conflicted because of the past litigation.

Every chance she got, then, she would say, "Eddie do this, say that, and you know what? Try and remember Berry on his birthday." (I do. It's November 28.) She would always promote it; it was so important to her.

But you know what? I didn't need to be reminded.

To this day, I love Berry so much and more than I ever have before.

Epilogue: Esther

There is one name, largely absent from these pages, who cannot and will not ever be forgotten – not by us, nor by any of the many people whose lives she touched.

Esther Gordy was the eldest of Berry's four sisters, nine years older than Berry himself, and she was integral to the birth of his dream. It was Esther who ran Ber-Berry, the Gordy family co-op that loaned him the money to launch Motown in the first place. Later, once the company was up and running, Esther was in charge of organising the label's most legendary tours. She was a company vice president and she also worked as chief executive officer.

Her most important role, however, was as a surrogate mother figure to so many of the young musicians and writers who peopled the label during those earliest years. Remember, the music business was a very different beast to the one we know today. There were no 'personal managers' or 'personal assistants' around in those days, no agents, no people that a young, uncertain and maybe even scared youngster could turn to in times of need; or who would forever be keeping a watchful eye open, to make certain things were all right.

That is the role that Esther took on – not officially, not because she was hired to do so. It was her personality that bade her take so many fledglings under her wing, and we loved her for it.

Eddie: Then I did a terrible thing. Something for which I'm not sure I can ever forgive myself. It was at the height of my first lawsuit against Motown. I make no excuses, but I was in a total haze, lost in the vortex of constantly shifting emotions, mindlessly reacting to the dramatics of litigation.

My lawyers were constantly bombarding me with names – should this person be included? Might we have a case against that person? And what about…? They were doing it for effect, dynamics – the more names they threw mud at, the more convincing they believed the case would be. And you notice I say 'the' case. Because it was no longer *my* case; it had taken on a life of its own.

Esther was one of those people who was caught up in the mess.

I was horrified when I realised, not only because she had no business being dragged into things but because Esther had never shown me anything but kindness and sincere friendship since the day I met her, back when I was a teenager. And I felt exactly the same way about her.

I remember one of the court sessions. Esther was there and, when it was over, she came up to me in the hallway of the court building and greeted me with such love and friendship and, of course, I greeted her in the same manner.

My lawyers, standing around watching, were astonished. In fact, one of them came up to me later and asked what was going on. "Man, if that's the way you all feel about one another, we could settle this thing right now."

But I was stubborn. And maybe thoughtless. My love for Esther, and hers for me, was a very special thing. It felt cheap and nasty to try and use that love to settle a lawsuit. So it dragged on until its ultimate conclusion, but all the while that moment stayed on my mind because I felt so guilty about it. Even after all the bridges were repaired, it continued to haunt me.

Time passed. Years passed. Esther, now in her eighties, was in poor health and Berry wanted to give something back to her while she was still around to enjoy it. On November 12, 2005, the 20th anniversary of the Motown Historical Museum of which Esther was director, Hitsville took over the Detroit Marriott Hotel for a celebration of her life.

Everybody was there – Stevie Wonder, Smokey Robinson, Martha Reeves, Thelma Houston. It was already set to be an amazing night. And then our office phone rang. It was Edna Anderson, asking if we would write a song for the evening. And, much to our surprise, asking if we would perform it, too.

Eddie: I told her we would do it but, to be perfectly honest, this was a very heavy emotional responsibility for me. This wasn't a pop song, it wasn't a theatrical song. It was a song for Esther, and that made it more important than any I had ever written in the past. For the first time in my life, I felt insecure about writing. I got cold feet.

I knew I had to deliver, though, because Edna had asked me to and I had promised. Brian was not so intimidated. He jumped right in on the melody. But I worked like crazy, feverishly, and it took me two weeks before I felt I had anything I could even show him.

I started adding certain melodies of my own, little passages that I felt. I wasn't writing a song, I was creating our ode to Esther, and it was structured to be dynamic in both melody and emotion.

It almost sounded like it had three parts that could be the chorus; it moved around almost like a folk song, it went into different changes, you could call them movements. I just immersed myself in this melody, helping my brother and adding to it and causing him to write certain melodies, until it was long enough and broad enough and involved enough that I could express everything I wanted to say, everything I felt for Esther. I remember Brian sitting at the piano saying, "You're going to have people crying with this song." I just ignored him.

The night we finished, I called McKinley Jackson, our bandleader back in the Invictus days, and told him we were on our way to

Detroit and needed him to put together a band and find us a rehearsal space to do this thing.

So he called around and found six or seven musicians, some from Motown and others from around the city, and we were all together in this basement space. Brian was orchestrating and I was singing, and Brian just looked at me, the emotion that I was pouring into it, and said, "You'd better sing on the microphone because you're going to make yourself hoarse with this song."

I did that, but there was another problem. All the while we'd been writing the song, and rehearsing it between ourselves, I had grown accustomed to the way Brian played it on the piano, the way he structured certain chords, hitting them in such a way that it reminded me of the lyric.

With the band, I didn't have that. They started playing and I was instantly lost.

"Brian, Brian, it's not going to work. You're going to have to play the piano."

Brian looked horrified. "I'm not playing it. I'm not a pianist."

"Man, you have to. It's the only way I'm going to remember the song."

"Okay, if I have to…"

We started again, and this time, it worked. Suddenly doors started opening and 10 or 12 other people in the building were coming in to see what was happening, who was singing – later, I laughed because it reminded me of my first ever audition for Berry. The same thing happened there, and I was just as uncomfortable now as I was back then.

But I got through it, and the next thing was a full dress rehearsal at the venue. And I suddenly realised, although I'd written the song, I'd never actually learned it. I didn't know the words. And that mattered because, yes, I was the one who would be singing it that evening, on stage, in front of a packed house. My first time performing live on a stage in 35 years and I didn't know the words to my own song.

Maybe I could place the lyrics on a music stand? The thought went through my head, but I knew it wouldn't work. This was a performance, not a reading.

Back to my hotel room, for however many hours I had until show time, rehearsing the lines, memorising the lyrics.

And when I thought I had finally got it, back to the venue. Smokey was there, Stevie, so many people performing, because Esther was so important to us all, and now I had to wait.

I was tense. I was tired. It was getting late, and I've never been one for staying up late. There was a tickle in the back of my throat. When I spoke, my voice sounded hoarse. Oh no, am I coming down with something?

I called over to Shirley Washington, my assistant. "When are we going on?"

"Hang on, I'll check." And then, "It'll be about an hour."

So I'd wait and then I'd ask her again. Same answer. About an hour.

Eddie and Brian's tireless executive administrator, actress and writer Shirley Washington. © Shirley Washington

Our cousin, Richard Davis, was there; I asked him if he could bring me a sip of brandy, just to calm my throat. I rarely drink alcohol… almost never, in fact. But I must have drunk about an ounce of brandy, and I was becoming sleepier and sleepier.

"Shirley, is it time yet?"

"No, about an hour." Always another hour. I didn't know an evening had so many hours in it! But finally, "Okay, Eddie, it's almost time, go and get ready…"

Harvey Fuqua wandered over. "Hey Eddie, so what are you going to be doing tonight?"

"We've got a song for Esther."

"Great! Who's going to be singing?"

"I am."

He just stared at me. "*You?*" And he walked away, probably scratching his head.

It was time. The MC announced me, we walked out on stage, the band struck up, we were into the song, everything was going so well… and then we got to a certain part of the song, a key part of the song, and my mind was blank. I couldn't remember the words.

I ad-libbed, shouting out to the crowd, "This is what we're here for! It's for Esther," and the entire place erupted. So I got through that part and now I was okay. I could sing the rest. Until we came to that same part again, and I had to shout out the same ad-lib again.

We got through it, though. Later, Harvey told me, "You stood there like a pro, one hand on the mic, one hand in your pocket, and you were belting the hell out of that song. You were hitting notes you should never have been able to make, it was great."

What made it even greater for me, though, was looking down about halfway through the song and seeing Berry standing in front of the stage, just looking up at me as I was singing, and suddenly, as the song moved towards its end, he was up on stage as well, picking up the microphone and saying "You know? This guy says he's just a songwriter, but he's a performer as well."

And just for a moment there, I was seventeen, eighteen years old, up on stage at a record hop somewhere, and Berry was there egging me on, telling me how good I was… "So-and-so's out in the crowd tonight. Show him you're the best, man."

Then, we were walking off stage together, singing together! It was almost like a gospel thing. I'd sing a line and Berry would sing it back, then I'd sing it back to him, back and forth, back and forth, as we were walking off the stage, and Berry loved it.

"This is your moment, this is your time, so shine, shine, shine," I'd sing, and Berry would echo back "shine, shine, shine", "this is your moment, this is your hour", "shine, shine, shine". We kept building, we kept going around, taking the song to a climax I had never even imagined. I loved it. It was truly magical.

I came off stage and people were running up to me, "Eddie, I had no idea you could sing like that…! Oh man, you have to go on the road with that song." Over and over again, "Are you going on the road with that song?" Thelma Houston even told me, "I want you to take me with you." I said, "Girl, I am *not* going on the road."

Making my way back to my seat, I heard someone say, "Who was that guy? I've not heard anyone sing like that since Jackie Wilson!" Suzanne de Passe came to me, she was crying, her mascara running down her cheeks. "Eddie Holland. Look what you made me do! Look at my face! Look what you've done to my mascara!"

So many people coming up to me, telling me what a great song it was, what a great performance. Berry saying, "You were fantastic tonight."

The most important thing, though, was two or three days later. Esther's granddaughter Robin called me and thanked me. She told me they'd recorded the song, and two or three times a day since the show, Esther had asked her to play the tape so she could hear it one more time. "You made my gran so happy."

Then Esther said something else. "I never knew they felt that way about me." She actually said that, and it doesn't happen very often, but that brought tears to my eyes.

More than that, though, it did my heart all the good in the world. Esther had been on my mind for so many years, and that's why I wrote the song.

It's why I did what I never thought I could do or would do – write a special song for a certain someone, go on stage, sing it, perform it and put everything I had into it. I didn't think I could do that, but suddenly that hole inside me that had been feeling so awful for so many years, I could feel it healing. All because of that one marvellous woman, and the opportunity I was given, when Edna Anderson made that call, to tell the world how I felt about her, and how I believed other people felt about her.

But it was never a typical song. It was an ode to Esther.

Ode To Esther

(Music by Brian Holland; lyrics by Eddie Holland)

When I look back over the early years
And oh, what magic years they were
I hold on to this memory of your smiling face
The presence of your grace

Were there struggles through the years?
There were many
Were there many hidden tears?
There were plenty

But through every struggle
Through every tear
you were always there
Never far, always near

I still remember all the young hopefuls
Reaching for the stars
Never realising all the days and nights you laboured
With our hopes in your heart

All the while we were reaching
Reaching for that touch of glory
You were always right there
You were a part of every story

So here we are
Sharing precious moments
Here with family and friends
Tonight we celebrate your life
Where it all began

Here I stand touched by old emotions
Wrapped in memories again
In celebration and devotion to you
Back where it all began

Heaven help me, Heaven help me

To be as strong as you
Then again
Oh, then again
It's not about me
Tonight
It's all about you
It's all about you
It's all about you
It's all about you

This is your moment, this is your time
So shine, shine, shine
This is your moment, this is your hour
So shine, shine, shine
This is your moment

Selected Discography

Highlights – Awards and Honours

1964 – BMI Songwriters of the Year

1965 – BMI Songwriters of the Year

1966 – BMI Songwriter of the Year (Eddie Holland only)
    HDH have received over 100 BMI awards for 30+ US Top 10 charting singles

1987 – Lifetime Achievement Award – National Academy of Songwriters

1988 – Songwriters Hall of Fame

1990 – Rock and Roll Hall of Fame

1998 – Grammy Trustees Award

2003 – BMI Icon Award

2004 – Special International Ivor Novello Award

2009 – Songwriters Hall of Fame – Johnny Mercer Award

2010 – HAL Awards gala honouring Holland–Dozier–Holland

2012 – Soul Music Hall of Fame

2015 – Hollywood Walk Of Fame

RIAA Gold Records

Note: Motown did not join the RIAA until 1976 (Diana Ross's 'Love Hangover' was the label's first certified million seller). Thus, while many Motown singles, including numerous HDH compositions, would ordinarily have qualified for the award in the years prior to that, only a tiny handful have in actuality been recognised by the organisation.

However, Motown did not allow its artists to go unrewarded. For every million seller the company registered, a privately produced gold record – in actuality, a regular single spray-painted gold – was given to the artist.

'Ain't Too Proud To Beg' The Temptations (Eddie Holland only)
 (awarded 1999)
'Ain't Too Proud To Beg'/'Beauty Is Only Skin Deep' The Temptations
 (Eddie Holland only) (awarded 1999)
'Baby Love' The Supremes (awarded 1997)
'Please Mr. Postman' The Carpenters (Brian Holland only)
 (awarded 1975)
'Please Mr. Postman' The Marvelettes (Brian Holland only)
 (awarded 2004)
'Reach Out I'll Be There' The Four Tops (awarded 1997)
'Stop! In The Name Of Love' The Supremes (awarded 1997)

All the Hits – HDH on the Hot 100

The following hits are arranged by the highest position reached in any one of the referenced charts. Peak positions in the others then follow.

Pop (US *Billboard*) chart positions taken from Joel Whitburn's *Top Pop Singles* (various editions). R&B (US *Billboard*) chart positions taken from Joel Whitburn's *Top R&B Singles* (various editions). UK chart positions taken from *The Complete Book of British Charts* by Neil Warwick, Jon Kutner and Tony Brown (various editions).

All songs composed by Holland–Dozier–Holland unless otherwise indicated. This list does not include songs to which HDH (or any combination thereof) are credited as co-writers through sampling, legal arrangements, translation etc. (i.e. N.W.A.'s '100 Miles And Runnin'', Len Barry's '1-2-3').

1 (Pop; 1 R&B; 1 UK) 'Baby Love' – The Supremes (1964)
1 (Pop; 1 R&B; 1 UK) 'Reach Out I'll Be There' – The Four Tops (1966)
1 (Pop; 1 R&B; 3 UK) 'Where Did Our Love Go' – The Supremes (1964)
1 (Pop; 1 R&B; 3 UK) 'You Can't Hurry Love' – The Supremes (1966)
1 (Pop; 1 R&B; 8 UK) 'You Keep Me Hangin' On' – The Supremes (1966)

1 (Pop; 1 R&B; 17 UK) 'Love Is Here And Now You're Gone' –
The Supremes (1967)

1 (Pop; 1 R&B; 23 UK) 'I Can't Help Myself (Sugar Pie Honey Bunch)' –
The Four Tops (1965)

1 (Pop; 1 R&B; 40 UK) 'Back In My Arms Again' – The Supremes (1965)

1 (Pop; 1 R&B) 'Please Mr. Postman' (*Georgia Dobbins, William Garrett,
Brian Holland, Robert Bateman, Freddie Gorman*) –
The Marvelettes (1961)

1 (Pop; 2 R&B; 7 UK) 'Come See About Me' – The Supremes (1964)

1 (Pop; 2 R&B; 7 UK) 'Stop! In The Name Of Love' – The Supremes (1965)

1 (Pop; 2 R&B; 39 UK) 'I Hear A Symphony' – The Supremes (1965)

1 (Pop; 2 UK) 'Please Mr. Postman' (*Georgia Dobbins, William Garrett, Brian
Holland, Robert Bateman, Freddie Gorman*) – The Carpenters (1974)

1 (Pop; 6 UK; 12 R&B) 'The Happening' (*HDH, Frank De Vol*) –
The Supremes (1967)

*Note: with the exception of The Marvelettes, each of the above also topped
the weekly *Cashbox* (US) chart.

1 (R&B; 3 Pop; 18 UK) 'Beauty Is Only Skin Deep' (*Eddie Holland,
Norman Whitfield*) – The Temptations (1966)

1 (R&B; 4 Pop) 'Heat Wave' – Martha & The Vandellas (1963)

1 (R&B; 8 Pop; 10 UK) '(I Know) I'm Losing You' (*Eddie Holland, Norman
Whitfield, Cornelius Grant*) – The Temptations (1966)

1 (R&B; 10 Pop; 17 UK) 'Jimmy Mack' – Martha & The Vandellas (1967)

1 (R&B; 13 Pop; 21 UK) 'Ain't Too Proud To Beg' (*Eddie Holland,
Norman Whitfield*) – The Temptations (1966)

1 (R&B; 47 Pop) 'All I Do Is Think Of You' (*Brian Holland, Michael
Lovesmith*) – Troop (1990)

1 (UK; 10 Pop) 'You Can't Hurry Love' – Phil Collins (1982)

1 (US; 2 UK) 'You Keep Me Hangin' On' – Kim Wilde (1986)

2 (Pop; 4 R&B; 5 UK) 'Reflections' – Diana Ross & The Supremes (1967)

2 (R&B; 5 Pop; 34 UK) 'It's The Same Old Song' – The Four Tops (1965)

2 (R&B; 6 Pop; 6 UK) 'Standing In The Shadows Of Love' –
The Four Tops (1966)

2 (R&B; 8 Pop; 60 UK) 'All I Need' (*Eddie Holland, Frank Wilson,
R. Dean Taylor*) – The Temptations (1967)
2 (R&B; 9 Pop; 22 UK) 'I'm Ready For Love' – Martha & The Vandellas (1966)
2 (R&B; 23 Pop) 'When The Lovelight Starts Shining Through His Eyes' –
The Supremes (1963)

3 (Pop) 'Baby I Need Your Loving' – Johnny Rivers (1967)

3 (R&B; 4 Pop; 8 UK) 'Bernadette' – The Four Tops (1967)
3 (R&B; 6 Pop; 49 UK) 'How Sweet It Is (To Be Loved By You)' –
Marvin Gaye (1964)
3 (R&B; 8 Pop) 'Mickey's Monkey' – The Miracles (1963)
3 (R&B; 14 Pop) '(Loneliness Made Me Realize) It's You That I Need'
(*Eddie Holland, Norman Whitfield*) – The Temptations (1967)
3 (R&B; 15 Pop) 'You're A Wonderful One' – Marvin Gaye (1964)
3 (R&B; 18 Pop; 22 UK) 'How Sweet It Is (To Be Loved By You)' –
Junior Walker & The All Stars (1966)
3 (R&B; 22 Pop) 'Can I Get A Witness' – Marvin Gaye (1963)
3 (R&B; 39 Pop) 'Everybody Needs Love' (*Eddie Holland,
Norman Whitfield*) – Gladys Knight & The Pips (1967)
3 (R&B; 54 Pop) 'Keep Holding On' (*Brian Holland, Eddie Holland*) –
The Temptations (1975)
3 (R&B) 'A Tear From A Woman's Eye' – The Temptations (1964)

3 (UK) 'Heaven Must Have Sent You' – The Elgins (1971 Reissue)
3 (UK) 'There's A Ghost In My House' (*HDH, R. Dean Taylor*) –
R. Dean Taylor (1974)
3 (UK) 'This Old Heart Of Mine (Is Weak For You)' (*HDH, Sylvia Moy*) –
The Isley Brothers (1968 Reissue)

4 (R&B; 7 Pop) 'Playboy' (*Brian Holland, Robert Bateman,
Gladys Horton, William Stevenson*) – The Marvelettes (1962)
4 (R&B; 11 Pop) 'Baby I Need Your Loving' – The Four Tops (1964)
4 (R&B; 12 UK; 20 Pop) '(I'm A) Road Runner' – Junior Walker & The All
Stars (1966)
4 (R&B; 17 Pop; 37 UK) '(Come 'Round Here) I'm The One You Need' –
The Miracles (1966)

4 (R&B; 23 Pop) 'Just A Little Bit Of You' (*Brian Holland, Eddie Holland*) – Michael Jackson (1975)

4 (R&B; 50 Pop) 'Take Me In Your Arms (Rock Me A Little While)' – Kim Weston (1965)

4 (UK; 83 Pop) 'This Old Heart Of Mine (Is Weak For You)' (*HDH, Sylvia Moy*) – Rod Stewart (1975)

5 (Pop; 10 R&B) 'My World Is Empty Without You' – The Supremes (1966)

5 (Pop; 51 UK) 'How Sweet It Is (To Be Loved By You)' – James Taylor (1975)

5 (Pop) 'Heat Wave' – Linda Ronstadt (1975)

5 (R&B; 8 Pop; 26 UK) 'Nowhere To Run' – Martha & The Vandellas (1965)

5 (R&B; 11 Pop) 'Too Many Fish In The Sea' (*Eddie Holland, Norman Whitfield*) – The Marvelettes (1964)

5 (R&B; 18 Pop) 'Shake Me, Wake Me (When It's Over)' – The Four Tops (1966)

5 (UK) 'He Was Really Sayin' Somethin'' (*Eddie Holland, Norman Whitfield, William Stevenson*) – Bananarama with Fun Boy Three (1982)

6 (Pop) 'You Keep Me Hangin' On' – Vanilla Fudge (1968 Reissue)

6 (R&B; 8 UK; 15 Pop) 'Where Did Our Love Go' – Donnie Elbert (1971)

6 (R&B; 11 Pop) 'Nothing But Heartaches' – The Supremes (1965)

6 (R&B; 12 Pop; 47 UK) 'This Old Heart Of Mine (Is Weak For You)' (*HDH, Sylvia Moy*) – The Isley Brothers (1966)

6 (R&B; 29 Pop) 'Come And Get These Memories' – Martha & The Vandellas (1963)

6 (R&B; 44 Pop) 'In My Lonely Room' – Martha & The Vandellas (1964)

6 (R&B; 60 Pop) 'Forever Came Today' – The Jackson 5 (1975)

7 (R&B; 8 Pop) 'Quicksand' – Martha & The Vandellas (1963)

7 (R&B; 9 Pop; 54 UK) 'Love Is Like An Itching In My Heart' – The Supremes (1966)

7 (R&B; 19 Pop; 26 UK) 'You Keep Running Away' – The Four Tops (1967)

7 (R&B; 33 Pop) 'Your Unchanging Love' – Marvin Gaye (1967)

7 (R&B; 46 UK; 54 Pop) 'We're Almost There' (*Brian Holland, Eddie Holland*) – Michael Jackson (1975)

7 (R&B; 50 Pop) 'Get The Cream Off The Top' (*Brian Holland, Eddie Holland*) – Eddie Kendricks (1975)

8 (R&B; 24 Pop; 51 UK) 'Come See About Me' – Junior Walker & The All Stars (1967)

8 (R&B) 'Someday, Someway' (*Brian Holland, Lamont Dozier, Freddie Gorman*) – The Marvelettes (1962)

9 (Pop; 13 UK; 16 R&B) 'In And Out Of Love' – The Supremes (1967)

9 (R&B; 19 Pop) 'Something About You' – The Four Tops (1965)

9 (R&B; 50 Pop) 'Heaven Must Have Sent You' – The Elgins (1966)

10 (Pop) 'This Old Heart Of Mine (Is Weak For You)' (*HDH, Sylvia Moy*) – Rod Stewart with Ronald Isley (1990)

10 (R&B; 12 UK; 14 Pop) 'Seven Rooms Of Gloom' – The Four Tops (1967)

10 (R&B; 22 Pop) 'You Lost The Sweetest Boy' – Mary Wells (1963)

10 (R&B; 42 Pop; 48 UK) 'Chairman Of The Board' (*Brian Holland, Lamont Dozier, Angelo Bond*) – Chairmen Of The Board (1971)

10 (R&B; 47 Pop; 50 UK) 'Little Darling (I Need You)' – Marvin Gaye (1966)

10 (R&B; 49 Pop) 'Strange I Know' (*Brian Holland, Lamont Dozier, Freddie Gorman*) – The Marvelettes (1962)

10 (R&B) 'Love Is Like An Itching In My Heart' – The Good Girls (1990)

10 (UK) 'I Can't Help Myself (Sugar Pie Honey Bunch)' – The Four Tops (1970 Reissue)

11 (Pop; 29 UK) 'Take Me In Your Arms (Rock Me A Little While)' – The Doobie Brothers (1975)

11 (Pop; 52 R&B) 'Heaven Must Have Sent You' – Bonnie Pointer (1979)

11 (R&B; 26 Pop) 'Girl (Why You Wanna Make Me Blue)' (*Eddie Holland, Norman Whitfield*) – The Temptations (1964)

11 (R&B; 42 Pop) 'Live Wire' – Martha & The Vandellas (1964)

11 (R&B; 44 Pop; 46 UK) 'Cherish What Is Dear To You (While It's Near To You)' (*Brian Holland, Lamont Dozier*) – Freda Payne (1971)

11 (UK; 14 R&B; 22 Pop) 'I Can't Help Myself (Sugar Pie Honey Bunch)' – Donnie Elbert (1972)

11 (UK) 'I Guess I'll Always Love You' – The Isley Brothers (1969 Reissue)

11 (UK) 'Reach Out I'll Be There' – The Four Tops (1988 Reissue)

13 (R&B; 34 Pop) 'Twistin' Postman' (*Robert Bateman, Brian Holland, William Stevenson*) – The Marvelettes (1962)

13 (R&B; 52 Pop) 'Don't Leave Me Starvin' For Your Love' – Holland & Dozier (1972)

13 (R&B; 56 Pop) 'Helpless' – Kim Weston (1966)

13 (UK) '(Come 'Round Here) I'm The One You Need' – Smokey Robinson & The Miracles (1971 Reissue)

13 (UK) 'Put Yourself In My Place' – The Isley Brothers (1969)

14 (R&B; 27 Pop) 'Baby Don't You Do It' – Marvin Gaye (1964)

14 (UK; 56 R&B; 60 Pop) 'Reach Out I'll Be There' – Gloria Gaynor (1975)

15 (UK) 'Can I Get A Witness' – Sam Brown (1989)

16 (R&B; 92 Pop) 'You Keep Me Hangin' On' – Wilson Pickett (1969)

16 (UK) 'A Love Like Yours (Don't Come Knocking Every Day)' – Ike & Tina Turner (1966)

17 (Pop) 'Ain't Too Proud To Beg' (*Eddie Holland, Norman Whitfield*) – The Rolling Stones (1974)

17 (R&B; 28 Pop; 28 UK) 'Forever Came Today' – The Supremes (1968)

17 (R&B; 29 Pop) 'Reach Out, I'll Be There' – Diana Ross (1971)

17 (R&B; 35 Pop) 'I Gotta Dance To Keep From Crying' – The Miracles (1963)

17 (R&B; 43 Pop) 'Without The One You Love (Life's Not Worth Living)' – The Four Tops (1964)

17 (R&B) 'Baby I Need Your Loving' – Carl Carlton (1982)

17 (UK) 'Gotta See Jane' (*Eddie Holland, R. Dean Taylor, Ronald Miller*) – R. Dean Taylor (1967)

18 (UK; 67 Pop) 'You Keep Me Hanging On' – Vanilla Fudge (1967)

19 (UK) 'It's The Same Old Song' – The Weathermen (1971)

20 (R&B) '(I Know) I'm Losing You' (*Eddie Holland, Norman Whitfield, Cornelius Grant*) – The Undisputed Truth (1970)

20 (UK) 'Working On A Building Of Love' – Chairmen Of The Board (1972)

21 (R&B; 52 Pop) 'You Brought The Joy' (*Brian Holland, Lamont Dozier*) – Freda Payne (1971)
21 (R&B; 64 Pop) 'He Was Really Sayin' Somethin'' (*Eddie Holland, Norman Whitfield, William Stevenson*) – The Velvelettes (1965)
21 (R&B; 100 Pop) 'Greetings (This Is Uncle Sam)' (*Brian Holland, Robert Bateman, Ronald Dunbar, The Valadiers*) – The Monitors (1966)

21 (UK) 'Jimmy Mack' – Martha & The Vandellas (1971 Reissue)

22 (R&B; 52 UK) 'Take Me In Your Arms (Rock Me A Little While)' – The Isley Brothers (1967)
22 (R&B; 70 Pop) 'Love (Makes Me Do Stupid Things)' – Martha & The Vandellas (1965)
22 (R&B; 93 Pop) 'Run, Run, Run' – The Supremes (1964)
22 (R&B) 'Darling Baby' – Jackie Moore (1972)

23 (R&B; 27 UK; 51 Pop) 'I'm In A Different World' (*Brian Holland, Lamont Dozier, R. Dean Taylor*) – The Four Tops (1968)

23 (UK) 'Bernadette' – The Four Tops (1972 Reissue)

24 (Pop) 'Too Many Fish In The Sea' (*Eddie Holland, Norman Whitfield*) – Mitch Ryder & The Detroit Wheels (1967)

24 (Pop) '(I Know) I'm Losing You' (*Eddie Holland, Norman Whitfield, Cornelius Grant*) – Rod Stewart (1971)

24 (R&B; 78 Pop) 'Forever' (*Brian Holland, Lamont Dozier, Freddie Gorman*) – The Marvelettes (1963)

24 (UK) 'Baby I Need Your Loving' – The Fourmost (1964)
24 (UK) 'Come See About Me' – Shakin' Stevens (1987)

25 (R&B; 40 Pop) 'I'm Gonna Let My Heart Do The Walkin''
(*Brian Holland, Eddie Holland*) – The Supremes (1976)
25 (R&B; 44 Pop) 'Locking Up My Heart' – The Marvelettes (1963)

27 (R&B; 76 Pop) 'Leaving Here' – Eddie Holland (1964)

28 (UK) 'Put Yourself In My Place' – The Elgins (1971 Reissue)

29 (Pop) 'Stop! In The Name Of Love' – The Hollies (1983)

29 (R&B; 58 Pop) 'Candy To Me' – Eddie Holland (1964)

30 (R&B; 35 Pop; 47 UK) 'It's The Same Old Song' – KC & The Sunshine Band (1978)
30 (R&B; 52 Pop) 'Baby I Need Your Loving' – O. C. Smith (1972)
30 (R&B) 'Everybody's Got A Song To Sing' – Chairmen Of The Board (1972)
30 (R&B) 'Forever' (*Brian Holland, Lamont Dozier, Freddie Gorman*) – Baby Washington & Don Gardner (1973)

30 (UK) 'There's A Ghost In My House' (*HDH, R. Dean Taylor*) – The Fall (1987)

31 (R&B; 45 UK; 61 Pop) 'I Guess I'll Always Love You' – The Isley Brothers (1966)
31 (R&B; 54 Pop) 'Just Ain't Enough Love' – Eddie Holland (1964)
31 (R&B; 67 Pop) 'This Old Heart Of Mine (Is Weak For You)' (*HDH, Sylvia Moy*) – Tammi Terrell (1969)

31 (UK) 'Third Finger, Left Hand' – The Pearls (1972)

32 (Pop) 'The Happening' (*HDH, Frank De Vol*) – Herb Alpert & The Tijuana Brass (1967)

33 (R&B) 'Free Your Mind' – The Politicians (1972)

34 (Pop) 'Baby Don't You Do It' – The Band (1972)

36 (R&B; 71 Pop; 95 UK) 'I Just Can't Walk Away' – The Four Tops (1983)

36 (UK) 'You Keep Me Hanging On' – Roni Hill (1977)

37 (UK; 73 Pop) 'Reach Out I'll Be There' – Michael Bolton (1992)

38 (R&B; 96 Pop) 'Stop! In The Name Of Love' – Margie Joseph (1971)

39 (Pop) 'Can I Get A Witness' – Lee Michaels (1971)

39 (R&B) 'The Girl's Alright With Me' (*Eddie Holland, Norman Whitfield and Eddie Kendricks*) – The Temptations (1964)

40 (Pop; 42 R&B) 'I Can't Help Myself (Sugar Pie Honey Bunch)' – Bonnie Pointer (1979)

40 (UK) 'Where Did Our Love Go' – Manhattan Transfer (1978)

41 (R&B) 'Love's Gone Bad' – Chris Clark (1966)
41 (R&B) 'Oh I Need Your Loving' (*Brian Holland, Eddie Holland*) – Eddie Kendricks (1981)

41 (UK) 'Little Darling (I Need You)' – Marvin Gaye (1971 Reissue)

42 (R&B) 'Stealing Moments From Another Woman's Life' (*Brian Holland, Lamont Dozier*) – Glass House (1970)

42 (UK) 'Nowhere To Run' – Martha & The Vandellas (1969 Reissue)

43 (R&B) 'I'm So Glad' (*Brian Holland*) – Junior Walker & The All Stars (1975)

46 (R&B) 'Slipping Away' – Holland–Dozier (1973)

47 (R&B) 'Baby I Need Your Loving' – Geraldine Hunt (1972)
47 (R&B) 'Thanks I Needed That' – Glass House (1972)

48 (Pop) 'Little Darling (I Need You)' – The Doobie Brothers (1977)
48 (Pop) 'Something About You' – LeBlanc & Carr (1977)

48 (R&B) 'Try On My Love For Size' (*Brian Holland, Lamont Dozier*) –
   Chairmen Of The Board (1971)

50 (R&B; 76 Pop) 'I'll Turn To Stone' – The Four Tops (1967)
50 (R&B) 'All I Do Is Think Of You' (*Eddie Holland, Michael Lovesmith*) –
   The Jackson 5 (1975)

51 (UK) 'A Love Like Yours (Don't Come Knocking Every Day)' –
   Dusty Springfield (1978)
51 (UK) 'This Old Heart Of Mine (Is Weak For You)' (*HDH, Sylvia Moy*) –
   The Isley Brothers (1976 Reissue)
51 (UK) 'Where Did Our Love Go' – Diana Ross & The Supremes
   (1974 Reissue)

52 (UK) 'This Old Heart Of Mine (Is Weak For You)' (*HDH, Sylvia Moy*) –
   Donnie Elbert (1972)

53 (R&B) 'Nowhere To Run' – The Dynamic Superiors (1976)

55 (R&B) 'I Need It Just As Bad As You' (*Brian Holland, Eddie Holland,
   Richard 'Popcorn' Wylie*) – Laura Lee (1974)

58 (UK) 'Baby Love' – Honey Bane (1981)

61 (R&B) 'New Breed Kinda Woman' – Holland–Dozier (1973)

61 (UK) 'Helpless' – Tracey Ullman (1984)

62 (Pop) 'Baby I Need Your Loving' – Eric Carmen (1979)

62 (R&B) '(I'm) Just Being Myself' (*HDH, Richard 'Popcorn' Wylie*) – Dionne Warwick (1973)

62 (UK) 'Stop! In The Name Of Love' – Diana Ross & The Supremes (1989 Reissue)

63 (Pop) 'All The Love I Got' (*Berry Gordy, Brian Holland, Janie Bradford*) – Marv Johnson (1960)

65 (Pop) 'Jimmy Mack' – Sheena Easton (1986)

66 (UK) 'Nowhere To Run' – Nu Generation (2000)

67 (Pop) 'Gotta See Jane' (*Eddie Holland, R. Dean Taylor, Ronald Miller*) – R. Dean Taylor (1971 Reissue)

68 (Pop) 'Where Did Our Love Go' – The J. Geils Band (1976)

71 (R&B) 'All I Do Is Think Of You' (*Brian Holland, Michael L. Smith*) – B5 (2005)

71 (UK) 'Where Did Our Love Go' – Tricia Penrose (1996)

74 (Pop) 'Come See About Me' – Nella Dodds (1964)
74 (Pop) 'Everything Is Good About You' (*Eddie Holland, James Dean*) – The Lettermen (1971)

75 (R&B) 'Love Gone Bad' (*Brian Holland, Eddie Holland*) – Mavis Staples (1984)

77 (R&B; 80 UK) 'It's The Same Old Song' – Third World (1989)

79 (Pop) 'Reach Out I'll Be There' – Merrilee Rush (1968)

86 (R&B) 'Love Is Like An Itching In My Heart' – Krystol (1986)

87 (Pop) '(I Know) I'm Losing You' (*Eddie Holland, Norman Whitfield, Cornelius Grant*) – Uptown (1986)

87 (Pop) 'My World Is Empty Without You' – José Feliciano (1969)

87 (R&B) 'Forever' (*Brian Holland, Lamont Dozier, Freddie Gorman*) – Chuck Cissel (1980)

89 (Pop) 'Ain't Too Proud To Beg' (*Eddie Holland, Norman Whitfield*) – Rick Astley (1989)

89 (R&B) 'Greetings (This Is Uncle Sam)' (*Brian Holland, Robert Bateman, Ronald Dunbar, The Valadiers*) – The Valadiers (1961)

91 (UK) 'You Keep Me Hangin' On' – Diana Ross & The Supremes (1986 Reissue)

92 (Pop) 'Back In My Arms Again' – Genya Ravan (1978)

92 (Pop) 'Please Mr. Postman' (*Georgia Dobbins, William Garrett, Brian Holland, Robert Bateman, Freddie Gorman*) – The Beatles (1964)

92 (Pop) 'Put Yourself In My Place' – The Elgins (1966)

93 (R&B) 'Standing In The Shadows Of Love' – Deborah Washington (1977)

93 (R&B) 'Where Do I Go From Here?' (*Brian Holland, Eddie Holland*) – The Supremes (1975)

96 (Pop) 'You Keep Me Hangin' On' – Jackie DeShannon (1970)

Chronology of Selected Compositions and Productions

Includes co-writers and original recording artists (where applicable).

This list does not include songs to which HDH (individually or collectively) are credited as co-writers through sampling, foreign language translations, legal/copyright arrangements, etc.

Key To Co-writers

AB – Angelo Bond	GM – Gwendolyne Murray	NYPA – New York Port Authority
AH – Anthony Hester	HB – Harold Beatty	
AW – Andre Williams	HC – Henry Cosby	RB – Robert Bateman
BA – Barney Ales	HE – Harold Edwards	RBr – Reginald A. Brown
BG – Berry Gordy	HW – Hugh Wyche	RD – R. Davis
BGa – B. Gaines	IB – Irving Biegel	RDu – Ronald Dunbar
BGo – Billy Gordon	IJH – Ivy Jo Hunter	RDT – R. Dean Taylor
BP – Bonnie Pointer	JB – Janie Bradford	RG – Robert Gordy
BPa – Barry Paine	JD – James Dorsey	RM – R. Miner
BS – Barrett Strong	JDe – James Dean	RMi – Ronald Miller
CC – C. Coulter	JG – Jack Goga	RoB – Rodney J. Brown
CD – Cleo Drake	JH – James Hendrix	RS – R. Stringer
CG – Cornelius Grant	JHa – Jerry Harris	RW – Richard Wylie
CJ – Cassandra Jordan	JT – John Thornton	SF – Stafford Floyd
CP – Clarence Paul	JY – James Young	SM – Sammy Mack
CS – Chester Scott	KC – K. Craighead	SO – Stanley Ossman
DC – D. Collins	KM – Kal Mann	SP – Scherrie Payne
DD – D. Dumas	LG – Linda Graves	SyM – Sylvia Moy
ED – Elizabeth Dozier	LH – Linda Holland	TH – Ty Hunter
EK – Eddie Kendricks	LM – Lee Moore	TK – T. Keane
ES – Earl Smiley	LP – Lesley R. Pierce	VS – Valerie Simpson
EW – Edythe Wayne	MC – Marty Coleman	VW – Vernon Williams
FDV – Frank De Vol	MD – Mack David	WG – William Garrett
FG – Freddie Gorman	MG – Marvin Gaye	WM – William Mitchell
FH – Fran Heard	MJ – Marv Johnson	WR – William 'Smokey' Robinson
FL – Frederick 'Shorty' Long	MM – M. Miller	
FP – Freda Payne	MLS – Michael L. Smith aka Michael Lovesmith	WS – William 'Mickey' Stevenson
FS – F. Stafford		
FW – Frank Wilson	MW – Marsha Woods	WT – W. Terry
GCl – George Clinton	MWo – Marlon Woods	WW – William Weatherspoon
GD – Georgia Dobbins	NA – Nickolas Ashford	
GF – George Fowler	NW – Norman Whitfield	
GH – Gladys Horton		

Brian Holland Compositions

* Denotes sessions produced/co-produced. Co-writers in brackets where applicable. Includes selected cover versions.

1959

'Don't Leave Me' (*RB, WR, BG*) – Marv Johnson
  also recorded by: Henry Lumpkin; The Miracles
'I'm Coming Home' (*RB, BG, GM*) – Marv Johnson

1960

'All The Love I've Got' (*BG, JB*) – Marv Johnson
  also recorded by: The Marvelettes*; James & Bobby Purify
'Continental Strut' (*RB, WM*) – Little Iva & Her Band
  also recorded by: The Satintones*
'I've Got A Notion' (*GF, RB*) – Henry Lumpkin
  also recorded by: Marv Johnson; Lynne Randell; Mary Wells*
'Oh Lover' (*WR, BG*) – Sherri Taylor & Singin' Sammy Ward
  also recorded by: Marvin Gaye & Mary Wells*

1961

'Because I Love You' (*RB, VW, CS*) – The Satintones
'Big Joe Moe' (*WS*) – Singin' Sammy Ward
'Even Though' (*RB*) – The Satintones
'Faded Letter' (*VW, SM, RB*) – The Satintones*
'Fire' (*AW, WS*) – Gino Parks
'I Know How It Feels' (*JB, RW, RB*) – The Marvelettes*
  also recorded by: The Satintones*
'I Want A Guy' (*BG, FG*) – The Marvelettes*
  also recorded by: The Supremes
'Just For You' (*JB, RB, FG*) – Freddie Gorman*
'My Kind Of Love' (*CS, VW, RB*) – The Satintones*
'Playboy' (*RB, GH, WS*) – The Marvelettes*
  also recorded by: Charity Brown; The Shrills; Dwight Yoakam
'Please Mr. Postman' (*GD, WG, RB, FG*) – The Marvelettes*
  also recorded by: The Beatles; The Carpenters; Richard Clayderman; Bern Elliott & The Fenmen; The Originals; Diana Ross; Helen Shapiro; Mike Sheridan & The Nightriders
'So Long Baby' (*RB, JY*) – The Marvelettes*

'Take A Chance' (*RB, MC*) – The Valadiers*
'Take A Chance On Me' (*FG, RB*) – Eddie Holland*
'The Last Laugh' (*JB*) – Eddie Holland
'(They Call Me) Cupid' (*BG, NW*) – Mickey Woods
'Three Months' (*RB, WS*) – The Marvelettes
'Twistin' Postman' (*RB, WS*) – The Marvelettes*
   also recorded by: Force Five (as 'Shaking Postman')
'What About Me' (*JB, WS*) – Eddie Holland*
'White House Twist' (*BG, BA*) – The Twistin' Kings
'Who Knows' (*JH, RB*) – Cornell Blakely
'You Broke My Heart' (*RB, FG*) – Cornell Blakely
'You Should Know' (*JB, SO*) – The Marvelettes
'Your Sweet Love' (*HE, RB*) – The Satintones

1962
'A Living Dream (Called A Girl)' (*MG, WS, HE*) – Freddie Gorman
'Come Into My Palace' (*WS-LM*) – Lee & The Leopards
   also recorded by: Patrice & Brenda Holloway; The Supremes; Mary Wells
'Gotta Have Your Love' (*JB*) – Eddie Holland
'He Gave Me You' (*WS, MJ*) – Marv Johnson
'If It's Love (It's Alright)' (*WS*) – Eddie Holland*
'Just Friends' (*JB*) – Freddie Gorman*
'Last Night I Had A Vision' (*WS*) – Eddie Holland
'Mashed Potato Time' (*WG, RB, FG, KM*) – The Marvelettes
'Uptight' (*BA, IB*) – Herman Griffin & Band*
'You'll Be Sorry Someday' (*RB, MC*) – The Valadiers*

1963
'To Think You Would Hurt Me' (*RG*) – Martha & The Vandellas

1964
'Do You Know What I'm Talking About' (*NW, EK*) – LaBrenda Ben
   also recorded by: The Downbeats; The Temptations

1967
'I Can't Give Back The Love I Feel For You' (*NA, VS*) – Rita Wright
   also recorded by: Jeff Beck; Vikki Carr; Diahann Carroll; Kiki Dee; Diana Ross; Suzee Ikeda; Diana Ross; The Supremes

1972
'Try It You'll Like It' (*WT, RM*) – The Barrino Brothers*

1974
'All I Do Is Think Of You' (*MLS*) – The Jackson 5*
   also recorded by: Troop; B5
'I'm So Glad' – Brian Holland*
'You Were Made Especially For Me' (*MLS*) – The Jackson 5*

1976
'I'm So Glad' – Junior Walker
'Love I Never Knew You Could Feel So Good' (*RBr, RD, FS*) –
The Supremes
'We Should Be Closer Together' (*BGa, FG, JB*) – The Supremes
'You're My Driving Wheel' (*HB, RBr, FS*) – The Supremes
   also recorded by: Eddie Holland

1977
'Three Thousand Miles From Home' (*RBr, SF*) – New York Port Authority
'You Are The Music In My Life' (*RD, SF, RBr*) – Donny Osmond
'You'll Be Glad' (*SF, RBr, MW, DC*) – Donny Osmond

1982
'I Can't Give Back The Way I Feel For You' (*NA, VS*) – Stephanie Mills

1984
'Johnny' (*BP, TK*) – Bonnie Pointer
'Tight Blue Jeans' (*BP*) – Bonnie Pointer

1990
'Another Lover' (*CJ*) – Cassandra
'I Miss You So Much' (*CJ, RD*) – Cassandra
'Overnight Success' (*CJ, RD*) – Cassandra

Brian Holland/Lamont Dozier Compositions

* Denotes sessions produced/co-produced. Co-writers in brackets where applicable. Includes selected cover versions.

1962

'A Little Bit Of Lovin'" (*HC*) – Eddie Holland
'Contract On Love' (*JB*) – Stevie Wonder*
   also recorded by: Martha & The Vandellas
'Dearest One' (*ED*) – Lamont Dozier
'Genuine Love' (*JB*) – Freddie Gorman*
'Goddess Of Love' (*FG*) – The Marvelettes*
'I Know Forever' (*FG*) – The Marvelettes*
'I Know His Name (Only His Name)' (*FG*) – Kim Weston*
   also recorded by: The Velvelettes
'Meet Me Half Way' – Kim Weston*
   also recorded by: Mable John
'Mr. Misery (Let Me Be)' (*FG*) – The Miracles*
'Old Love (Let's Try It Again)' (*FG*) – Mary Wells*
   also recorded by: The Four Tops; Brian Holland; Martha & The Vandellas; Mary Wells; Kim Weston
'Past Time Lover' (*FG*) – Freddie Gorman*
   *also recorded by: Marvin Gaye**
   'So Great Is My Love' (*JD, FG*) – Eddie Holland
'Someday, Someway' (*FG*) – The Marvelettes*
   also recorded by: Martha & The Vandellas
'Strange I Know' (*FG*) – The Marvelettes*
'There He Is (At My Door)' (*FG*) – The Vells*
   *also recorded by: Martha & The Vandellas**
'Time Changes Things' (*JB*)* – The Supremes
   *also recorded by: Martha & The Vandellas**
'Too Strong To Be Strung Along' (*FG*) – The Marvelettes*
'Twin Brother' (*WR*) – Eddie Holland*

1963

'A Little Bit Of Sympathy, A Little Bit Of Love' (*AH*) – The Marvelettes*
'All That Glitters Isn't Gold' (*BG*) – Martha & The Vandellas

'Forever' (*FG*) – Martha & The Vandellas*
    also recorded by: Baby Washington & Don Gardner; Chuck Cissel;
    Marvin Gaye; The Marvelettes*; The Orlons; Stevie Wonder**
'I Had A Vision' (*FG*) – Freddie Gorman*
'I'll Always Take You Back' (*JB*) – Sammy Turner*
'Pa (I Need A Car)' (*FG*) – The Contours*

1964
'Just Like In The Movies' (*RDT*) – R. Dean Taylor
'Surfer's Call' (*RDT*) – R. Dean Taylor

1970
'Chairman Of The Board' – Chairmen Of The Board
'Stealing Moments From Another Woman's Life' – Glass House
'The World Don't Owe You A Thing' – Freda Payne

1971
'Cherish What Is Near To You' (*AB*) – Freda Payne
    also recorded by: The Blossoms
'Heaven Is There To Guide Us' (*SP*) – Glass House
    also recorded by: the 8th Day
'How Does It Feel' (*EW, RDu*) – Honey Cone
'I Had It All' – The Barrino Brothers
'I Shall Not Be Moved' (*AB*) – Freda Payne
    also recorded by: The Barrino Brothers
'I'm Not Getting Any Better' – Freda Payne
'It's Not What You Fall For, It's What You Stand For' – Laura Lee
'Prelude' – Freda Payne
'Savannah Lady' (*DD*) – General Johnson
'Suddenly It's Yesterday' – Freda Payne
'The Road We Didn't Take' (*DD*) – Freda Payne
'Touch Me Jesus' (*AB*) – Glass House
    also recorded by: The Sylvers
'Try On My Love For Size' – Chairmen Of The Board
    also recorded by: Danny Woods
'When Love Was A Child' – The Barrino Brothers
'You Brought The Joy' – Freda Payne

1972
'Come Back' – The Jones Girls
'Don't Let It Rain On Me' (*SP*) – Glass House
'Funky Toes' – The Politicians Ft. McKinley Jackson
'Horse And Rider' (*SP*) – Glass House
'I Don't See Me In Your Eyes Anymore' (*SP*) – Glass House
'If I'm Good Enough To Love (I'm Good Enough To Marry)' (*AB*) –
    Laura Lee
'If You Can Beat Me Rockin' (You Can Have My Chair)' (*RDu*) – Laura Lee
    also recorded by: Elkie Brooks
'Let It Flow' (*SP*) – Glass House
'Let Me Ride' – Danny Woods
'Roller Coaster' (*RM*) – Danny Woods
'The Judgement Day' – Warlock
'Two Can Be As Lonely As One' (*AB*) – Danny Woods
'Your Love Controls Me' (*RDu, EW*) – The Jones Girls
'You've Been My Rock' – Warlock

1973
'When Love Was A Child' – The Barrino Brothers

1975
'You Are There' – Michael Jackson

1976
'Hot Shot' – Junior Walker & The All Stars
'Probe Your Mind' – Junior Walker & The All Stars

Brian Holland/Eddie Holland Compositions and Productions

* Denotes sessions produced/co-produced. Co-writers in brackets where
applicable. Includes selected cover versions.

1962
'True Love Will Go A Mighty Long Way' (*WS*) – Eddie Holland
'You Deserve What You Got' (*WS*) – Eddie Holland*

1974

'I Can't Make It Alone' – Laura Lee
'(If You Want To Try Love Again) Remember Me' – Laura Lee
'I Need It Just As Bad As You' (*RW*) – Laura Lee
   also recorded by: Marcia Hines
'Let's Get Together' – Brian Holland
'Superwoman (You Ain't No Ordinary Woman)' – Brian Holland
'Touch Me' – Eloise Laws
'We've Come Too Far To Walk' – Laura Lee

1975

'Early Morning Love' (*HB*) – The Supremes
'Get The Cream Off The Top' – Eddie Kendricks
   also recorded by: Sterling Harrison
'Honey Love' (*RW*) – The Jackson 5
'Just A Little Bit Of You' – Michael Jackson
   also recorded by: Deborah Holland; Evelyn 'Champagne' King (as
   'Just A Little Bit Of Love')
'Keep Holding On' – The Temptations
'Take Me Back' – Michael Jackson
'We're Almost There' – Michael Jackson
   also recorded by: Alicia Keys; Wali Ali
'Where Do I Go From Here' – The Supremes

1976

'Come Into My Life' (*RD*) – The Supremes
'Don't Lose What You Got (Trying To Get Back What You Had)' – Junior
   Walker
'High Energy' (*HB*) – The Supremes
   also recorded by: Susaye Greene (solo rerecording)
'I Don't Want To Be Tied Down' (*RD*) – The Supremes
'I Need You Right Now' – Junior Walker
   also recorded by: Thelma Houston
'I'm Gonna Let My Heart Do The Walking' (*HB*) – The Supremes
   also recorded by: High Inergy
'Just Can't Get Enough' (*AB*) – Junior Walker

'Let Yourself Go' (*HB*) – The Supremes
   also recorded by: Eddie Holland; Hot Chocolate
'Love (Keep Us Together)' – Junior Walker
'My Piece Of The Rock' (*CC*) – 100 Proof Aged In Soul
'Only You (Can Love Me Like You Love Me)' (*HB*) – The Supremes
   also recorded by: Eddie Holland
'Someone Just Like You' (*HB*) – Chairmen Of The Board Ft. Prince Harold
'Sweet Dream Machine' (*HB*) – The Supremes
'Till The Boat Sails Away' (*HB, BPa*) – The Supremes
   also recorded by: Hiromi Iwasaki
'You Ain't No Ordinary Woman' – Junior Walker
'You Keep Me Moving On' (*HW, RW*) – The Supremes
'You're What's Missing In My Life' (*HB*) – The Supremes
   also recorded by: G. C. Cameron; Virginia McDonald
'You've Got Extra Added Power In Your Love' (*HB*) – Chairmen Of The
   Board Ft. Prince Harold

1977
'Ain't It Good Feeling Good' (*MM, RD*) – Eloise Laws
'All You Can Do With Love' (*HB*) – The Dynamic Superiors
'Camouflage' (*MM, RD*) – Eloise Laws
'Give It All Up' (*JB*) – The Dynamic Superiors
'Here Comes That Feeling Again' (*HB, MW*) – The Dynamic Superiors
'I Believe In You Baby' (*AB*) – Eloise Laws
'I Can't Go On Living Without Your Love' (*RD*) – Thelma Houston
   also recorded by: Eddie Holland
'I Can't Stand It' (*HB*) – Donny Osmond
'I Discovered You (You Discovered Me)' (*HB, MW*) – Donny Osmond
'I Got It' (*DC*) – New York Port Authority
'I Haven't Had A Heartache All Day' (*HB*) – Donny Osmond
'I Need You Now' – Táta Vega
'I'm Mad As Hell (Ain't Gonna Take No More)' (*HB*) – 100 Proof Aged In
   Soul & New York Port Authority
'In The Middle Of The Feeling' (*HB*) – Three Ounces Of Love
'I've Got A Right To Be Loved' (*HB, MW*) – Three Ounces Of Love
'Love Goes Deeper Than That' (*HB*) – Eloise Laws
'Make It Last Forever' (*HB, MM*) – Eloise Laws

'Oh, It Must Be Love' (*HB*) – Donny Osmond
'Put A Little Love Into It (When You Do It)' (*HB*) – Eloise Laws
'Some Kind Of Woman' – Jermaine Jackson
'Somebody Is Always Messing Up A Good Thing' (*MLS*) – Honey Cone
   Ft. Sharon Cash
'The More I Live, The More I Love' (*HB, MW*) – Donny Osmond
'Truth Will Come Out' (*HB*) – Honey Cone Ft. Sharon Cash
'Where Did We Go Wrong' – Eloise Laws
'You Got Me Loving You Again' (*MM*) – Eloise Laws

1978
'Bare Back' (*HB*) – The Temptations
'Ever Ready Love' (*HB*) – The Temptations
'Fire Don't Burn' (*MD, RMi*) – Diana Ross
'I Just Don't Know How To Let You Go' (*MW*) – The Temptations
'Mystic Woman (Love Me Over)' (*RD*) – The Temptations
'Take A Trip To My Tomorrow (Let's Encounter For The First Time)' (*MW*)
   – Jermaine Jackson
    also recorded by: Sterling Harrison
'That's When You Need Love' (*RD*) – The Temptations
'Wake Up To Me' (*HB, MW*) – The Temptations
'We Can Never Relight That Old Flame Again' (*MD*) – Diana Ross
'You Build Me Up To Tear Me Down' – Diana Ross
'You Gave Me Something To Believe In' (*MW*) – Jermaine Jackson
    also recorded by: Eddie Holland
'You're So Easy To Love' (*HB*) – The Temptations

1979
'Let's Say Goodbye To Goodbye' (*MW*) – Energetics

1981
'(Oh I) Need Your Loving' – Eddie Kendricks
    also recorded by: Wali Ali
'One Size Fits All' – Sterling Harrison

1983
'Body Buddy' (*HB*) – the 8th Day

'Call Me Up' (*HB*) – the 8th Day
'Don't Blow It' (*HB*) – the 8th Day
'(He Puts Me In) The Right Mood' (*RD*) – the 8th Day
'In The Valley' (*HB*) – the 8th Day
'It Ain't Funny No More' (*HB*) – the 8th Day
'Let My Heart Do The Walking' (*HB*) – Jayne Edwards
'Love Gone Bad' – Mavis Staples

1984
'I Bet She Does It Like She Dances' – Hard Cover

1985
'It's A Tight Fit' – Lipstick
'Women Out There' (*HB*) – Sam Bostic

1986
'Can't Shake You Loose' (*LP, LH*) – Liquid Heat
'Caught Up In the Magic' (*RD*) – Liquid Heat
'Deep In It' (*JDe*) – Heavy Traffic
'Dr. Please' (*LP, LH*) – Liquid Heat
'Hand Made Love' (*RD*) – Heavy Traffic
'Jealousy' (*LP*) – Heavy Traffic
'Promises In The Dark' – Heavy Traffic
'Show Me The Way To Love' (*LP, LH*) – Liquid Heat
'The Fire Is Gone' – Heavy Traffic

1990
'Kilimanjaro' (*RD*) – Cassandra
'You Make It Easy' (*CJ*) – Cassandra

1991
'Love Don't Walk Away' – Keisha Jackson

2005
'Ode To Esther' – Eddie Holland

2009–2015 – selected *First Wives Club* compositions
'I'm Not That Type Of Girl'
'My Heart Wants To Try One More Time'
'Old Me, New Me'
'One Sweet Moment'
'Shoulder To Shoulder'
'Stir It Up'
'Whirlpool Of Emotions'

Eddie Holland Compositions

Co-writers in brackets where applicable. Includes selected cover versions.

1961
'Thank You (For Loving Me All The Way)' (*CP, WS*) – Stevie Wonder
   also recorded by: Andre Williams

1962
'Just A Few More Days' – Eddie Holland
'Throw A Farewell Kiss' (*NW*) – Freddie Gorman
   also recorded by: The Christians; The Velvelettes

1963
'A Need For Love' – The Marvelettes
'Brenda' – Eddie Holland
   also recorded by: The Four Tops
'Bright Lights, Big City' (*NW*) – Marvin Gaye
'Dance A While, Cry A While' (*NW*) – The Marvelettes
'Happy Go Lucky' (*NW*) – Eddie Holland
'Heart Broken, Heart Breaker (And The Clock)' (*NW*) – Eddie Holland
'He Who Picks A Rose' (*NW, EK, ES*) – The Temptations
   also recorded by: The Carstairs; Jimmy Ruffin; Edwin Starr
'I Couldn't Cry If I Wanted To' (*NW*) – Eddie Holland
   also recorded by: The Temptations
'I Couldn't Dance' – Freddie Gorman

'I'm Grateful' (*CD, GF*) – Eddie Holland
   also recorded by: The Four Tops
'I'm On The Outside Looking In' – Eddie Holland
'It's Best To Be Sure' – Eddie Holland
'Johnny Do Right' (*NW*) – The Marvelettes
'(Loneliness Made Me Realize) It's You That I Need' (*NW*) –
   Eddie Holland
   also recorded by: The Persuasions; Jimmy Ruffin; The Temptations
'(Talkin' 'Bout) Nobody But My Baby' (*NW*) – The Temptations
   also recorded by: The Miracles
'This Little Girl' (*HC, WS*) – Stevie Wonder
   also recorded by: The Roulettes
'True, True Loving (The World's Greatest Thing)' (*NW*) – Marvin Gaye
'Welcome Back' – Eddie Holland
'You're Sweeter As The Days Go By' – Eddie Holland

1964
'A Tear For The Girl' – Martha & The Vandellas
'Beauty Is Only Skin Deep' (*NW*) – The Miracles
   also recorded by: Aswad; Herman Brood & His Wild Romance; Paul
   Carrack; Jimmy Ruffin; The Temptations
'Don't Fool Around' (*RDT*) – R. Dean Taylor
'Everybody Needs Love' (*NW*) – Mary Wells
   also recorded by: Lloyd Charmers; John Holt; Gladys Knight & The
   Pips; The Miracles; Lloyd Parks; Jimmy Ruffin; Doreen Schaeffer; Slim
   Smith; The Temptations; The Velvelettes; Delroy Wilson
'Girl (Why You Wanna Make Me Blue)' (*NW*) – The Temptations
   also recorded by: Phil Collins
'He Was Really Sayin' Somethin'' (*NW, WS*) – The Velvelettes
   also recorded by: Bananarama with Fun Boy Three; The Marvelettes;
   Shakespears Sister; Shalamar; Earl Van Dyke
'I Gotta Know Now' (*NW*) – The Temptations
   also recorded by: The Isley Brothers; The Supremes
'I Want Her Love' (*NW*) – Jimmy Ruffin
'Oh Little Boy (What Did You Do To Me)' (*WS*) – Mary Wells
'Poor Girl' (*RDT*) – R. Dean Taylor

'The Girl's Alright With Me' (*NW, EK*) – The Temptations
  also recorded by: Derrick Harriott; The Spinners;
  The Undisputed Truth
'Too Many Fish In The Sea' (*NW*) – The Marvelettes
  also recorded by: Phil Collins; Gwen Guthrie; Bette Midler;
  Mitch Ryder, The Tremeloes; Earl Van Dyke; The Young Rascals

1965
'A Bird In The Hand (Is Worth Two In The Bush)' (*NW*) – The Velvelettes
  also recorded by: Gladys Knight & The Pips
'I Got Heaven Right Here On Earth' (*NW, EK*) – The Temptations
  also recorded by: The Temptations (rerecording)
'Let's Go Somewhere' (*RDT*) – R. Dean Taylor
  also recorded by: David Garrick; Beryl Marsden
'Lonely Lonely Girl Am I' (*NW, EK*) – The Velvelettes
  also recorded by: Dave & Ansel Collins; Chuck Jackson (as 'Lonely
  Lonely Man Am I'); The Temptations (as 'Lonely Lonely Man Am I')
'No Time For Tears' (*NW*) – The Marvelettes
  also recorded by: The Elgins; Marvin Gaye
'Since You've Been Loving Me' (*MJ*) – The Velvelettes
'The Boy From Crosstown' (*NW*) – The Velvelettes
  also recorded by: Gladys Knight & The Pips; The Marvelettes;
  Edwin Starr (as 'The Girl From Crosstown')

1966
'Ain't Too Proud To Beg' (*NW*) – The Temptations
  also recorded by: Dennis Alcapone; Rick Astley; Count Basie & His
  Orchestra; Don Carlos; The Drifters; The Groovers; Half Japanese;
  Hall & Oates; Z. Z. Hill; J. J. Jackson; The Mystics; Sandy Nelson;
  The Rolling Stones; Slim Smith; The Supremes & The Temptations;
  Westlife
'Everything Is Good About You' (*JD*) – The Supremes
  also recorded by: Chris Clark; The Lettermen; Barbara McNair
'Function At The Junction' (*FL*) – Shorty Long
  also recorded by: Huey Lewis & The News; Little Richard;
  Ramsey Lewis; The Supremes & The Four Tops

'(I Know) I'm Losing You' (*NW, CG*) – The Temptations
  *also recorded by: The Commodores; The Jackson 5; Gladys Knight
  & The Pips; The Marmalade; The Mods; Rare Earth; Dave Stewart &
  Barbara Gaskin; Diana Ross & The Supremes & The Temptations; The
  SoulSations; Rod Stewart; Undisputed Truth; Uptown; Junior Walker
  & The All Stars; Baby Washington*
'No Man Can Love Her Like I Do' (*NW, EK*) – The Temptations
'So Long' (*NW, RDT*) – Marvin Gaye

1967
'All I Need' (*FW, RDT*) – The Temptations
  also recorded by: The Supremes; Bobby Taylor & The Vancouvers
'Every Now And Then' (*FW*) – Marvin Gaye
'Gotta See Jane' (*RM, RDT*) – R. Dean Taylor
  also recorded by: Andy Scott; The Messengers; Obi-Men; Rare Earth
'I Gotta Find A Way To Get You Back' (*NW, EK, CG*) – Tammi Terrell
  also recorded by: The Temptations
'It Must Be Love Baby' (*RDT*) – R. Dean Taylor
  also recorded by: Chris Clark
'Sorry Is A Sorry Word' (*IJH*) – The Temptations
  also recorded by: Ivy Jo Hunter

1968
'Bring Back The Love' (*JG, JD, WW*) – The Monitors

1972
'Superstar (Remember How You Got Where You Are)' (*NW*) –
  The Temptations

1976
'You Are The Heart Of Me' (*MLS*) – The Supremes

1977
'I Used To Hate It (Till I Ate It)' (*SF, RBr, RoB*) – New York Port Authority
'Once Is Just Not Enough' (*MWo, RBr, SF*) – The Dynamic Superiors
'Twilight Zone' (*NYPA*) – New York Port Authority

1983
'Hot On The Heels Of Love' (*HB*) – the 8th Day

1985
'Baby Gives Good Phone' (*HB, MWo*) – Sam Bostic
'Built For Love' (*HB*) – Sam Bostic

1986
'Coming Down With Love' (*HB*) – Heavy Traffic
'I Can't Keep Pretending' (*LP, LH, RD*) – Liquid Heat
'I'm So Hot' (*LP, LK, RD*) – Liquid Heat
'Let's Go Crazy' (*HB*) – Heavy Traffic
'You Can't Hurt Me No More (It's Gone With The Wind)' (*KC*) –
    Heavy Traffic

1988
'(I've Got) Female Trouble' (*HB*) – The Boys From Detroit

Eddie Holland/Lamont Dozier Compositions
Co-writers in brackets where applicable. Includes selected cover versions.

1962
'Day Dreamer' (*FH*) – Eddie Holland

1965
'Don't Compare Me With Her' (*JB*) – Brenda Holloway
also recorded by: Gladys Knight & The Pips; Kim Weston

Holland–Dozier–Holland Compositions and Productions
Co-writers in brackets where applicable. Includes selected cover versions.

1962
'Darling, I Hum Our Song' – Eddie Holland
        also recorded by: The Four Tops; Martha & The Vandellas
'Guarantee (For A Lifetime)' – Mary Wells

1963

'A Love Like Yours (Don't Come Knocking Everyday)' –
 Martha & The Vandellas
  also recorded by: Kim Weston

'Build Him Up' – Kim Weston
  also recorded by: Martha & The Vandellas

'Call On Me' – Bruce Channel
  also recorded by: The Four Tops; Shorty Long

'Can I Get A Witness' – Marvin Gaye
  *also recorded by: Blinky; Sam Brown; Lee Michaels; Barbara
  Randolph; The Rolling Stones; Dusty Springfield; Steampacket; The
  Supremes; The Temptations; Earl Van Dyke; Stevie Wonder; Z. Z. Hill*

'Can You Fix It (My Broken Heart)' – Mary Wells

'Come And Get These Memories' – Martha & The Vandellas
  *also recorded by: Ray Godfrey; Anna King; Hattie Littles;
  The Supremes; Kim Weston*

'Come On Home' (*JB*) – Holland–Dozier

'Do-Da Do-Da Day' – The Miracles

'Follow Me Home' – Marvin Gaye

'Gotta Say It, Gonna Tell It Like It Is' – Marvin Gaye
  also recorded by: The Four Tops

'Heat Wave' – Martha & The Vandellas
  *also recorded by: The Animals; Choker Campbell; Phil Collins;
  The Jam; Juice Newton; Nazareth; Joan Osborne; Linda Ronstadt;
  Dusty Springfield; The Supremes; Ike & Tina Turner; The Who*

'He Holds His Own' – Mary Wells
  also recorded by: The Supremes

'He Won't Be True (Little Girl Blue)' – The Marvelettes

'I Gotta Dance To Keep From Crying' – The Miracles

'I'm Gonna Make It To The Top' – Freddie Gorman

'Jealous Lover' – Martha & The Vandellas

'Knock On My Door' – The Marvelettes

'Lead Me And Guide Me' – LaBrenda Ben

'Leaving Here' – Eddie Holland
  *also recorded by: The Birds; Brownsville Station; Lars Frederiksen &
  The Bastards; Tommy Good; The Isley Brothers; The Messengers;
  Motörhead; Pearl Jam; The Rationals; The Volts; The Who*

'Live Wire' – Martha & The Vandellas
'Locking Up My Heart' – Martha & The Marvelettes
'Mickey's Monkey' – The Miracles
    also recorded by: Choker Campbell; The Hollies; John Mellencamp;
    Mother's Finest; The Supremes; Martha & The Vandellas;
    The Young Rascals
'One Block From Heaven' – Mary Wells
'Pretty Little Angel Face' – Eddie Holland
'Quicksand' – Martha & The Vandellas
'Run, Run, Run' – The Supremes
'Standing At The Crossroads Of Love' – The Supremes
'This Is When I Need You Most' – Martha & The Vandellas
'Tie A String Around Your Finger' (*JB*) – The Marvelettes
'Too Hurt To Cry, Too Much In Love To Say Goodbye' – The Darnells/
    The Marvelettes
    also recorded by: The Supremes
'Too Late To Cry' – Eddie Holland
'What Goes Up Must Come Down' – Holland–Dozier
    also recorded by: The Four Tops
'When The Lovelight Starts Shining Through His Eyes' – The Supremes
    also recorded by: Beryl Marsden; Bonnie Pointer; Dusty Springfield;
    The Zombies
'You Lost The Sweetest Boy' – Mary Wells
    also recorded by: The Marvelettes; Dusty Springfield; The Velvelettes

1964

'A Tear From A Woman's Eyes' – The Temptations
'Any Girl In Love (Knows What I'm Going Through)' – Kim Weston
    also recorded by: Gladys Knight & The Pips; The Supremes
'Ask Any Girl' – Kim Weston
    also recorded by: Chris Clark; Tony Martin (as 'Ask Any Man');
    The Supremes
'Baby Don't You Do It' – The Supremes
    also recorded by: The Band; The Black Crowes; Marvin Gaye;
    The Isley Brothers; The Poets; Barbara Randolph; Small Faces;
    The Who; Stevie Wonder

'Baby I Need Your Loving' – The Four Tops
   also recorded by: Bob Andy; Choker Campbell; Carl Carlton; Eric
   Carmen; Double Exposure; The Fourmost; Marvin Gaye & Kim
   Weston; Geraldine Hunt; Marvin Gaye & Tammi Terrell; Eddie
   Kendricks; Gladys Knight & The Pips; Shorty Long; Lulu; Virginia
   McDonald; Johnny Rivers; O. C. Smith; The Supremes
'Baby Love' – The Supremes
   also recorded by: Honey Bane; Choker Campbell; Tony Martin;
   Royal Philharmonic Orchestra
'Back In My Arms Again' – The Supremes
   also recorded by: The Jam; Genya Raven
'Beach Ball' – The Supremes
'Candy To Me' – Eddie Holland
   also recorded by: The Four Tops; Martha & The Vandellas
'Come See About Me' – The Supremes
   also recorded by: The Afghan Whigs; Choker Campbell;
   The Contours; Nella Dodds; Mark Farner; Barbara Mason;
   The Originals; Bonnie Pointer; Earl Van Dyke; Shakin' Stevens;
   Junior Walker; Yo La Tengo
'Finders Keepers Losers Weepers' – The Marvelettes
'Honey Boy' – Mary Wells
   also recorded by: Little Lisa; The Supremes
'How Sweet It Is (To Be Loved By You)' – Marvin Gaye
   also recorded by: Michael Bublé; Karen Dalton; The Elgins;
   The Grateful Dead; The Isley Brothers; Liz Lands; Joan Osborne;
   Rare Earth; James Taylor; Ruby Turner; Earl Van Dyke; Junior Walker
   & The All Stars
'If You Don't Want My Love' – Eddie Holland
   also recorded by: The Four Tops; Martha & The Vandellas
'If You Were Mine' – The Andantes
'I Like Everything About You' – Eddie Holland
   also recorded by: Chris Clark; Dennis Edwards; The Four Tops;
   Chuck Jackson
'I'll Take Care Of You' – The Four Tops
   also recorded by: Marvin Gaye
'I'm Giving You Your Freedom' – The Supremes
'I'm In Love Again' – The Supremes

'In My Lonely Room' – Martha & The Vandellas
 also recorded by: The Action; The Supremes
'It's All Your Fault' – The Supremes
'Jimmy Mack' – Martha & The Vandellas
 also recorded by: James Brown; Sheena Easton; Lani Hall;
 Bettye LaVette; Laura Nyro & Labelle; Bonnie Pointer
'Just Ain't Enough Love' – Eddie Holland
 also recorded by: The Isley Brothers
'(Like A) Nightmare' – The Andantes
'Love Has Gone' – The Four Tops
'Love (Makes Me Do Foolish Things)' – Kim Weston
 also recorded by: Jean Carn; Martha & The Vandellas; The Supremes
'My Lady Bug Stay Away From That Beatle' (*HDH, RDT*) – R. Dean Taylor
'Nowhere To Run' – Martha & The Vandellas
 also recorded by: The Dynamic Superiors; Sterling Harrison; The
 Isley Brothers; Hattie Littles; The Messengers; Laura Nyro & Labelle;
 Nu Generation; Tower Of Power; Ruby Turner; Earl Van Dyke
'Penny Pincher' – The Supremes
'Send Me No Flowers' – The Supremes
'Surfer Boy' – The Supremes
'Take Me In Your Arms (Rock Me A Little While)' – Eddie Holland
 also recorded by: Blood, Sweat & Tears; Chris Clark; The Doobie
 Brothers; The Isley Brothers; Jermaine Jackson; Mother Earth;
 Martha & The Vandellas; Kim Weston
'The Only Time I'm Happy' – The Supremes
'Third Finger, Left Hand' – Martha & The Vandellas
'Treat Her Right' – Eddie Holland
'Where Did Our Love Go' – The Supremes
 also recorded by: Adam Ant; Choker Campbell; Donnie Elbert;
 The J. Geils Band; Manhattan Transfer; Tricia Penrose; The Pussycat
 Dolls; Soft Cell; Three Ounces Of Love
'Where Did You Go' – The Four Tops
 also recorded by: Chuck Jackson
'Whisper You Love Me Boy' – Mary Wells
 also recorded by: Chris Clark; The Supremes
'Without The One You Love' – The Four Tops
 also recorded by: The Supremes & The Four Tops

'Your Love Is Amazing' – The Four Tops
   also recorded by: Byron Lee & The Dragonaires; Shorty Long
'You're A Wonderful One' – Marvin Gaye
   also recorded by: Don Bryant; Art Garfunkel; Earl Van Dyke
'You're Gone (But Always In My Heart)' – The Supremes
   also recorded by: Gladys Knight & The Pips

1965

'Can't Break The Habit' – Martha & The Vandellas
'Darling Baby' – The Supremes
   also recorded by: Rose Banks; The Elgins; Jackie Moore
'He's All I Got' (*JD*) – The Supremes
'Helpless' – The Four Tops
   also recorded by: Chuck Jackson; Manhattan Transfer; Tracey Ullman; Kim Weston
'I Can't Help Myself (Sugar Pie Honey Bunch)' – The Four Tops
   also recorded by: Axe; Donnie Elbert; Gloria Lynne; Robert Parker; Bonnie Pointer; The Real Thing; Johnny Rivers; Johnny Ross & The Soul Explosions; The Supremes; Earl Van Dyke; Delroy Wilson
'I Got A Weak Heart' – Kim Weston
'I Hear A Symphony' – The Supremes
   also recorded by: High Inergy; The Isley Brothers; Quincy Jones; Barbara McNair; Diana Ross & The Supremes & The Temptations; Royal Philharmonic Orchestra; Stevie Wonder
'(I'm A) Road Runner' – Junior Walker & The All Stars
   also recorded by: The Animals; Fleetwood Mac; Peter Frampton; Jerry Garcia; Albert Lee; Geno Washington & The Ram Jam Band; Steppenwolf; James Taylor
'(I'm So Glad) Heartaches Don't Last Always' – The Supremes
'I'm Willing To Pay The Price' – Martha & The Vandellas
'It's The Same Old Song' – The Four Tops
   also recorded by: Bob Andy; Claude François; KC & The Sunshine Band; The Supremes; Third World; The Weathermen
'Just As Long As You Need Me' – The Four Tops
'Little Darling (I Need You)' – Marvin Gaye
   also recorded by: The Doobie Brothers

'Lonely Lover' – Marvin Gaye
  also recorded by: The Four Tops
'Love Feels Like Fire' – The Four Tops
'Love Is Like An Itching In My Heart' – The Supremes
  also recorded by: Christian Death (as 'Love Is Like A Bitching In My Heart'); The Good Girls; Krystol
'Mother Dear' – The Supremes
'My World Is Empty Without You' – The Supremes
  also recorded by: The Afghan Whigs; José Feliciano; Diamanda Galás; The Heptones; Barbara McNair; The Miracles; The Originals; Della Reese; Mary Wilson; Stevie Wonder
'Nothing But Heartaches' – The Supremes
'Put Yourself In My Place' (*JT*) – The Elgins
  also recorded by: Chris Clark; The Isley Brothers; Byron Lee & The Dragonaires; Ken Parker; The Supremes
'Remove This Doubt' – The Supremes
'Since You've Been Gone' – The Four Tops
  also recorded by: Martha & The Vandellas
'Something About You' – The Four Tops
  also recorded by: Debbie Dean; Byron Lee & The Dragonaires; Sisters Love
'Stay In My Lonely Arms' – The Four Tops
  also recorded by: The Elgins; The Supremes
'Stop! In The Name Of Love' – The Supremes
  also recorded by: Gloria Gaynor; The Hollies; The Isley Brothers; Margie Joseph; Diana Ross & The Supremes & The Temptations; Talas; Kim Weston
'There's No Love Left' (*JD*) – The Four Tops
  also recorded by: The Isley Brothers
'True Fine Boy' – Saundra Edwards
'Until You Love Someone' – The Four Tops
  also recorded by: Chris Clark
'Who Could Ever Doubt My Love' – The Supremes
  also recorded by: Brenda Holloway; The Isley Brothers
'Your Unchanging Love' – Marvin Gaye
'You've Been A Long Time Coming' – Marvin Gaye

1966

'Baby, That's A Groove' (*JH, GCI*) – Roy Handy

'Can't Satisfy' (*SyM*) – The Impressions

'(Come 'Round Here) I'm The One You Need' – The Miracles
   also recorded by: The Cowsills; The GPs; The Jackson 5

'Don't Let True Love Die' (*JD*) – The Supremes

'Going Down For The Third Time' – The Supremes

'Heaven Must Have Sent You' – The Elgins
   also recorded by: Bonnie Pointer; The Supremes

'I Got A Feeling' – The Four Tops
   also recorded by: Barbara Randolph

'I Guess I'll Always Love You' – The Supremes
   also recorded by: The Isley Brothers

'I Hope You Have Better Luck Than I Did' – The Marvelettes
   also recorded by: Martha & The Vandellas

'I'll Turn To Stone' (*RDT*) – The Supremes
   also recorded by: Dennis Edwards; The Four Tops; Barbara Randolph

'I'm Ready For Love' – Martha & The Vandellas
   also recorded by: High Inergy; June Pointer; The Temptations

'It's A Good Feeling' (*WR*) – The Miracles

'I Understand My Man' – The Elgins

'Just One Last Look' – The Temptations
   also recorded by: The Four Tops

'Love Is Here And Now You're Gone' – The Supremes
   also recorded by: Donnie Elbert; Michael Jackson

'Love Is In Our Hearts' (*JD*) – The Supremes

'Love's Gone Bad' – Chris Clark
   also recorded by: Michael Jackson; The Underdogs; Rita Wright

'Mother You, Smother You' (*RDT*) – The Supremes
   also recorded by: Christine Schumacher & The Supremes

'Nothing But Soul' – Junior Walker & The All Stars

'One Way Out' – Martha & The Vandellas

'Overture' – The Supremes

'Reach Out I'll Be There' – The Four Tops
   *also recorded by: Michael Bolton; Petula Clark; Gloria Gaynor;
   Joe Harnell; Eddie Holland; Thelma Houston; The Impact Of Brass;
   The Jackson 5; Gary Private; Diana Ross; Merrilee Rush;*

San Remo Golden Strings; Snuff; Sunday Funnies;
Bobby Taylor & The Vancouvers
'Shake Me, Wake Me (When It's Over)' – The Four Tops
  also recorded by: Claude François; The Hollies; Chuck Jackson;
  Barbra Streisand; The Supremes
'Standing In The Shadows Of Love' – The Four Tops
  also recorded by: Sterling Harrison; The Jackson 5; Rod Stewart;
  Joe Stubbs; Deborah Washington; Barry White
'Suspicion' – The Originals
'There's A Ghost In My House' (*RDT*) – R. Dean Taylor
  also recorded by: The Fall; The Positives
'There's No Stopping Us Now' – The Supremes
'The Wheels Of The City' – Barbara McNair
'This Old Heart Of Mine (Is Weak For You)' (*SyM*) – The Isley Brothers
  also recorded by: The Contours; Donnie Elbert; Byron Lee &
  The Dragonaires; Mizz; Rod Stewart; Rod Stewart & Ronald Isley;
  The Supremes; Tammi Terrell; Wild Cherry; Delroy Wilson
'You Can't Hurry Love' – The Supremes
  also recorded by: Phil Collins; Dixie Chicks; The Four Tops;
  The Jackson 5; Stray Cats
'You Keep Me Hangin' On' – The Supremes
  also recorded by: Rose Banks; Brass Monkey; Cuddly Toys;
  Jackie DeShannon; Sam Harris; Ron Hill; Jonah Jones; Eloise Laws;
  Hugh Masekela; Reba McEntire; Wilson Pickett; Rod Stewart;
  Diana Ross & The Supremes & The Temptations; Vanilla Fudge;
  Kim Wilde; Mary Wilson

1967
'7 Rooms Of Gloom' – The Four Tops
  also recorded by: Pat Benatar; Blondie
'All I Know About You' (*FDV*) – The Supremes
'Bernadette' – The Four Tops
  also recorded by: Claude François; Lionel Richie
'I Can't Get Along Without You' (*BS*) – Martha & The Vandellas
'I Can't Go On Sharing Your Love' – The Isley Brothers
  also recorded by: Chuck Jackson
'I Can't Make It Alone' – The Supremes

'In And Out Of Love' – The Supremes
'Leave It In The Hands Of Love' (*JD*) – Martha & The Vandellas
'Reflections' – The Supremes
  also recorded by: The Four Tops; Sterling Harrison; Michael
  McDonald; Leo Sayer; The Sweet; The Temptations; Luther Vandross;
  Syreeta Wright
'Stay In My Lonely Arms' – The Supremes
  also recorded by: The Elgins; The Four Tops
'The Happening' (*FDV*) – The Supremes
  also recorded by: Herb Alpert & The Tijuana Brass
'We Couldn't Get Along Without You' – The Supremes
'We've Got A Way Out Love' – The Originals
  also recorded by: The Undisputed Truth
'You Keep Running Away' – The Four Tops
  also recorded by: Chuck Jackson; The Messengers

1968
'Detroit Is Happening' (*FDV*) – Willie Horton
'Forever Came Today' – The Supremes
  also recorded by: The Commodores; The Jackson 5;
  Sterling Harrison
'I'm In A Different World' – The Four Tops
  also recorded by: Jermaine Jackson

1971
'If It's Good To You (It's Good For You)' – The Flaming Ember
'It's Instrumental To Be Free' – the 8th Day
'Who's It Gonna Be' – Honey Cone
'Working On A Building Of Love' – Chairmen Of The Board

1972
'Everybody's Got A Song To Sing' (*RM*) – Chairmen Of The Board
'Free Your Mind' – The Politicians Ft. McKinley Jackson
'Giving Up The Ring' (*TH*) – Glass House
'Growing Pains' – Brotherly Love
'I Gotta Get Home (Can't Let My Baby Get Lonely)' – the 8th Day
'It Didn't Take Long' – Danny Woods

'Livin' High Off The Goodness Of Your Love' (*FP, RS*) –
   The Barrino Brothers
'Playing Games' – Glass House
'Rocks In My Head' – the 8th Day
'Thanks I Needed That' – Glass House
'Tighten Him Up' – Eloise Laws
'Why Can't We Be Lovers' – Holland–Dozier
   also recorded by: Coke Escovedo
'You Made Me An Offer I Can't Refuse' (*RM*) – Eloise Laws

1973
'Can't Get Enough' – Holland–Dozier
'Don't Leave Me' – Holland–Dozier
'If You Don't Want To Be In My Life' – Holland–Dozier
'I'm Gonna Hijack Ya, Kidnap Ya, Take What I Want' – Holland–Dozier
'Love Factory' (*HDH, RW*) – Eloise Laws
'Mother Misery's Favorite Child' – Freda Payne
'New Breed Kinda Woman' – (*RW*) Holland–Dozier Ft. Lamont Dozier
'Slipping Away' – Holland–Dozier
'Stay With Me' – Eloise Laws
'Two Wrongs Don't Make A Right' (*RW*) – Freda Payne
'Well Worth Waiting For Your Love' (*RW*) – The Barrino Brothers
'We've Gotta Find A Way Back To Love' – Freda Payne
'You Took Me From A World Outside' – Holland–Dozier
   also recorded by: Tyrone Edwards

1974
'Can't Get Enough Of You' – Tyrone Edwards
'Don't Leave Me Starving For Your Love' – Laura Lee
'Don't Stop Playing Our Song' – Lamont Dozier
'Enough Of Your Love' – Lamont Dozier
'If You Want To Try Love Again (Remember Me)' – Laura Lee
'The Picture Will Never Change' – Lamont Dozier

1976–1980
'Don't Let My Teardrops Bother You' (*RW*) – The Supremes

The following demo recordings were issued within the Jobete Music Co. *Yesterday, Today, Forever* promotional release. Three LPs featured abridged versions of 37 contemporary rerecordings of 'classic' (LP one, *Yesterday*) and recent (LP two, *Today*) material (see individual song listings). The following titles, from LP three, *Forever*, remain unique to this release. All compositions are credited to Holland–Dozier–Holland.

'Can't Wait For Your Love' – Virginia McDonald
'Get On The Right Track' – Sterling Harrison
'Help Me To Sing My Song' – Aja
'I Want Her' – Wali Ali
'It Can Never Be The Same' – Adrenne Williams
'Magic Touch' – Eddie Holland
'Memories (They Dance With Me)' – Kathy McFarland
'Run For Cover' – Eddie Holland
'Showin' Off' – Sterling Harrison
'(There You Go) Testing My Love' – Adrenne Williams
'Traveling With Love In Mind' – Virginia McDonald
'You Can't Stop My Loving' – Family Affair
'You're Heaven Sent' – Darnell McFarland

1981
'Common Ground' (*LG*) – Margo Michaels & NiteLite
'I Ain't Changing' – Margo Michaels & NiteLite
'I Can't Live Without You' – Margo Michaels & NiteLite
'Listen To My Heart' – Margo Michaels & NiteLite
'Make It Like Music' – Margo Michaels & NiteLite
'Take My Everything' – Margo Michaels & NiteLite
    also recorded by: Darnell McFarland
'Thank You For The Love' – Margo Michaels & NiteLite
'The Good Stuff's Coming In' – Margo Michaels & NiteLite

1983
'Back Where I Belong' – The Four Tops
'I Just Can't Walk Away' – The Four Tops
'Make Yourself Right At Home' – The Four Tops
'Sail On' – The Four Tops

Selected Productions

Brian Holland

Brian Holland productions of other artists' compositions, unless otherwise indicated.

1961
'Angel' – The Marvelettes
'Happy Days' – The Marvelettes
'Oh I Apologize' – The Marvelettes
'The Day Will Come' – Freddie Gorman
'Way Over There' – The Marvelettes
'What Is A Man (Without A Woman)' – Henry Lumpkin
'Zing Went The Strings Of My Heart' – The Satintones

1962
'Fortune Teller (Tell Me)' – Lamont Dozier
'Is It Yes Or Is It No' – Johnny Powers
'It's Now Or Never' – Johnny Powers
'The Day Will Come' – Mary Wells

1974
'Moving Violation' – The Jackson 5

1977
'All In Love Is Fair' – The Dynamic Superiors
'Don't Tear Down What Took So Long To Build' – G. C. Cameron
'Fly Into The Wind' – Donny Osmond
'Happy Song' – The Dynamic Superiors
'I'll Be Your Servant' – G. C. Cameron
'I'll Love You Forever' – G. C. Cameron
'I'm Sorry' – Donny Osmond
'Kiss Me When You Want To' – G. C. Cameron
'Let's Run Away Together' – G. C. Cameron
'Nothing's Sweeter Than Love' – G. C. Cameron
'This Will Make You Dance' – G. C. Cameron
'You Need A Strong Dose Of Love' – G. C. Cameron

'You're What I Need' – The Dynamic Superiors
'You've Got Me Dangling On A String' – Donny Osmond

1978
'I See My Child' – The Temptations

1983
'Blow Your Own Horn' – Herb Alpert
'True Confessions' – Herb Alpert

Brian Holland/Lamont Dozier

Brian Holland/Lamont Dozier productions of other artists' compositions, unless otherwise indicated.

1963
'A Need For Love' – The Marvelettes
'Dance What You Wanna' – The Miracles
'Dancin' Holiday' – The Miracles
'Do You Love Me' – The Miracles
'Forget About Me' – Carolyn Crawford
'Hello Stranger' – Martha & The Vandellas
'Hey There Lonely Boy' – Martha & The Vandellas
'I Got A Woman' – Marvin Gaye
'If I Had A Hammer' – Martha & The Vandellas
'I've Been Good To You' – Hattie Littles
'Just One Look' – Martha & The Vandellas
'Land Of A Thousand Dances' – The Miracles
'Mockingbird' – Martha & The Vandellas
'More (Theme From Mondo Cane)' – Martha & The Vandellas
'My Boyfriend's Back' – Martha & The Vandellas
'No Longer A Rebel' – R. Dean Taylor
'Old Time Lovin'' – The Show Stoppers
'Respectable Distance Away' – R. Dean Taylor
'That Won't Do' – Sammy Ward
'The Bird's The Word' – The Miracles
'The Monkey Time' – The Miracles

'The Twist' – The Miracles
'The Wah Watusi' – The Miracles
'Then He Kissed Me' – Martha & The Vandellas
'Twist And Shout' – The Miracles
'Wait Till My Bobby Gets Home' – Martha & The Vandellas
'Who Wouldn't Love A Man Like That' – Mable John

1964
'A Tear For The Girl' – Martha & The Vandellas
'All Grown Up' – R. Dean Taylor
'Little Girl, I'm Going To Marry You' – R. Dean Taylor

1965
'(All Of A Sudden) My Heart Sings' – The Supremes
'A Lover's Concerto' – The Supremes
'Give Me Something' – R. Dean Taylor
'Stranger In Paradise' – The Supremes
'Unchained Melody' – The Supremes
'With A Song In My Heart' – The Supremes
'Without A Song' – The Supremes
'Wonderful, Wonderful' – The Supremes
'Yesterday' – The Supremes
'You're What's Happening Baby' – The Four Tops

1966
'634-5789' – The Elgins
'A Taste Of Honey' – The Four Tops
'Baby A Go-Go' – Barbara McNair
'Barefootin'' – The Marvelettes
'Black Is Black' – Jimmy Ruffin
'Blowin' In The Wind' – The Supremes
'Bluesette' – The Four Tops
'Break Away' – The Lewis Sisters
'Countin' On You, Babe' – Barbara McNair
'For Your Precious Love' – The Elgins
'Good Lovin'' – The Elgins
'If I Were A Carpenter' – The Four Tops

'In The Midnight Hour' – The Elgins
'In The Still Of The Night' – The Four Tops
'It's A Man's Man's Man's World (But It Wouldn't Be Without A Woman)'
   – The Elgins
'Last Train To Clarksville' – The Four Tops
'Let The Music Play' – The Supremes
'Matchmaker, Matchmaker' – The Four Tops
'Message To Michael' – The Marvelettes
'Michelle' – The Four Tops
'On A Clear Day (You Can See Forever)' – The Four Tops
'Once Upon A Time' – The Four Tops
'Quiet Nights Of Quiet Stars (Corcovado)' – The Four Tops
'Strangers In The Night' – The Supremes
'Sweet Talkin' Guy' – The Marvelettes
'Tender Is The Night' – The Supremes
'The Shadow Of Your Smile' – The Supremes
'The Sound Of Music' – The Supremes
'What Now My Love' – The Supremes
'What The World Needs Now Is Love' – The Supremes
'When A Man Loves A Woman' – The Elgins
'Who Can I Turn To (When Nobody Needs Me)' – The Supremes
'Wives And Lovers' – The Four Tops

1967
'Cherish' – The Four Tops
'Crying In The Chapel' – Chris Clark
'If I Ruled The World' – The Supremes
'I'm A Believer' – The Four Tops
'Night Fo' Last' – Shorty Long
'Ode To Billie Joe' – The Supremes
'Something On My Mind' – Rita Wright
'The Sweetheart Tree' – The Four Tops
'Up, Up And Away' – The Supremes
'Walk Away, Renee' – The Four Tops

1968
'Nothing But Trouble' – Billy Eckstine
'Try It Baby' – Chris Clark

1971
'Bring The Boys Back Home' – Freda Payne
'Mama's Gone' – Freda Payne
'Odds And Ends' – Freda Payne
'You've Got To Love Somebody (Let It Be Me)' – Freda Payne

Solo Recordings

Eddie Holland Singles

1958
Mercury 71290: 'Little Miss Ruby'/'You (You You You You)'

Kudo 667: '(Where's The Joy) In Nature Boy'/'Shock'
   (*label credits Briant Holland & Band*)

1959
Tamla 102/United Artists 172: 'Merry-Go-Round'/'It Moves Me'

United Artists 191: 'Because I Love Her'/'Everything's Going'

1960
United Artists 207: 'Magic Mirror'/'Will You Love Me'

1961
United Artists 280: 'Why Do You Want To Let Me Go'/'The Last Laugh'*
   (*B-side Brian Holland/Janie Bradford*)

Motown 1021: 'Jamie'/'Take A Chance On Me'
   (*B-side Brian Holland/Freddie Gorman/Robert Bateman. Produced
   by Brian Holland/Robert Bateman*)

1962
Motown 1026: 'You Deserve What You Got'/'Last Night I Had A Vision'
   (*A-side Brian Holland/Eddie Holland/William Stevenson. B-side Brian
   Holland/William Stevenson. Both sides produced by Brian Holland/
   William Stevenson*)

Motown 1030: 'If Cleopatra Took A Chance'/'What About Me'
(*B-side Brian Holland/William Stevenson/Janie Bradford. Produced by Brian Holland*)

Motown 1031: 'If It's Love (It's Alright)'/'It's Not Too Late'
(*A-side Brian Holland/William Stevenson. Produced by Brian Holland/William Stevenson*)

1963

Motown 1036: 'Darling, I Hum Our Song'/'Just A Few More Days'
(*A-side HDH. B-side Eddie Holland. Both sides produced by Brian Holland/Lamont Dozier*)

Motown 1043: 'Baby Shake'/'Brenda'
(*B-side Eddie Holland. Produced by Brian Holland/Lamont Dozier*)

Motown 1049: 'I'm On The Outside Looking In'/'I Couldn't Cry If I Wanted To'
(*A-side Eddie Holland. B-side Eddie Holland/Norman Whitfield. Both sides produced by Brian Holland/Lamont Dozier*)

Motown 1052: 'Leaving Here'/'Brenda'
(*A-side HDH. B-side Eddie Holland. Both sides produced by Brian Holland/Lamont Dozier*)

1964

Motown 1058: 'Just Ain't Enough Love'/'Last Night I Had A Vision'
(*A-side HDH. Produced by Brian Holland/Lamont Dozier. B-side Brian Holland/William Stevenson. Produced by Brian Holland/William Stevenson*)

Motown 1063: 'Candy To Me'/'If You Don't Want My Love'
(*both sides HDH. Both sides produced by Brian Holland/Lamont Dozier*)

Eddie Holland Albums

1962

Motown MT 604: *Eddie Holland*

'Jamie'/'True Love Will Go A Mighty Long Way' (*Brian Holland/ Eddie Holland/William Stevenson*)/'If It's Love (It's Alright)'/'What About Me'/'It's Not Too Late'/'If Cleopatra Took A Chance'/'Take A Chance On Me'/'Last Night I Had A Vision'/'A Little Bit Of Lovin'' (*Brian Holland/Lamont Dozier/Henry Cosby*)/'Gotta Have Your Love' (*Brian Holland/Janie Bradford*)

1977

Yesterday Today & Forever

Jobete Music promotional three-LP set includes the following demonstration recordings. These performances were not intended for public release.

'I Can't Go On Living Without Your Love'

'Let Yourself Go'

'Magic Touch'

'Only You (Can Love Me Like You Do)'

'Reach Out I'll Be There'

'Run For Cover'

'You Gave Me Something To Believe In'

'You're My Driving Wheel'

2012

It Moves Me: The Complete Recordings 1958–1964

Includes MT604, plus the following rare and unissued recordings:

'Action Speaks Louder Than Words' (*recorded 1958*)

'Bashful Kind' (*recorded 1958*)

'Rain And Thunder' (*home recording, 1958*)

'Happy Days' (*home recording, 1958*)

'I'm So Glad I Learned To Do The Cha-Cha' (*home recording, 1958*)

'Love Is What You Make It' (*recorded 1962*)

'Day Dreamer' (*Brian Holland/Lamont Dozier/Fran Heard. Produced by Brian Holland/Lamont Dozier. Recorded 1962*)

'So Great Is My Love' (*Brian Holland/Lamont Dozier/Freddie Gorman/ James Dorsey. Produced by Brian Holland/Lamont Dozier. Recorded 1962*)

'Twin Brother' (*Brian Holland/Lamont Dozier/William Stevenson. Produced by Brian Holland/Lamont Dozier. Two versions, recorded 1962*)

'Welcome Back' (*Eddie Holland. Produced by Brian Holland/ Lamont Dozier. Recorded 1963*)

'(Loneliness Made Me Realize) It's You That I Need' (*Eddie Holland/ Norman Whitfield. Recorded 1963*)

'I'm Grateful' (*Eddie Holland/George Fowler/Cleo Drake. Produced by Brian Holland/Lamont Dozier. Recorded 1963*)

'Heart Broken, Heart Breaker (And The Clock)' (*Eddie Holland/ Norman Whitfield. Recorded 1963*)

'You're Sweeter As The Days Go By' (*Eddie Holland. Produced by Brian Holland/Lamont Dozier. Recorded 1963*)

'It's Best To Be Sure' (*Eddie Holland. Produced by Brian Holland/ Lamont Dozier. Recorded 1963*)

'Happy Go Lucky' (*Eddie Holland/Norman Whitfield. Recorded 1963*)

'Too Late To Cry' (*HDH. Produced by Brian Holland/Lamont Dozier. Recorded 1963*)

'Pretty Little Angel Face' (*HDH. Produced by Brian Holland/ Lamont Dozier. Recorded 1963*)

'Take Me In Your Arms (Rock Me A Little While)' (*HDH. Produced by Brian Holland/Lamont Dozier. Recorded 1964*)

'I Like Everything About You' (*HDH. Produced by Brian Holland/ Lamont Dozier. Recorded 1964*)

Brian Holland Singles

1974

Invictus ZS7 1265: 'I'm So Glad' (parts one and two)
   (*both sides Brian Holland. Both sides produced by Brian Holland*)

Invictus ZS8 1272: 'Super Woman (You Ain't No Ordinary Woman)'/ 'Let's Get Together'
   (*both sides Brian Holland/Eddie Holland. Produced by Brian Holland*)

Brian Holland/Lamont Dozier Singles

1963
Motown 1045: 'What Goes Up Must Come Down'/'Come On Home'
(*both sides HDH. Produced by Brian Holland/Lamont Dozier*)

1972
Invictus Is-9125: 'Why Can't We Be Lovers'/'Don't Leave Me (Instrumental)'
(*label credits Holland–Dozier Ft. Lamont Dozier. Both sides HDH. Holland–Dozier–Holland Prod Inc*)

Invictus Is-9133: 'Don't Leave Me Starvin' For Your Love' (parts one and two)
(*label credits Holland–Dozier Ft. Brian Holland. Both sides HDH*)

1973
Invictus ZS7-1253: 'Slipping Away'/'Can't Get Enough'
(*label credits Holland–Dozier Ft. Brian Holland. Both sides HDH. Holland–Dozier–Holland Prod Inc*)

Invictus ZS7-1254: 'New Breed Kinda Woman'/'If You Don't Want To Be In My Life'
(*label credits Holland–Dozier ft. Lamont Dozier. Both sides HDH*)

Invictus ZS7-1258: 'I'm Gonna Hijack Ya, Kidnap Ya, Take What I Want'/'You Took Me From A World Outside'
(*both sides HDH. Produced by Brian Holland*)

Collected Listening

If you want to hear the music exactly as we originally intended, untouched by modern technology, you cannot do better than to seek out the original recordings, on 45 and LP.

Considerably less time- and money-consuming options are readily available, however. The Motown and Invictus/Hot Wax/Music Merchant catalogues are undergoing constant reappraisal in both CD and digital form. Series such as Motown's multi-volume *Complete Motown Singles* and *Motown Unreleased* collections, expanded editions of many original albums, and a multitude of straightforward reissues and compilations also abound.

The following collections are of particular interest.

Heaven Must Have Sent You – The Holland–Dozier–Holland Story (Hip-O Records, 2005)
Three-CD box set includes major Motown and Invictus/Hot Wax hits, solo recordings, cover versions and more.

Holland–Dozier–Holland: The Complete 45s Collection (Harmless, 2014)
Fourteen-CD, 288-track box set featuring both sides of every Invictus/ Hot Wax/Music Merchant 45, plus rarities and remixes.

The Supremes Sing Holland–Dozier–Holland (Expanded Edition) (Universal, 2018)
Two-CD collection includes mono and stereo mixes of original album, plus previously unreleased, alternate, extended and live versions.

Eddie Holland – It Moves Me: The Complete Recordings 1958–1964 (Ace Records, 2012)
Two-CD collection includes singles, LP tracks and unreleased material (see page 362 for details).

Holland–Dozier – The Creative Corporation (Demon Records, 2012)
Single disc compilation of Invictus-era material recorded and released by Brian Holland and Lamont Dozier.

About the Co-Author

Dave Thompson is the author of over 150 books. His co-written memoirs include *There's No Bones in Ice Cream: Sylvain Sylvain's Story of the New York Dolls* and *The Spirit of Hawkwind* with Nik Turner. A columnist for Goldmine magazine, his work has also appeared in *Rolling Stone*, *Alternative Press*, *Mojo*, *Record Collector* and many other major publications. Born in the UK, Thompson is now a resident of Delaware, USA.